Praise for *Key p*

'Marr has collected and described a great set of metrics that managers can select from when choosing the performance measures for their business and especially for translating their strategy map into a Balanced Scorecard.'

Robert S. Kaplan, Baker Foundation Professor at the Harvard Business School and co-author of *The Balanced Scorecard* and *The Execution Premium*

'All the KPIs you need to consider are here, from the familiar (net profit, ROI) to the emergent (Klout score). If you care about performance measurement, you need to leaf through Marr's book from cover to cover – don't miss a page!'

Thomas H. Davenport, President's Distinguished Professor, Babson College and co-author of *Competing on Analytics and Analytics at Work*

'Once again, Bernard Marr shows why he is the leading thinker in business performance. With *Key Performance Indicators* he delivers another must-read book for anyone in business. This book will help you focus on the metrics that really matter to answer your key management questions. It provides an essential toolset critical for the effective running of any organisation.'

Gerry Pimm, Strategy, Planning & Performance Manager, Citizens Advice

'Bernard Marr's new book is an incredibly valuable resource for any manager. Marr has again hit the bull's eye with a book that is extremely clear, concise, well-organised, and, most importantly, immensely practical.'

Dean R. Spitzer, PhD and author of *Transforming Performance Measurement*

'In *Key Performance Indicators*, Bernard Marr has identified the most meaningful measures that companies and organisations should look at. I've so often seen people fumbling around trying to define the right measures for their business strategy and they often do a poor job of reinventing the very measures defined in this book. I will be using this book with my clients so they stop wasting time choosing measures and start using them instead.'

Stacey Barr, Performance Measurement Expert, Samford, Australia

'I love the set of 75 KPIs outlined in this book – their breadth and the highly-readable format makes it a much needed contribution to the field of management!'

Gary Cokins, Principal, Business Consulting, SAS and author of *Performance Management: Integrating Strategy Execution, Methodologies, Risk, and Analytics*

'Bernard Marr continues to establish himself as the leader in the field of performance measurement. His latest book *Key Performance Indicators* is a great resource for managers to select the measure that actually matter.'

Todd Scaletta, Vice President, Research and Innovation, CMA Canada

Key performance indicators

PEARSON

At Pearson, we believe in learning – all kinds of learning for all kinds of people. Whether it's at home, in the classroom or in the workplace, learning is the key to improving our life chances.

That's why we're working with leading authors to bring you the latest thinking and the best practices, so you can get better at the things that are important to you. You can learn on the page or on the move, and with content that's always crafted to help you understand quickly and apply what you've learned.

If you want to upgrade your personal skills or accelerate your career, become a more effective leader or more powerful communicator, discover new opportunities or simply find more inspiration, we can help you make progress in your work and life.

Pearson is the world's leading learning company. Our portfolio includes the Financial Times, Penguin, Dorling Kindersley, and our educational business, Pearson International.

Every day our work helps learning flourish, and wherever learning flourishes, so do people.

To learn more please visit us at: **www.pearson.com/uk**

BERNARD MARR

Key performance indicators

The 75 measures every manager needs to know

PEARSON

Harlow, England • London • New York • Boston • San Francisco • Toronto • Sydney • Auckland • Singapore • Hong Kong
Tokyo • Seoul • Taipei • New Delhi • Cape Town • São Paulo • Mexico City • Madrid • Amsterdam • Munich • Paris • Milan

PEARSON EDUCATION LIMITED

Edinburgh Gate
Harlow CM20 2JE
Tel: +44 (0)1279 623623
Fax: +44 (0)1279 431059
Website: www.pearson.com/uk

First published in Great Britain in 2012

© Bernard Marr 2012

The right of Bernard Marr to be identified as author of this work has been asserted by him in accordance with the Copyright, Designs and Patents Act 1988.

Pearson Education is not responsible for the content of third-party internet sites.

ISBN: 978-0-273-75011-6

British Library Cataloguing-in-Publication Data
A catalogue record for this book is available from the British Library

Library of Congress Cataloging-in-Publication Data
Innes, James, 1975–
Marr, Bernard.
  Key performance indicators : the 75 measures every manager needs to know / Bernard Marr. -- 1st ed.
    p. cm.
  Includes bibliographical references and index.
  ISBN 978-0-273-75011-6 (pbk.)
  1. Performance technology--Management. 2. Performance standards. 3. Organizational effectiveness. I. Title.
  HF5549.5.P37M37 2012
  658.4'013--dc23
                              2011050789

All rights reserved. No part of this publication may be reproduced, stored in a retrieval system, or transmitted in any form or by any means, electronic, mechanical, photo-copying, recording or otherwise, without either the prior written permission of the publisher or a licence permitting restricted copying in the United Kingdom issued by the Copyright Licensing Agency Ltd, Saffron House, 6–10 Kirby Street, London EC1N 8TS. This book may not be lent, resold, hired out or otherwise disposed of by way of trade in any form of binding or cover other than that in which it is published, without the prior consent of the publisher.

All trademarks used herein are the property of their respective owners. The use of any trademark in this text does not vest in the author or publisher any trademark ownership rights in such trademarks, nor does the use of such trademarks imply any affiliation with or endorsement of this book by such owners.

11
17

Typeset in 9.25pt Swiss Light by 3
Printed and bound in Malaysia, CTP-PJB

Numbers are the product of counting, but there is so much more to life that we can't count.

I dedicate this book to the four people who give me meaning and happiness beyond measure:

My wife Claire and our three children Sophia, James and Oliver

Contents

Introduction xxv

PART ONE Financial perspective 1

1 Net profit 3
Why is this indicator important? 3
How do I measure it? 4
Cost/effort in collecting the data 4
Target setting/benchmarks 4
Tips/warnings 7
References 7

2 Net profit margin 9
Why is this indicator important? 9
How do I measure it? 10
Cost/effort in collecting the data 10
Target setting/benchmarks 10
Tips/warnings 11
References 11

3 Gross profit margin 13
Why is this indicator important? 13
How do I measure it? 14
Cost/effort in collecting the data 14
Target setting/benchmarks 14
Tips/warnings 15
References 16

4 Operating profit margin 17
Why is this indicator important? 17
How do I measure it? 18
Cost/effort in collecting the data 18
Target setting/benchmarks 18

Tips/warnings 19
References 19

5 EBITDA 21
Why is this indicator important? 21
How do I measure it? 22
Cost/effort in collecting the data 22
Target setting/benchmarks 22
Tips/warnings 23
References 24

6 Revenue growth rate 25
Why is this indicator important? 25
How do I measure it? 26
Cost/effort in collecting the data 26
Target setting/benchmarks 27
Tips/warnings 27
References 28

7 Total shareholder return (TSR) 29
Why is this indicator important? 29
How do I measure it? 30
Cost/effort in collecting the data 30
Target setting/benchmarks 30
Tips/warnings 31
References 31

8 Economic value added (EVA) 33
Why is this indicator important? 33
How do I measure it? 34
Cost/effort in collecting the data 35
Target setting/benchmarks 35
Tips/warnings 37
References 37

9 Return on investment (ROI) 39
Why is this indicator important? 39
How do I measure it? 40
Cost/effort in collecting the data 41
Target setting/benchmarks 41
Tips/warnings 42

References 43

10 Return on capital employed (ROCE) 45
Why is this indicator important? 45
How do I measure it? 46
Cost/effort in collecting the data 46
Target setting/benchmarks 46
Tips/warnings 48
References 48

11 Return on assets (ROA) 49
Why is this indicator important? 49
How do I measure it? 50
Cost/effort in collecting the data 50
Target setting/benchmarks 50
Tips/warnings 51
References 51

12 Return on equity (ROE) 53
Why is this indicator important? 53
How do I measure it? 54
Cost/effort in collecting the data 54
Target setting/benchmarks 54
Tips/warnings 55
References 55

13 Debt-to-equity (D/E) ratio 57
Why is this indicator important? 57
How do I measure it? 58
Cost/effort in collecting the data 58
Target setting/benchmarks 59
Tips/warnings 60
References 60

14 Cash conversion cycle (CCC) 61
Why is this indicator important? 61
How do I measure it? 62
Cost/effort in collecting the data 63
Target setting/benchmarks 63
Tips/warnings 65
References 65

15 | Working capital ratio 67
Why is this indicator important? 67
How do I measure it? 68
Cost/effort in collecting the data 69
Target setting/benchmarks 69
Tips/warnings 70
References 70

16 | Operating expense ratio (OER) 71
Why is this indicator important? 71
How do I measure it? 72
Cost/effort in collecting the data 72
Target setting/benchmarks 72
Tips/warnings 73
References 73

17 | CAPEX to sales ratio 75
Why is this indicator important? 75
How do I measure it? 76
Cost/effort in collecting the data 76
Target setting/benchmarks 76
Tips/warnings 77
References 77

18 | Price/earnings ratio (P/E ratio) 79
Why is this indicator important? 79
How do I measure it? 80
Cost/effort in collecting the data 80
Target setting/benchmarks 80
Tips/warnings 81
References 81

PART TWO Customer perspective 83

19 | Net promoter score (NPS) 85
Why is this indicator important? 85
How do I measure it? 86
Cost/effort in collecting the data 87
Target setting/benchmarks 87

Tips/warnings 89
References 89

20 Customer retention rate 91
Why is this indicator important? 91
How do I measure it? 92
Cost/effort in collecting the data 93
Target setting/benchmarks 93
Tips/warnings 94
References 95

21 Customer satisfaction index 97
Why is this indicator important? 97
How do I measure it? 98
Cost/effort in collecting the data 99
Target setting/benchmarks 99
Tips/warnings 100
References 101

22 Customer profitability score 103
Why is this indicator important? 103
How do I measure it? 104
Cost/effort in collecting the data 105
Target setting/benchmarks 105
Tips/warnings 106
References 106

23 Customer lifetime value 107
Why is this indicator important? 107
How do I measure it? 108
Cost/effort in collecting the data 109
Target setting/benchmarks 110
Tips/warnings 110
References 111

24 Customer turnover rate 113
Why is this indicator important? 113
How do I measure it? 114
Cost/effort in collecting the data 115
Target setting/benchmarks 116
Tips/warnings 116

References 116

25 Customer engagement 117
Why is this indicator important? 117
How do I measure it? 118
Cost/effort in collecting the data 119
Target setting/benchmarks 119
Tips/warnings 120
References 120

26 Customer complaints 121
Why is this indicator important? 121
How do I measure it? 122
Cost/effort in collecting the data 123
Target setting/benchmarks 123
Tips/warnings 125
References 125

PART THREE Marketing and sales perspective 127

27 Market growth rate 129
Why is this indicator important? 129
How do I measure it? 130
Cost/effort in collecting the data 130
Target setting/benchmarks 130
Tips/warnings 131
References 131

28 Relative market share 133
Why is this indicator important? 133
How do I measure it? 134
Cost/effort in collecting the data 135
Target setting/benchmarks 135
Tips/warnings 136
References 137

29 Brand equity 139
Why is this indicator important? 139
How do I measure it? 140

Cost/effort in collecting the data 141
Target setting/benchmarks 141
Tips/warnings 142
References 142

30 Cost per lead 143
Why is this indicator important? 143
How do I measure it? 144
Cost/effort in collecting the data 144
Target setting/benchmarks 144
Tips/warnings 146
References 146

31 Conversion rate 147
Why is this indicator important? 147
How do I measure it? 148
Cost/effort in collecting the data 149
Target setting/benchmarks 149
Tips/warnings 150
References 150

32 Search engine rankings (by keyword) and click-through rate 151
Why is this indicator important? 151
How do I measure it? 152
Cost/effort in collecting the data 152
Target setting/benchmarks 152
Tips/warnings 153
References 153

33 Page views and bounce rates 155
Why is this indicator important? 155
How do I measure it? 156
Cost/effort in collecting the data 157
Target setting/benchmarks 157
Tips/warnings 158
References 158

34 Customer online engagement level 159
Why is this indicator important? 159
How do I measure it? 160

Cost/effort in collecting the data 162
Target setting/benchmarks 162
Tips/warnings 163
References 163

35 Online share of voice (OSOV) 165
Why is this indicator important? 165
How do I measure it? 166
Cost/effort in collecting the data 166
Target setting/benchmarks 167
Tips/warnings 168
References 168

36 Social networking footprint 169
Why is this indicator important? 169
How do I measure it? 170
Cost/effort in collecting the data 171
Target setting/benchmarks 171
Tips/warnings 172
References 173

37 Klout score 175
Why is this indicator important? 175
How do I measure it? 176
Cost/effort in collecting the data 176
Target setting/benchmarks 176
Tips/warnings 177
References 177

PART FOUR Operational processes and supply chain perspective 179

38 Six Sigma level 181
Why is this indicator important? 181
How do I measure it? 182
Cost/effort in collecting the data 183
Target setting/benchmarks 183
Tips/warnings 184
References 184

39 | Capacity utilisation rate (CUR) 185
Why is this indicator important? 185
How do I measure it? 186
Cost/effort in collecting the data 186
Target setting/benchmarks 187
Tips/warnings 187
References 187

40 | Process waste level 189
Why is this indicator important? 189
How do I measure it? 190
Cost/effort in collecting the data 191
Target setting/benchmarks 192
Tips/warnings 192
References 192

41 | Order fulfilment cycle time (OFCT) 193
Why is this indicator important? 193
How do I measure it? 194
Cost/effort in collecting the data 194
Target setting/benchmarks 194
Tips/warnings 195
References 195

42 | Delivery in full, on time (DIFOT) rate 197
Why is this indicator important? 197
How do I measure it? 198
Cost/effort in collecting the data 198
Target setting/benchmarks 199
Tips/warnings 200
References 200

43 | Inventory shrinkage rate (ISR) 201
Why is this indicator important? 201
How do I measure it? 202
Cost/effort in collecting the data 202
Target setting/benchmarks 202
Tips/warnings 203
References 203

44 | Project schedule variance (PSV) 205
Why is this indicator important? 205
How do I measure it? 206
Cost/effort in collecting the data 207
Target setting/benchmarks 207
Tips/warnings 207
References 208

45 | Project cost variance (PCV) 209
Why is this indicator important? 209
How do I measure it? 210
Cost/effort in collecting the data 210
Target setting/benchmarks 211
Tips/warnings 211
References 211

46 | Earned value (EV) metric 213
Why is this indicator important? 213
How do I measure it? 214
Cost/effort in collecting the data 214
Target setting/benchmarks 214
Tips/warnings 215
References 216

47 | Innovation pipeline strength (IPS) 217
Why is this indicator important? 217
How do I measure it? 218
Cost/effort in collecting the data 218
Target setting/benchmarks 218
Tips/warnings 220
References 220

48 | Return on innovation investment (ROI^2) 221
Why is this indicator important? 221
How do I measure it? 222
Cost/effort in collecting the data 222
Target setting/benchmarks 223
Tips/warnings 223
References 223

49 Time to market 225
Why is this indicator important? 225
How do I measure it? 226
Cost/effort in collecting the data 227
Target setting/benchmarks 227
Tips/warnings 228
References 228

50 First pass yield (FPY) 229
Why is this indicator important? 229
How do I measure it? 230
Cost/effort in collecting the data 230
Target setting/benchmarks 231
Tips/warnings 231
References 232

51 Rework level 233
Why is this indicator important? 233
How do I measure it? 234
Cost/effort in collecting the data 235
Target setting/benchmarks 235
Tips/warnings 236
References 236

52 Quality index 237
Why is this indicator important? 237
How do I measure it? 238
Cost/effort in collecting the data 239
Target setting/benchmarks 239
Tips/warnings 239
References 240

53 Overall equipment effectiveness (OEE) 241
Why is this indicator important? 241
How do I measure it? 242
Cost/effort in collecting the data 242
Target setting/benchmarks 243
Tips/warnings 244
References 245

54 | Process or machine downtime level 247
Why is this indicator important? 247
How do I measure it? 248
Cost/effort in collecting the data 248
Target setting/benchmarks 249
Tips/warnings 249
References 249

55 | First contact resolution (FCR) 251
Why is this indicator important? 251
How do I measure it? 252
Cost/effort in collecting the data 253
Target setting/benchmarks 253
Tips/warnings 254
References 254

PART FIVE Employee perspective 255

56 | Human capital value added (HCVA) 257
Why is this indicator important? 257
How do I measure it? 258
Cost/effort in collecting the data 258
Target setting/benchmarks 258
Tips/warnings 259
References 259

57 | Revenue per employee (RPE) 261
Why is this indicator important? 261
How do I measure it? 262
Cost/effort in collecting the data 262
Target setting/benchmarks 262
Tips/warnings 263
References 264

58 | Employee satisfaction index 265
Why is this indicator important? 265
How do I measure it? 266
Cost/effort in collecting the data 267
Target setting/benchmarks 267

Tips/warnings 268
References 268

59 Employee engagement level 269
Why is this indicator important? 269
How do I measure it? 270
Cost/effort in collecting the data 271
Target setting/benchmarks 271
Tips/warnings 272
References 272

60 Staff advocacy score 273
Why is this indicator important? 273
How do I measure it? 274
Cost/effort in collecting the data 275
Target setting/benchmarks 275
Tips/warnings 276
References 276

61 Employee churn rate 277
Why is this indicator important? 277
How do I measure it? 278
Cost/effort in collecting the data 278
Target setting/benchmarks 278
Tips/warnings 279
References 280

62 Average employee tenure 281
Why is this indicator important? 281
How do I measure it? 282
Cost/effort in collecting the data 282
Target setting/benchmarks 282
Tips/warnings 283
References 284

63 Absenteeism Bradford factor 285
Why is this indicator important? 285
How do I measure it? 286
Cost/effort in collecting the data 287
Target setting/benchmarks 287
Tips/warnings 288

References 288

64 360-degree feedback score 289
Why is this indicator important? 289
How do I measure it? 290
Cost/effort in collecting the data 291
Target setting/benchmarks 291
Tips/warnings 292
References 293

65 Salary competitiveness ratio (SCR) 295
Why is this indicator important? 295
How do I measure it? 296
Cost/effort in collecting the data 297
Target setting/benchmarks 297
Tips/warnings 297
References 298

66 Time to hire 299
Why is this indicator important? 299
How do I measure it? 300
Cost/effort in collecting the data 300
Target setting/benchmarks 300
Tips/warnings 301
References 301

67 Training return on investment 303
Why is this indicator important? 303
How do I measure it? 304
Cost/effort in collecting the data 306
Target setting/benchmarks 306
Tips/warnings 307
References 307

PART SIX Corporate social responsibility perspective 309

68 Carbon footprint 311
Why is this indicator important? 311
How do I measure it? 312

Cost/effort in collecting the data 313
Target setting/benchmarks 313
Tips/warnings 315
References 315

69 | **Water footprint** 317
Why is this indicator important? 317
How do I measure it? 318
Cost/effort in collecting the data 319
Target setting/benchmarks 319
Tips/warnings 320
References 320

70 | **Energy consumption** 321
Why is this indicator important? 321
How do I measure it? 322
Cost/effort in collecting the data 322
Target setting/benchmarks 322
Tips/warnings 323
References 323

71 | **Savings levels due to conservation and improvement efforts** 325
Why is this indicator important? 325
How do I measure it? 326
Cost/effort in collecting the data 326
Target setting/benchmarks 326
Tips/warnings 327
References 327

72 | **Supply chain miles** 329
Why is this indicator important? 329
How do I measure it? 330
Cost/effort in collecting the data 330
Target setting/benchmarks 330
Tips/warnings 331
References 331

73 | **Waste reduction rate** 333
Why is this indicator important? 333
How do I measure it? 334

Cost/effort in collecting the data 335
Target setting/benchmarks 335
Tips/warnings 335
References 336

74 | Waste recycling rate 337
Why is this indicator important? 337
How do I measure it? 338
Cost/effort in collecting the data 338
Target setting/benchmarks 338
Tips/warnings 339
References 339

75 | Product recycling rate 341
Why is this indicator important? 341
How do I measure it? 342
Cost/effort in collecting the data 342
Target setting/benchmarks 342
Tips/warnings 343
References 343

Index 344

Introduction

KPIs are vital management tools

Key performance indicators (KPIs) are the vital navigation instruments used by managers to understand whether their business is on a successful voyage or whether it is veering off the prosperous path. The right set of indicators will shine light on performance and highlight areas that need attention. 'What gets measured gets done' and 'if you can't measure it, you can't manage it' are just two of the popular sayings used to highlight the critical importance of metrics. Without the right KPIs managers are sailing blind.

The problem is that most managers are struggling to understand and identify the vital few management metrics and instead collect and report a vast amount of everything that is easy to measure. As a consequence they end up drowning in data while thirsting for information.

Effective managers and decision makers understand the performance of all key dimensions of their business by distilling them down into the critical KPIs. Not understanding key metrics can often cause anxiety and can hold people back. This book will demystify and explain in simple terms the most important KPIs in use today. It will equip you with the skills to understand, measure and interpret the most important aspects of any business.

How to use this book

You can use this book in two ways: as an essential reference guide that allows you to look up the KPIs you want to understand and learn more about as and when you need it; or you can use it to help you complete your performance management framework, business dashboard, balanced scorecard or business intelligence strategy.

Performance frameworks, dashboards or scorecards are used by companies to group KPIs together into displays or reports so that they provide at-a-glance overviews of how the business (or business units) is performing. To facilitate the design of dashboards and scorecards, the KPIs in this book are grouped into the following key business perspectives that are shared across most organisations, irrespective of type or industry sector:

- Financial perspective
- Customer perspective
- Marketing and sales perspective

- Operational processes and supply chain perspective
- Employee perspective
- Corporate social responsibility perspective

Each KPI in this book is described using the same framework outlining why the KPI is important and what it measures, how the data are collected and how it is calculated. Each KPI description also includes a practical example as well as tips on data sources, target setting and benchmarking, measurement frequency, pitfalls, cost and effort of creating the data, and references.

KPIs have to measure what matters

For KPIs to be the vital navigation instruments that help you understand whether your business is on the right track or not, we have first to define the strategy and then closely link our KPIs to that. Too many organisations fall into the trap of retrofitting objectives to existing and established metrics: which is simply back to front. KPI development has to start with your strategy and the objectives the business is aiming to achieve.

I spend most of my life helping organisations define their strategy, develop dashboards and scorecards, and develop the KPIs they need to monitor and manage their business. If you would like practical step-by-step guidance on how to develop and use a performance management system, I would refer you to my most recent books, *The Intelligent Company* (for commercial companies) and *More with Less* (for government and not-for-profit organisations). They will guide you through the process and make a perfect companion to this book.

One important point I make in my other books that is worth repeating here is that KPIs need to give us information and answers to what we need to know. What we have to make sure is that we know what our information needs are and what questions we want answered before we introduce any KPIs. This is why I have developed the concept of Key Performance Questions or KPQs for short. A KPQ is a management question that captures exactly what it is that managers need to know. The rationale for KPQs is that they focus our attention on what actually matters most and therefore provide guidance for choosing the most meaningful KPIs.

Many of my clients now use the concept of KPQs in anger to guide their KPI selection and to provide context for their KPI reporting. Take Google for instance – one of today's most successful and most admired companies. Google's executive chairman Eric Schmidt now says: 'We run the company by questions, not by answers. So in the strategy process we've so far formulated 30 questions that we have to answer […] You ask it as a question, rather than a pithy answer, and that stimulates conversation.'

In this book I have created a KPQ for each KPI that is included. This gives you further context for each KPI and provides you with a starting point for using KPQs in your own business.

Your unique set of KPIs

I have always stressed the importance of designing KPIs based on your own unique circumstances and information needs. However, what I have learnt over the many years of helping leading companies and government organisations with their performance management and business intelligence is that there are some important (and innovative) KPIs everyone should know about. They will give you a solid base of knowledge. However, there will be other, more specialised measures designed for your specific strategy or industry context. Take, for example, the network performance KPIs for a telecom operator or the quality indicators for healthcare providers. These will have to be included in your list of KPIs but will not be found in this book, at least not in their industry-specific format. For a wide-ranging list of business metrics I would like to refer you to the online KPI Library of the Advanced Performance Institute (**www.ap-institute.com**). There you will also find relevant white papers and case studies on the topic.

A final note: management is not a numbers game

It might seem strange to end the introductory chapter of this book by stating that KPIs should *not* primarily be about measurement. Rather, the focus should be on selecting a robust set of value-adding indicators that serve as the beginning of a rich performance discussion focused on the delivery of your strategy.

Let me make the point that management is not a numbers game. There is a real temptation that managers will run their company on the KPI data they are receiving. What I want you to remember is that behind every number are real people, such as customers who have purchased goods or services or employees who are satisfied or not. Always make sure you look behind the face value of your KPIs to get a real sense of their meaning.

Publisher's acknowledgements

We are grateful to the following for permission to reproduce copyright material:

Example on p36 adapted from 'Building and Communicating Shareholder Value', *Business Intelligence* (2000), with kind permission of James Creelman; Example on p60 adapted from KPI 13 (D/E ratio), www.fool.com/investing/value/2007/06/20/using-the-debt-to-equity-ratio.aspx, © 2007 The Motley Fool, LLC (www.fool.com); Table on p134 adapted from www.bcg.com. Adapted from The BCG Portfolio Matrix. From the Product Portfolio Matrix, © 1970, The Boston Consulting Group; Table on pp 141–2 adapted from www.interbrand.com, Interbrand, 2010; Example on p162 adapted from http://marketingroi.wordpress.com/2007/10/02/customer-engagement-is-measurable/, with kind permission of Ron Shevlin; Extract on p190 from www.sprickstegall.com/blog-the-laboratory-strategy-space. 8 Lean Wastes-3 Optional Metrics for Each. Author: Susan Stegall. Posted January 27, 2010, Susan Stegall and Leslie Sprick (Sprickstegall); Example on p195 adapted from http://Satistar.com/Whitepapers/Cycle%20Time%20Reduction.pdf, with kind permission of SatiStar Corporation; Table on p235 adapted from www.oee.com, Vorne Industries, Inc.; Example on p306 adapted from Building and Developing an HR Scorecard, *Business Intelligence* (James Creelman 2001), with kind permission of James Creelman; Table on p323 adapted from www.ntu.ac.uk/ecoweb/document_uploads/94617.pdf

In some instances we have been unable to trace the owners of copyright material, and we would appreciate any information that would enable us to do so.

[PART ONE]

Financial perspective

Net profit

Strategic perspective

Financial perspective

Key performance question this indicator helps to answer

To what extent are we generating bottom-line results?

Why is this indicator important?

Profits are important for all businesses regardless of whether they are in the private or public sector. Simply put: the very nature of business is to produce goods or services that you can sell for a financial return or reward. Taking away the costs of producing goods and providing services from the revenue or sales you are generating will leave you with your profits.

For any business, net profit (also referred to as net income) typically represents the most important measure of performance. Net profit shows us whether there is still any money left over after deducting all costs and expenses. The profits can then be reinvested to grow the company (called retained earnings) and used to pay a return to the company's owners or shareholders (called dividends).

It is vital for managers and investors to know whether their company's activities translate into bottom-line performance. For instance, a company can have great sales figures but if they don't generate a surplus then the company will soon be in trouble.

How do I measure it?

Data collection method

The data for the net profit metric are collected from the income statement (see the example on the next page).

Formula

$$\text{Net profit (\$)} = \text{Sales revenue (\$)} - \text{Total costs (\$)}$$

Here is how you reach net profit on a P&L (Profit & Loss) account:

1. Sales revenue = Price (of product) × Quantity sold
2. Gross profit = Sales revenue − Cost of sales and other direct costs
3. Operating profit (EBIT, earnings before interest and taxes) = Gross profit − Overheads and other indirect costs
4. Pretax profit (EBT, earnings before taxes) = Operating profit − One-off items and redundancy payments, staff restructuring − Interest payable
5. **Net profit** = Pre-tax profit − Tax
6. Retained earnings = Net profit − Dividends

Frequency

Net profit is usually measured each month as part of income statement preparation.

Source of the data

The net profit data are extracted from the readily available accounting data.

Cost/effort in collecting the data

The costs of producing the net profit measure are usually low as long as a company has the relevant accounting information available. As most companies hold this data in existing accounting systems it is just a matter of adding a calculation routine to the existing system.

Target setting/benchmarks

Net profit margins vary by industry, but all else being equal, the higher a company's net profits the better.

Example Consider the following two examples. The first explains in narrative form how Donna Manufacturing (a fictitious company) calculates net profit, while the second provides an income statement example from Grande Corporation (also fictitious).

In 2011, Donna Manufacturing sold 100,000 widgets for $5 each, with a cost of goods sold of $2 each. It had $150,000 in operating expenses, and paid $52,500 in income taxes.

To calculate the net profit the organisation first needs to find the revenue or total sales. If Donna's sold 100,000 widgets at $5 each, it generated a total of $500,000 in revenue. The company's cost of goods sold was $2 per widget; 100,000 widgets at $2 each is equal to $200,000 in costs. This leaves a gross profit of $300,000 ($500k revenue − $200k cost of goods sold). Subtracting $150,000 in operating expenses from the $300,000 gross profit leaves us with $150,000 income before taxes. Subtracting the tax bill of $52,500, we are left with a net profit of $97,500.

Grande Corporation

Income Statement for Year Ending 31 December 2011	
Figures in 1,000s	
Gross sales revenues	33,329
Less returns & allowances	346
Net sales revenues	32,983
Cost of goods sold	
Direct materials	6,320
Direct labour	6,100
Manufacturing overhead	
Indirect labour	5,263
Depreciation, mfr equip	360
Other mfr overhead	4,000
Net mfr overhead	9,623
Net cost of goods sold	22,043
Gross profit	10,940
Operating expenses	
Selling expenses	

Income Statement for Year Ending 31 December 2011

Sales salaries	4,200
Warranty expenses	730
Depreciation, store equip	120
Other selling expenses	972
Total selling expenses	6,022
General & admin expenses	
Administration salaries	1,229
Rent expenses	180
Depreciation, computers	179
Other gen'l & admin exp	200
Total gen'l & admin exp	1,788
Total operating expenses	7,810
Operating income before taxes	3,130
Financial revenue & expenses	
Revenue from investments	118
Less interest expense	511
Net financial gain (expense)	(393)
Income before tax & extraordinary items	2,737
Less income tax on operations	958
Income before extraordinary items	1,779
Extraordinary items	
Sale of land	610
Less initial cost	145
Net gain on sale of land	465
Less income tax on gain	118
Extraordinary items after tax	347
Net profit (income)	**2,126**

Tips/warnings

Net profit is one of a range of profitability metrics designed to answer questions such as: 'is the company profitable?', 'is it making good use of its assets?', 'is it producing value for its shareholders?' and 'is the company able to survive and grow?'. On its own it will not give you the full picture and other important profitability metrics such as profit margins, operating profit, return on assets and return on equity will have to be looked at too.

Also, net profit can be measured by business unit or even by product or service, which often gives more interesting insights. The main complication with this is when overhead costs (such as head office staff costs, rent, utility costs, etc.) need to be allocated across business units. Almost by definition, overheads are costs that cannot be directly allocated to any specific business unit, product or service. Companies have to find the most suitable way of splitting overhead costs while avoiding overcomplicating the calculations.

Finally, proponents of economic profit calculations, such as economic value added (EVA, see later in this part), argue that conventional accounting metrics (such as net profit and other traditional profitability metrics) give a distorted view of an organisation's value-creation capabilities and underlying performance. The main argument is that a traditional profit figure does not take into account the cost of capital, and therefore essentially treats capital as being 'free'. What they are highlighting is that if an organisation is driving performance purely from a profit viewpoint then capital is a critical resource to the business that is not being reflected in the value calculation. An organisation might be generating profit and not creating any value because it is not covering the cost of the investment to generate those resources, they argue.

References

www.investopedia.com/terms/n/netincome.asp

Net profit margin 2

Strategic perspective
Financial perspective

Key performance question this indicator helps to answer
How much profit are we generating for each dollar in sales?

Why is this indicator important?

With the previous KPI we looked at net profit as a total number. In order to make net profits more comparable and to understand how much profit a company makes for each dollar in revenue we can produce the net profit margin (also referred to as return on sales or net income margin), which takes the net profit of a company as a ratio over its total sales or revenues.

The net profit margin is therefore a key indicator of how well a company is run (i.e. how efficient it is and how well it controls its costs), as a low net profit margin could indicate too high operating costs or a wrong pricing structure.

Low net profit margins mean that a company has a lower 'margin of safety' and that small changes such as a slight decline in sales or a rise in operating expenses, e.g. higher fuel or electricity bills or a hike in raw material prices, could quickly diminish any returns and turn the company from a profitable business to a loss-maker.

For managers, net profit margins are particularly useful when compared over time and relative to other companies in the same sector. Investors often compare net profit margins across industries to identify the most profitable and attractive sectors and companies to invest in.

How do I measure it?

Data collection method

The data for the net profit margin metric are collected from the income statement (see previous KPI).

Formula

$$\text{Net profit margin} = \left(\frac{\text{Net profit}}{\text{Revenues}}\right) \times 100$$

Frequency

Usually measured each month as part of the income statement preparation.

Source of the data

The net profit and revenue data are extracted from the accounting data.

Cost/effort in collecting the data

The costs of producing the net profit measure are usually low as long as a company has the relevant accounting information available. As most companies hold this data in existing accounting systems it is just a matter of adding a calculation routine to the existing system.

Target setting/benchmarks

Net profit margins vary by industry, but all else being equal, the higher a company's profit margin compared to its competitors, the better. As a very general ball-park benchmark (which will depend a lot on the industry), a net profit margin of between 20% and 40% is considered to be very good. Here are some examples of the most profitable companies in the S&P 500 (a listing of the biggest and best public companies in America):

- Public Storage (NYSE:PSA) = 46.14%
- Corning Incorporated (NYSE:GLW) = 45.65%
- Altera Corporation (NASDAQ:ALTR) = 40.97%
- Linear Technology Corporation (NASDAQ:LLTC) – 39.14%
- CME Group Inc. (NASDAQ:CME) = 37.20%

The average net profit margin for all S&P 500 companies is around 10%.

Example In the previous KPI description we calculated the net profit and net sales revenues for Grande Corporation based on its income statement (see pages 5–6).

To get to the net profit margin we simply divide the two numbers as follows:

$$\text{Net profit margin} = \frac{\text{Net profit}}{\text{Net sales revenues}}$$

$$\text{Net profit margin} = \frac{\$2,126,000}{\$32,983,000}$$

Net profit margin = 6.4%

Tips/warnings

As with net profits, net profit margins can also be measured by business unit or even by product or service, which often gives more interesting insights.

References

www.investopedia.com/terms/p/profitmargin.asp

www.in-business.org.uk/formula-for-calculating-net-profit-margin/

www.ccdconsultants.com/documentation/financial-ratios/net-profit-margin-interpretation.html

Gross profit margin   3

> **Strategic perspective**
> Financial perspective
>
> **Key performance question this indicator helps to answer**
> How much profit are we generating for each dollar in sales?

Why is this indicator important?

Another profitability ratio which is widely used is the gross profit margin. Instead of the net profit margin, where we are deducting all costs from the revenue, here we are only deducting the cost of goods sold (sometimes referred to as cost of sales). Costs of goods are the direct production and distribution costs a company incurs for supplies, inventory, production and distribution of their products or services.

Looking at how much it costs a company to produce its goods and services and putting this in relation to sales revenue gives us a ratio of production efficiency. A gross profit margin of 30% would indicate that for each dollar in sales, the company spent 70 cents in direct costs to produce the good or service that the firm sold.

The gross profit margin basically shows us how much from each dollar of a company's revenue is left after taking away the cost of goods sold, and therefore how much money is available to cover overhead, other expenses and of course retained earnings and dividends. This also means that gross profit margin should be much higher than the net profit margin (see previous KPI).

A high gross profit margin would indicate that a company is likely to make a reasonable profit as long as it keeps the remaining costs under control. A low gross profit margin on the other hand would indicate that the production costs are too high and that its production efficiency is not managed to an appropriate level.

For managers, gross profit margins are particularly useful when compared over time and relative to other companies in the same sector. Investors often compare gross profit margins across industries to identify the most profitable and attractive sectors and companies to invest in.

How do I measure it?

Data collection method

The data for gross profit margin are captured through the monthly management accounting process and reported in the Profit and Loss statement.

Formula

$$\text{Gross profit margin} = \left(\frac{\text{(Revenue} - \text{Cost of goods sold)}}{\text{Revenues}}\right) \times 100$$

Frequency

Total gross profit margin is calculated monthly as part of the normal management reporting cycle.

Source of the data

The revenue and cost of goods sold are extracted from the accounting data.

Cost/effort in collecting the data

Calculating gross profit margin is a standard measurement within commercial organisations and there is no cost or effort required in collecting the data above, which are needed for monthly and other period accounting purposes.

Target setting/benchmarks

Gross profit margins vary by industry, but all else being equal, the higher a company's profit margin compared to its competitors, the better. In some industries, like clothing for example, gross profit margins are expected to be near the 40% mark, as the goods need to be bought from suppliers at a certain rate before they are resold. In other industries such as software product development, where the cost of duplication is negligible, the gross profit margin can be higher than 80%.

Also, a company's gross profit margin should be stable. It should not fluctuate much from one period to another, unless the industry in which it operates has been undergoing drastic changes which will affect the cost of goods sold or pricing policies.

> **Example** Simply put, gross profit margin represents the difference between total sales and the cost of those sales.
> For example: If total sales equal $1,000 and cost of sales equals $300, then the margin equal $700.
> Gross profit margin can be expressed as a monetary value or as a percentage. As a percentage, the gross profit margin is stated as a percentage of revenues.
> The equation: (Revenue − Cost of goods sold)/Revenue = Gross profit margin. Using the preceding example, the margin would be 70%.
>
> $$\frac{(\$1,000 - \$300)}{\$1,000} \times 100 = 70\%$$
>
> Basically, 70% gross profit margin means that for every dollar generated in sales, the company has 70 cents left over to cover other expenses and profit.

Tips/warnings

Although an important corporate measure, better performance insights can be gleaned by analysing gross profit margin at the business unit, department or product level. This can provide useful data on the real drivers of profit within the enterprise.

It is also worth bearing in mind that markup and gross profit margin on a single product, or group of products, are not, as many erroneously believe, the same thing. Gross profit margin is a percentage of the selling price, while markup is traditionally figured as a percentage of the seller's cost.

Using the numbers from the preceding example, if an organisation purchases goods for $300 and prices them for sale at $1,000, the markup is $700. As a percentage, this markup comes to 233%:

$$\frac{(\$1,000 - \$300)}{\$300} \times 100 = 233\%$$

In other words, if your business requires a 70% margin to show a profit, your average markup will have to be 233%.

This example shows that although markup and margin may be the same in dollars ($700), they represent two different concepts as percentages (233% versus 70%). More than a few new businesses have failed to make their expected profits because the owners assumed that if their markup is X%, their margin will also be X%. This is not the case.

References

www.investopedia.com/articles/fundamental/04/042804.asp#axzz1U9QWeAQD

http://bizfinance.about.com/od/financialratios/a/Profitability_Ratios.htm

http://beginnersinvest.about.com/od/incomestatementanalysis/a/gross-profit-margin.htm

www.ccdconsultants.com/documentation/financial-ratios/gross-profit-margin-interpretation.html

Operating profit margin
4

> **Strategic perspective**
> Financial perspective
>
> **Key performance question this indicator helps to answer**
> To what extent are we operating our business efficiently?

Why is this indicator important?

Another profitability measure used in companies is the operating profit margin (or operating margin for short). It can provide insights into a company's operating efficiency and pricing strategy. By dividing the operating income by revenue it measures the proportion of revenue that remains after deducting the costs of operating the business, including costs for labour, raw material, overhead, depreciation, amortisation, selling, advertising, admin, etc.).

Because operating income includes only the sales revenue from regular business operations (and not revenues from extraordinary items, taxes, and interest on long-term liabilities), the ratio provides an insight into the profitability of sales generated from regular operations of the business.

Basically, it tells how much money a company makes (before interest and taxes) on each dollar of sales. The operating profit margin can be used to understand whether the costs of operating a business are too high for the production or sales volume (especially when compared to similar companies in the same sector). If companies have a high operating profit margin compared to competitors, this can often indicate that it was able to create a lower-cost operating model. The example that is often used is Wal-Mart, which owing to its warehouse and distribution efficiency is able to reduce the costs of getting products into its shops.

High operating profit margins show that a company is managing its operating costs well. If management is able to increase the operating profit margin over time then this shows that the company is earning more per dollar of sales, or that sales are increasing faster than operating costs.

How do I measure it?

Data collection method

The data for the operating profit margin are captured through the monthly management accounting process and reported in the income statement.

Formula

$$\text{Operating profit margin} = \left(\frac{\text{Operating profit}}{\text{Revenue}}\right) \times 100$$

Where the Operating profit = EBIT (Earnings before interest and taxes).

Frequency

Operating profit margin is usually calculated monthly or quarterly as part of the normal management reporting cycle.

Source of the data

The revenue and cost of goods sold are extracted from the accounting data.

Cost/effort in collecting the data

Calculating operating profit margin is a standard measurement within commercial organisations and there is no cost or effort required in collecting the data above, which are needed for monthly and other period accounting purposes.

Target setting/benchmarks

Operating profit margins vary by industry, but all else being equal, the higher a company's operating profit margin compared to its competitors, the better. Here are some benchmarks from some of the most profitable companies in the S&P 500:

- Public Storage (NYSE:PSA) = 42.17%
- Corning Incorporated (NYSE:GLW) = 24.96%

- Altera Corporation (NASDAQ:ALTR) = 45.46%
- Linear Technology Corporation (NASDAQ:LLTC) = 51.42%
- Visa Inc. (NYSE:V) = 57.93%

Overall, S&P 500 companies average an operating profit margin of around 15%.

Example Here is an example calculation with figures taken from the Consolidated Statements of Income:

(In millions)	
Revenue	$20,000
EBIT	$4,000

$$\text{Operating Profit Margin} = \left(\frac{4,000}{20,000}\right) \times 100 = 20\%$$

Tips/warnings

Operating profit margin is a measure that can be used to compare companies that do not issue a separate disclosure of their cost of goods sold figures (which are needed to calculate the gross profit margin).

References

http://beginnersinvest.about.com/od/incomestatementanalysis/a/operating-income-operating-margin.htm

www.investopedia.com/articles/stocks/08/operating-margins.asp#axzz1UA03Rbu5

www.wikinvest.com/metric/Operating_Margin

www.investopedia.com/articles/fundamental/04/042804.asp#axzz1U9QWeAQD

EBITDA

5

> **Strategic perspective**
> Financial perspective
>
> **Key performance question this indicator helps to answer**
> To what extent are we operating our business efficiently to generate profits?

Why is this indicator important?

Another financial performance indicator is EBITDA, or Earnings Before Interest, Taxes, Depreciation and Amortisation. It is essentially taking sales revenue and subtracting all expenses other than interest, taxes, depreciation and amortisation.

EBITDA is therefore a measure of a company's operational profitability over time, but taking out the potentially distorting effects of changes in interest, taxes, depreciation and amortisation, which can all be manipulated by financing and accounting decisions. The argument for using EBITDA is that it allows us to better compare companies and their operational profitability without taking into account their capital structure.

First used in the 1980s, EBITDA has grown to be of particular interest to organisations that have large amounts of fixed assets which are subject to heavy depreciation charges (such as manufacturing companies) or in the case where a company has a large amount of acquired intangible assets on its books and is thus subject to large amortisation charges (such as a company that has purchased a brand or a company that has recently made a large acquisition). Depreciation and amortisation are defined in the working example on pages 22–23.

How do I measure it?

Data collection method

EBITDA can be calculated using the company's income statement and accounting data.

Formula

EBITDA = Revenue − Expenses (excluding interest, tax, depreciation and amortisation)

Frequency

As with any earnings or cash-flow metric, EBITDA is usually calculated on a quarterly or monthly basis. But organisations will typically project EBITDA over a 12-month period and report over the previous 12-month period.

Source of the data

The EBITDA data can be extracted from the income statement.

Cost/effort in collecting the data

The cost of collecting the data for the EBITDA metric is small as the data has to be collected anyway for accounting purposes. Therefore the effort to populate the metric is also low.

Target setting/benchmarks

Many organisations will set EBITDA targets and report these to the investment community. The actual figure will depend on the industry and comparing performance will be against others in the same industry. Like any profitability measure, as long as the number is positive you are off the hook, and the bigger the better.

> **Example** The EBITDA calculation can be made as follows:
> 1. Calculate net income. To calculate net income obtain total income and subtract total expenses.
> 2. Determine income taxes. Income taxes are the total amount of taxes paid to the government.

3   Compute interest charges. Interest is the fee paid to companies or individuals that reimburses the individual or companies for the use of credit or currency.

4   Establish the cost of depreciation. Depreciation is the term used to define a cash (machines or property) or non-cash asset (a copyright, a trademark or brand name recognition) that loses value over time whether through ageing, wear and tear, or the assets becoming obsolete. To explain, most assets lose their value over time (in other words, they depreciate), and must be replaced once the end of their useful life is reached. There are several accounting methods that are used in order to write off an asset's depreciation cost over the period of its useful life. Because it is a non-cash expense, depreciation lowers the company's reported earnings while increasing free cash flow (the cash that a company is able to generate after laying out the money required to maintain or expand its asset base).

5   Ascertain the cost of amortisation. Amortisation is a method of decreasing the amounts of financial instruments over time, including interest and other finance charges. As an example of amortisation, suppose XYZ Biotech spent $30 million on a piece of medical equipment and that the patent on the equipment lasts 15 years; this would mean that $2 million would be recorded each year as an amortisation expense. While amortisation and depreciation are often used interchangeably, technically this is an incorrect practice because amortisation refers to intangible assets and depreciation refers to tangible assets.

6   Add all previously defined components. The resulting figure is then subtracted from total expense. This final figure is then subtracted from total revenue to arrive at EBITDA.

Tips/warnings

A common misconception is that EBITDA represents cash earnings. EBITDA is a good metric to evaluate profitability, but not cash flow.

EBITDA also leaves out the cash required to fund working capital and the replacement of old equipment, which can be significant. Therefore EBITDA often comes in for criticism as it doesn't tell the full story of an organisation's financial performance. It is recommended, as with most of the financial measures, that to get a fuller picture of a company's financial health it is important to use EBITDA alongside other financial metrics.

As EBITDA is a non-GAAP (Generally Accepted Accounting Principles – a set of rules that accountants follow) measure, it allows a greater amount of discretion as to what is (and is not) included in the calculation. This also means that companies often change the items included in their EBITDA calculation from one reporting period to the next, which can cause confusion.

In general, EBITDA is a useful measure only for large companies with significant assets, and/or for companies with a significant amount of debt financing. It is rarely a useful measure for evaluating a small company with no significant loans.

Because it is difficult to compare companies using actual numbers, analysts and investors often deploy the EBITDA margin, a ratio which makes profitability more comparable by dividing EBITDA by Revenue.

References

www.investopedia.com/terms/e/ebitda.asp

http://moneyterms.co.uk/ebitda/

Revenue growth rate 6

Strategic perspective
Financial perspective

Key performance question this indicator helps to answer
How well are we growing the business?

Why is this indicator important?

It is the basic fact of business that commercial organisations exist to make money. And although there are a number of factors to consider, the primary driver of 'making money' is to grow revenues.

Revenue (sometimes referred to as turnover or sales) is simply the income that a company receives from its normal business activities, usually the sale of goods and/or services.

In accounting terms revenue represents the 'top line', to denote how it is reported on an income statement (at the very top). The 'bottom line' denotes net profit (what is left from the revenues once all expenses are deducted).

Generally, revenue might be understood as income received by an organisation in the form of cash or cash equivalents. However, sales revenue can be described as income received from selling goods or services over a given period of time.

Although revenue growth is a simple measure (in that all that is being measured is the rate of increase in the growth of revenues), its importance cannot be underestimated. Growth figures are, of course, a primary focus of senior management teams as they denote how well an organisation's strategic and operational goals are being realised.

Moreover, growth figures are of enduring interest to the investment community. Simply put, if a company can demonstrate solid 'top-line growth', analysts might view this as positive, even if bottom-line growth is sluggish. It has long been recognised that consistent revenue growth is considered essential for a company's publicly traded stock to be attractive to investors.

Analysts (and indeed senior teams and even competitors) will look at revenue growth compared to a previous period (most likely a quarter or series of quarters). The current quarter's sales figure will also usually be compared on a year-over-year basis. Such analyses provide insights into how much a company's sales are increasing over time and therefore how well the organisation is performing, especially in comparison to the competition.

How do I measure it?

Data collection method

Sales revenue data are collected from an organisation's general ledger (the main accounting record of a business) and will be summarised periodically under the heading Revenue or Revenues on an income statement. Revenue account names describe the type of revenue, such as 'Repair service revenue', 'Rent revenue earned' or 'Sales'.

Formula

Revenue growth is simply this quarter's (or any other time period) revenue compared to that of a previous quarter (or any other time period).

Frequency

Revenues are calculated monthly and reported in the monthly management accounts. Growth rates might be reported on a quarterly basis with multi-quarter and/or year-on-year comparisons.

Source of the data

This data can be extracted from the general ledger and captured in the income statement.

Cost/effort in collecting the data

By law, organisations must capture and report revenue data, so there's no cost in collecting this data apart from the normal cost of doing business. The simplicity of calculating growth rates means that there is little cost or effort in collecting this data.

Target setting/benchmarks

For publicly traded organisations it is straightforward to compare the revenue growth of different companies (especially those in the same or similar industries/sectors), as all data are publicly available and most organisations will report growth rates (if not, it is simple to calculate).

Most commercial organisations will set growth targets as a key part of their annual budgeting process. Wherever possible, this should be based on an understanding of competitor targets.

Below are some example growth rates for well-known companies across different industries.

Company	Average revenue growth rates (over 5 years between 2007 and 2011)
Bank of America	Just over **3%**
Walt Disney	Just over **4%**
Wal-Mart Stores	About **5.5%**
Colgate-Palmolive	Just under **7%**
Exxon-Mobile	About **8.5%**
Pfizer	Just under **10%**
The Coca-Cola Company	About **15%**
Apple	Over **40%**

Example Revenue growth is remarkably simple to measure. For example, if Company X generated $91.3 billion in revenue during its fourth quarter of 2010 and $82.2 billion in the third quarter that year, the company would have seen quarterly revenue growth of 11% sequentially. If Company X generated $80.2 billion in the fourth quarter of 2009, the company would have seen its revenue increase 13.8% on a year-over-year basis.

Tips/warnings

Although revenue and, in particular, revenue growth is a critical measure of business performance, business success also requires attention to be paid to other financial barometers such as expenses as a company's overall performance is measured by the extent to which its asset inflows (revenues) compare with its asset outflows (expenses). Net income is the result of this equation.

In start-up mode, or in entering a new market, for example, an organisation might decide to drive revenues while sacrificing net income. This is a normal business strategy. When doing so, organisations must pay close attention to cash flow, another of the key barometers of an organisation's financial health. Healthy cash flow is critical to driving growth.

References

CNNMoney – **http://money.cnn.com/**

http://money.cnn.com/magazines/fortune/fortunefastestgrowing/2010/companies/salesgrowth/

Total shareholder return (TSR)

7

Strategic perspective
Financial perspective

Key performance question this indicator helps to answer
To what extent are we delivering value to shareholders?

Why is this indicator important?

The reason why most shareholders invest in a company is to maximise the return on their investment. Total shareholder return (TSR) is a key measure as it represents the change in capital or value of a listed or quoted company over a period of time (typically one year).

TSR combines share price appreciation and dividends (the portion of corporate profits paid out by a corporation to its shareholders) to show the total return to shareholders.

TSR is a valuable metric because it represents a readily understood figure of the overall financial benefits generated for shareholders. The figure can be interpreted as a measure of how the market evaluates the overall performance of a company over a specified period. Moreover, given that TSRs are expressed in percentage terms, the figures are readily comparable between companies in the same sector.

Furthermore, as TSR is an easy way to compare performance of similar companies, it is a metric that is followed closely by present and potential investors and is one gauge of the effectiveness (or not) of how the organisation is competing and creating value in the marketplace. As a result, it can be safely argued that leaders of publicly traded organisations should pay close attention to TSR.

How do I measure it?

Data collection method

The data can be easily collected from the available stock price of a company and from accounting information.

Formula

Total shareholder value = ((Share price at the end of period t − Share price at beginning of period t) + Dividends)/Share price at beginning of period

Note: dividends include not only regular dividend payments but also any cash payments to shareholders, and also special or one-time dividends and share buyback (the reacquisition by a company of its own stock).

The importance of the dividend component of the total return calculation is typically more significant in traditionally higher-yielding areas of the stock market such as utilities, tobacco companies and beverage producers.

Frequency

Typically yearly, but some organisations will assess TSR twice per year. A full 12-month period is generally preferable as it provides a more accurate snapshot of the performance of the stock. Analysing a full calendar year will allow for seasonal ups and downs, and also allow time for temporary factors that may have caused a short-term rise or fall in the value of the shares.

Source of the data

These data can be extracted from the accounting data and share price information.

Cost/effort in collecting the data

It is relatively inexpensive to collect these data as they are easily retrievable.

Target setting/benchmarks

TSR can easily be compared from company to company and benchmarked against industry or market returns as the data are publicly available. It is usual that organisations will compare their TSR against organisations within a similar risk profile. TSR performance against peers is typically tracked on a rolling basis.

Example In the later 1990s Unilever introduced a TSR target that was measured over a three-year rolling period against a peer group of 20 fast-moving consumer goods (FMCG) organisations. These companies were in similar markets to Unilever with a comparable food, home care and personal care portfolio.

In the report *Building and Communicating Shareholder Value*, one of Unilever's financial planning managers said: 'The principle is that if those are the businesses we have to beat competitively, then we should also look to deliver superior financial returns and therefore greater shareholder value compared to the same companies. We don't compare ourselves with companies in very different industries, such as information technology, primarily because of the very different risk/reward profile.'

He also stressed that a key reason for choosing TSR was that it is the ultimate test of creating shareholder value, one which tells you much more about the returns an organisation delivers to its shareholders than typical financial metrics such as earnings growth. Unilever implemented TSR as a corporate measure in 1997 with the goal of being in the top third of its peer group, a target that was achieved for the three years to 1999.

Tips/warnings

Companies often use TSR as a key measure to determine senior executive compensation, because TSR focuses not just on improving the financial/stock performance of the firm but on putting it in relation to a peer group. The argument is that a company's stocks might do very well over a period of time but lag behind those of competitors or other organisations with a similar profile. Therefore a significant percentage of incentive-compensation is dependent on performance comparative to a tightly defined peer group.

Owing to its nature, TSR cannot be calculated at divisional or business unit level, neither is it applicable to privately owned enterprises.

A downside of the TSR calculation is that it is not 'forward looking', in that it reflects only the past overall return to shareholders and so provides little or no insight into likely future returns.

References

www.qfinance.com

James Creelman, *Building and Communicating Shareholder Value*, London: Business Intelligence, 2000.

Economic value added (EVA)

8

> **Strategic perspective**
> Financial perspective
>
> **Key performance question this indicator helps to answer**
> How well are we delivering value to our shareholders?

Why is this indicator important?

Conceived by the New York headquartered consultancy Stern-Stewart, EVA is an estimate of a company's economic profit. It is basically the profit earned by a company less the costs of financing the company's capital.

It is used as an internal governance mechanism for ensuring that meeting, and exceeding, investor expectations is central to directing all operational activities and investment decisions within the organisation.

EVA is a measure of economic profit that exceeds investor expectations, and as such is a performance measure that, by removing accounting anomalies, enables a direct comparison of companies of similar risk profiles. As examples of anomalies, through the EVA calculation expenses such as research and development and training are expensed: according to the theory these are investments and should be treated as such.

Central to the ability to compare performance accurately is the focus on the cost of capital. According to the EVA approach, organisations only make a profit when they take the cost of capital into the calculation of their financial performance.

Capital is not free. There is an opportunity cost of capital, in that investors can put their money in many places (for instance into government bonds, the bank or equity markets). It is important to deduct the cost of capital in order to see the actual profitability of the enterprise, so a charge for the cost of capital is made. Capital accounts for both debt and equity. Capital is a measure of all the cash that has been deposited in a company over its lifetime, irrespective of its financing source.

EVA is also used extensively as a measure by which to set and assess incentive-compensation payments to managers. Particularly interesting in this post-credit-crunch world is that the bonus structure encourages the careful balancing of the delivering of short-term financial results and longer-term performance (thus safeguarding the interests of shareholders that have made long-term investments in the enterprise). Moreover, the incentive-compensation approach has been shaped to ensure that managers share the 'pain and gain' of investors. As the CEO of one organisation that deploys the EVA incentive-compensation scheme says: 'We want to make sure that the people who work at [this company] have the same objectives as those who invest in it.'

The incentive-compensation model is based on a bonus bank. Essentially, the bonus bank works like this: each year a bonus is declared depending on EVA improvement versus target and that bonus is deposited into the bonus bank. Typically, one-third of the declared bonus is paid out in that year, with the remainder held 'at risk' against future years' EVA performance.

It should be stressed that employees should be incentivised for EVA improvement over the previous year's figure, thus ensuring that the focus is on continuous EVA improvement. Also, an important point is that bonuses are not necessarily paid when a positive EVA figure is reported, if the underlying performance has declined. Conversely, a business unit starting from a significant negative-EVA position may be incentivised for improving the figure, although at the end of the year it is still in negative territory.

How do I measure it?

Data collection method

The data are derived directly from the profit and loss statement, while taking into account the charge for the cost of capital and making amendments based on the capitalising of line items that are expensed according to conventional accounting rules.

Formula

EVA equals net operating profit after taxes, minus cost of capital, multiplied by the total capital employed

$$EVA = NOPAT - (C \times K)$$

Where:

- NOPAT is net operating profit after tax

- C is the weighted average cost of capital (WACC), which represents the rate that a company is expected to pay on average to all its security holders to finance its assets
- K is the economic capital employed

Normally, the equity cost of capital for an organisation is measured through the Capital Asset Pricing Model (CAPM). A firm's nominal equity cost of capital is calculated as a base risk-free rate plus 'beta' – the latter being a general equity risk premium adjusted for a firm-specific risk measure. In short, therefore, the equity rate is the return investors are seeking to achieve when buying a company's common shares. This is expressed as: the firm's equity investors' expected return (future) = risk-free return (future) + the firm's beta (a relative measure of volatility) × general equity risk premium (history).

The equity risk premium represents the excess return above the risk-free rate that investors demand for holding risky securities. So, with a risk-free rate of 7%, a beta of 1.1 and an assumed equity risk premium of 4%, a company would have the following cost of equity: Cost of equity = 7% + (1.1 × 4%) = 11.4%.

The cost of debt is the rate of return that debt-holders require in order to hold debt. To determine this rate the yield has to be calculated. This is typically worked out using discounted cash flow analysis, i.e. the internal rate of return. The cost of tax should be calculated after tax as follows: Cost of debt after tax = Cost of tax before tax × (100 − marginal tax rate).

Frequency

The EVA calculation is made on a monthly basis. The WACC can be done annually.

Source of the data

The EVA calculation can be extracted from the profit and loss accounts.

Cost/effort in collecting the data

Collecting data for the EVA metric requires a little more effort than other financial indicators. The more of the required data that are already available, the quicker and cheaper EVA can be calculated. If the data are readily available EVA only requires creating a new formula in the accounting system. However, if important data are missing then it can become very expensive to create processes and systems to collect missing pieces of data.

Target setting/benchmarks

Performance to EVA can be assessed by comparing it with those organisations that have similar risk profiles.

Example Consider this example from a company that designs, manufactures and markets household furniture (quoted from a case study written by James Creelman for the report *Building and Communicating Shareholder Value*, London: Business Intelligence, 2000). All figures are in thousands of US dollars:

Operating incomes	$224,313
Interest expense on non-capitalised leases	$4,071
Goodwill amortisation	$3,001
Other	$4,621
Increase (decrease) in reserves	($4,293)
Capitalised design and research	$3,657
Adjusted operating profit	$235,370
Cash taxes	($73,607)
NOPAT	$151,763
Weighted average cash employed	$551,600
WACC	11%
Cost of capital	$60,676
Economic Value Added	$91,087

EVA is used as a way to evaluate the investments that this organisation makes. Taking its packaging line as an example, the line could no longer fully meet customers' demands and package mix. A new state-of-the-art line would help the organisation gain additional sales and also reduce packaging costs. The combined effect will be a £2.0 million increase in profit after tax (net income). But additional operating capital of £7.5 million is required. Assuming a cost of capital of 11%, the impact on economic added value will be:

Increase in net income (NOPAT) £2.0m

Minus: Capital charge of additional operating capital (11% of £7.5m) £0.8m

Economic value added: £1.2m

Tips/warnings

Implementing EVA is as much a cultural change as it is financial. Organisations must ensure that they create a culture where economic performance is more important than simple profit and loss.

Detractors of EVA state that changing the 'accounting distortions' makes it overly complex. For this reason, some companies do not rectify the 'distortions', and simply deduct the cost of capital figure from NOPAT, making this a very straightforward metric.

Moreover, making decisions based on calculated likely EVA returns might put managers off making 'risky' investments. Organisations need to understand their risk appetite as well as the projected EVA number.

References

www.sternstewart.com

www.investopedia.com/university/EVA/

Return on investment (ROI)   9

> **Strategic perspective**
> Financial perspective
>
> **Key performance question this indicator helps to answer**
> How well are we generating sustainable profits?

Why is this indicator important?

Return on investment (ROI), also referred to as the rate of return or rate of profit, is a financial performance measure that is used to evaluate the efficiency of an investment (after or during the investment period) or to compare the efficiency of a number of different investments (before capital is allocated).

ROI is a calculation of the most tangible financial gains or benefits that can be expected from a project versus the costs for implementing the suggested programme or solution. In short, it is the ratio of money gained or lost (realised or unrealised) on an investment relative to the amount of money invested.

ROI is a very popular metric within organisations because its versatility and simplicity are powerful aids to the decision-making process. By running an ROI projection organisations can determine the likely ROI on an investment. If there are other opportunities with a higher ROI, then it is probable that the lower ROI-yielding investment will not be undertaken or at least will become less of a priority.

Estimating ROI for a proposed expenditure will go a long way in aiding management to make a 'go' or 'no go' decision. ROI can be separated into two categories: micro and macro ROI.

Micro ROI is focused on elements of any project or programmes a company may become involved in. Most such initiatives would have a shorter time-frame (maybe up to a year). These may include such things as:

- a direct mail programme
- a print advertising programme
- a sales promotion.

Micro ROI can include almost anything a company would spend money on where they would expect a positive financial result in less than a year.

Macro ROI concerns the overall performance of major company initiatives. These may include:

- adding a new assembly line
- creating the company's own truck delivery system
- building a new production facility

The payout for these types of initiative is probably more than a year and could extend for several years.

Although calculating ROI can be more difficult for intangible investments (such as knowledge development etc.), it has been applied successfully to areas such as training.

Naturally, the ROI metric is a key metric tracked by the investment community, which looks for businesses that can demonstrate that they are adept at generating positive returns on their investments on an ongoing basis.

How do I measure it?

Data collection method

The data are collected from analysis of the accounting data.

Formula

Return on investment is calculated in several ways. For example:

$$ROI = \frac{(\text{Gain from investment} - \text{Cost of investment})}{\text{Cost of investment}}$$

In the above formula 'Gains from investment' refers to the proceeds obtained from selling the investment of interest.

ROI can also be calculated as net benefits / net costs or as profit / cost × year days / period.

Frequency

ROI can then be measured at the end of a programme (such as a marketing effort, where it is straightforward to calculate the ROI based on known and complete costs and benefits).

However, ROI is also measured as a percentage of return over a period of a year (most useful for longer-term projects), thus giving a calculation of how long it will take the organisation to cover its investment and then make a profit from that investment.

If the rate of return (ROR) is 33.3% in one year, then it will take three years to recover the complete investment (100%/33.3% = 3).

If ROR is 50%, then payback is two years; if 200%, then six months.

Source of the data

These data can be extracted from the accounting data.

Cost/effort in collecting the data

The cost and effort of calculating ROI depend on the complexity of calculating the benefits of the investments. This can be complex if data for the financial benefits are not already available or when more complex formulas are being used to e.g. convert intangible benefits into financial returns. However, if simple financial formulas are used, the cost and effort will go down as the data should be readily available in the accounting system.

Target setting/benchmarks

Organisations will set their own ROI targets, and where possible will base these on industry benchmarks. In general, the higher the investment risk, the greater the potential investment return and the greater the potential investment loss (such an understanding will influence the setting of an ROI target).

Moreover, profitability ratios such as ROI are typically used by financial analysts to compare a company's profitability over time or compare profitability between companies. The investment community might be a good mechanism for identifying benchmark targets.

Example Let's look at a simple ROI calculation. Take a parcel-mapping project that costs $50,000 to implement, and you demonstrate $25,000 in net benefits, then the calculation would appear as follows.

$$ROI = \left(\frac{25,000}{50,000}\right)$$

As a further example, consider this 90-day promotion:

- Period: 90 days
- Sales: $320,000
- Profit: $120,000
- Programme cost: $200,000
- $\text{ROI} = \left(\dfrac{\text{profit}}{\text{cost}}\right) \times \dfrac{\text{year days}}{\text{period}}$
- $\left(\dfrac{\$120{,}000}{\$200{,}000}\right) \times \left(\dfrac{360}{90}\right)$
- ROI = 60% × 4 = 240% annual rate of return

In this example, the company recouped its initial investment of $200,000 from its sales of $320,000, leaving a profit of $120,000.

Since the promotion was over a 90-day period, the company got 60% return on its investment in 90 days. Annually, the return is four times the 60% or 240% for annualised ROI.

Tips/warnings

It is worth keeping in mind that the calculation for return on investment and, therefore, the definition, can be modified to suit the situation. Basically, it all depends on what the organisation (or part of it) decides to include as returns and costs. The definition of the term in the broadest sense just attempts to measure the profitability of an investment and, as such, there is no one 'right' calculation.

For example, a marketer may compare two different products by dividing the gross profit that each product has generated by its respective marketing expenses. A financial analyst, however, may compare the same two products using an entirely different ROI calculation, perhaps by dividing the net income of an investment by the total value of all resources that have been employed to make and sell the product.

This flexibility has a downside, as ROI calculations can be easily manipulated to suit the user's purposes, and the result can be expressed in many different ways. When using this metric, an organisation must have a clear understanding of what inputs are being used.

Furthermore, care must be taken not to confuse annual and annualised returns. An annual rate of return is a single-period return, while an annualised rate of return is a multi-period, average return.

An annual rate of return is the return on an investment over a one-year period, such as 1 January through 31 December. An annualised rate of return is the return on an investment over a period other than one year (such as a month, or two years) multiplied or divided to give a comparable one-year return. For instance, a one-month ROI of 1% could be stated as an annualised rate of return of 12%. Or a two-year ROI of 10% could be stated as an annualised rate of return of 5%.

References

The ROI Institute **www.roiinstitute.net**

www.investopedia.com

Jack J. Phillips and Patti P. Phillips, *The Business Case for ROI, Measuring the Return on Investment in Human Resources*, paper by Jack Phillips Center for Research, 2001

http://agencyroundtable.com/uploaded/articles/AAF%20luncheon%20 handout.pdf

Patricia Pulliam Phillips and Jack J. Phillips, *Return on Investment (ROI) Basics* (ASTD Training Basics), 2006.

Return on capital employed (ROCE)

10

> **Strategic perspective**
> Financial perspective
>
> **Key performance question this indicator helps to answer**
> How well are we generating earnings from our capital investments?

Why is this indicator important?

Clearly, the prime objective of making an investment in a business is to obtain a satisfactory return on capital invested. One of the most popular metrics for assessing the success of a business in realising this objective is return on capital employed (ROCE).

The main elements of ROCE are operating profit and capital employed. ROCE compares earnings with the capital employed in the company. There are a number of ways that we can reach the earnings (or operating profit) ratio, but a common approach is to use as the denominator Earnings before interest and tax (EBIT), a variation on the earnings before interest, tax, depreciation and amortisation metric (EBITDA, see page 21), while capital employed is the capital investment necessary for the company to function and grow.

ROCE uses the reported (period end) capital numbers. A variation of this metric is Return on average capital employed (ROACE), which uses the average of the opening and closing capital for the period.

Many in the accounting and investing professions consider ROCE to be one of the best measures of profitability in order to assess the overall performance of the business. It indicates how well the management has used the investment made by owners and creditors into the business. It is commonly used as a basis for various managerial decisions (for instance, using the ROCE target as the basis for deciding which projects to finance). As the primary objective of business is to earn profit, the higher the return on capital employed, the more efficient the firm is in using its funds.

The ratio can be measured for a number of years in order to find a trend as to whether the profitability of the company is improving or otherwise. Put another way, ROCE shows how much a business is gaining for its assets, or how much it is losing from its liabilities.

How do I measure it?

Data collection method

The data for ROCE are derived from an analysis of the accounting data.

Formula

ROCE is calculated by taking the earnings before interest and tax and dividing them by the capital employed:

$$ROCE = \frac{EBIT}{Total\ capital\ employed}$$

Frequency

Usually measured on an annual basis.

Source of the data

These data can be extracted from the accounting data.

Cost/effort in collecting the data

The data for the ROCE metrics are easily accessible in the accounting data so there is little additional cost involved.

Target setting/benchmarks

It is common for organisations to compare ROCE targets against companies in the same industry or with similar profiles. Accessing the comparative data is relatively straightforward as they will be publicly reported or straightforward to calculate.

Example This example of calculating ROCE is from ExxonMobil, although it actually uses the ROACE calculation (and uses the terms interchangeably). The corporation's total ROCE is net income excluding the after-tax cost of financing, divided by total corporate average capital employed. The corporation has applied its ROCE definition consistently for many years and views it as the best measure of historical capital productivity in such a capital-intensive, long-term industry, both to evaluate management's performance and to demonstrate to shareholders that capital has been used wisely over the long term. Additional measures, which are more cash-flow-based, are used to make investment decisions.

(Millions of dollars)	2008	2007	2006	2005	2004
Return on average capital employed					
Net income	45,220	40,610	39,500	36,130	25,330
Financing costs (after tax)					
Gross third-party debt	(343)	(339)	(264)	(261)	(461)
ExxonMobil share of equity companies	(325)	(204)	(156)	(144)	(185)
All other financing costs – net	1,485	268	499	(35)	378
Total financing costs	817	(275)	79	(440)	(268)
Earnings excluding financing costs	44,403	40,885	39,421	36,570	25,598
Average capital employed	129,683	128,760	122,573	116,961	107,339
Return on average capital employed – corporate total	34.2%	31.8%	32.2%	31.3%	23.8%

Source: ExxonMobil quarterly report, filed 11 March 2009

Tips/warnings

An often-cited drawback of ROCE is that it measures return against the book value of assets in the business. As these are depreciated the ROCE will increase, even though cash flow has remained the same. Thus, older businesses with depreciated assets will tend to have higher ROCE than newer, possibly better businesses. In addition, while cash flow is affected by inflation, the book value of assets is not. Consequently revenues increase with inflation while capital employed generally does not.

Another criticism is that if an organisation has a cost of capital of, say, 10% (see EVA on page 33) and has an ROCE target of 30%, it might turn down a potential investment that promises a return of 20% because it falls short of the ROCE target. Critics argue that this is still an investment that should be pursued as it is adding value to the investor.

References

www.accountingformanagement.com/return_on_capital_employed.htm

www.wikinvest.com/stock/Exxon_Mobil_(XOM)/Return_Average_Capital_Employed_Roce

Return on assets (ROA)

Strategic perspective
Financial perspective

Key performance question this indicator helps to answer
To what extent are we able to generate profits from the assets we control?

Why is this indicator important?

Companies make investments in assets (such as machinery, equipment, buildings, etc.) in order to generate a return. Companies want to make sure that they maximise the income they generate from the assets they own. Return on assets (ROA) assesses a company's profitability relative to the assets it controls and is therefore a measure of how efficiently a company is using the assets at its disposal.

If the ROA is low it indicates that the income has been low compared to the amount of assets owned. ROA is a particularly useful KPI if compared to other similar companies in the same sector. If the ROA of a company is below the industry average, it indicates an inefficient use of business assets.

How do I measure it?

Data collection method

Simply take the data from the income statement of a company and divide the income by the asset value.

Formula

The simple (and maybe too simplistic) formula for return on assets is:

$$\text{ROA} = \left(\frac{\text{Net income during period } t}{\text{Total assets at the end of period } t}\right) \times 100$$

The problem with this simple formula is twofold:

1. Companies can fund their assets in two ways – through debt or through equity. Funding assets by taking on large debts will result in higher interest payments. To take this capital structure into account it is sensible to add interest expenses to the net income before calculating the ratio.

2. Taking the total assets at the end of the period (e.g. the fiscal year) can be misleading because the net income was earned using the assets the company owned earlier. This is why it makes sense to take the average total assets for that period.

This means that a more advanced formula for ROA is:

$$\text{ROA} = \left[\frac{(\text{Net income in period } t + \text{Interest expense in period } t)}{(\text{Average assets during period t})}\right] \times 100$$

Frequency

ROA is usually calculated on an annual basis but reported on a rolling quarterly basis, i.e. calculated for the past four quarters each quarter.

Source of the data

The data will come directly from the income statements of a company.

Cost/effort in collecting the data

Because the data are readily available, the effort of collecting the data is minimal.

Target setting/benchmarks

There are no generic benchmarks available as the ROA varies significantly by industry and sector. Some sectors are very asset- or capital-intensive (e.g.

steel companies, mining companies, manufacturing companies) while others are capital-light (e.g. software companies, advertising companies and service sector companies in general).

Example Let's take a company that earned $10 million in net income in a given period and paid $1 million in interest expenses in the same period. Its assets at the beginning of the period were $15 million, and at the end of the period $22 million.

$$ROA = \left[\frac{\text{(Net income in period } t + \text{Interest expense in period } t\text{)}}{\text{(Average assets during period } t\text{)}}\right] \times 100$$

$$ROA = [(\$10m + \$1m) / ((\$15m + \$22m) / 2)] \times 100$$

$$ROA = \left(\frac{\$11m}{\$18.5m}\right) \times 100$$

$$ROA = 59\%$$

Tips/warnings

Earlier we discussed the influence of capital structure (debt versus equity) and its influence on ROA. However, even with the extended formula there is an influence left because of the way interest payments are taxed: a company with high debt generally pays fewer taxes compared to a company with no debt. This means that net income is higher for companies with higher debt to equity ratios.

Also worth noting is that ROA can only be calculated for companies that are making a profit. The ROA comparison across industries with different profitability levels can therefore be misleading.

References

www.wikinvest.com/metric/Return_on_Assets_(ROA)

www.investopedia.com/terms/r/returnonassets.asp

http://beginnersinvest.about.com/od/incomestatementanalysis/a/return-on-assets-roa-income-statement.htm

www.buzzle.com/articles/return-on-assets-ratio.html

Return on equity (ROE)

12

Strategic perspective
Financial perspective

Key performance question this indicator helps to answer
How efficiently are we using the investments that shareholders have made to generate profits?

Why is this indicator important?

Following on from the previous KPIs, return on equity (ROE) is another common measure of company profitability. ROE measures how much profit a company is generating from the money shareholders have invested.

Many analysts consider ROE the single most important financial ratio for investors and the best measure of management team performance.

Companies with a high ROE (especially if they have little or no debt – see also ROA or the debt to equity ratio) are able to grow without large capital expenditures which in turn allows managers to reinvest the capital to improve business operations without the owners of the business (shareholders) having to invest more capital. A high ROE also means that there is less of a need to take on debt and borrow money elsewhere.

As with many other profitability measures, ROE is most useful when comparisons are made between similar companies in the same sector.

How do I measure it?

Data collection method

Measuring ROE is a straightforward calculation of data that are readily available from the financial systems and financial statements.

Formula

ROE is measured by dividing the net income by the shareholder equity:

$$\text{Return on equity} = \left(\frac{\text{Net income for period } t}{\text{Average shareholder's equity over period } t} \right) \times 100$$

where shareholder equity is calculated from the balance sheet by taking total assets and subtracting total liabilities. This leaves the amount of money owned by the shareholders.

Frequency

ROE is usually calculated on an annual basis, but reported on a rolling quarterly basis.

Source of the data

The data will come directly from the income statements of a company.

Cost/effort in collecting the data

Because the data are readily available, the effort of collecting the data is minimal.

Target setting/benchmarks

As with any profitably and efficiency measure, the more the better. Getting a higher return for the money invested is desirable. For most of the last decade, companies in the S&P 500, a measure of the biggest and best public companies in America, averaged ROEs of 10% to 15%. In the 1990s, the average return on equity was in excess of 20%. As a general ball-park benchmark, an ROE of between 15% and 20% is considered good.

Example Let's look at a simple example (adapted from **www.buffetsecrets.com/return-on-equity.htm**): An investor who buys a business for $100,000 has an equity of $100,000 in that investment. This sum represents the total capital provided by the investor.

If the investor then makes a net profit each year from the business of $10,000, the return on equity is 10%:

$$\text{ROE} = \left(\frac{\$10k}{\$100k}\right) \times 100 = 10\%$$

If, however, the investor has borrowed $50,000 from a bank and pays an annual amount of interest to the bank of $3,500, the calculations change. The total capital in the business remains at $100,000 but the equity in the business (the capital provided by the investor) is now only $50,000 ($100,000 − $50,000).

The profit figures also change. The net profit now is only $6,500 ($10,000 − $3,500).

The return on capital (total capital employed, equity plus debt) remains at 10%. The return on equity is different and higher. It is now 13%:

$$\text{ROE} = \left(\frac{\$6,500}{\$50,000}\right) \times 100 = 13\%$$

Tips/warnings

To compare the change in profitability over a given period, companies could calculate the ROE using the equity figure from the beginning of a period and then calculate it again using the shareholder equity at the end of the period.

References

http://beginnersinvest.about.com/od/incomestatementanalysis/a/understanding-return-on-equity.htm

www.fool.com/investing/beginning/return-on-equity-an-introduction.aspx

www.wikinvest.com/metric/Return_on_Equity_(ROE)

www.buffetsecrets.com/return-on-equity.htm

Debt-to-equity (D/E) ratio 13

> **Strategic perspective**
> Financial perspective
>
> **Key performance question this indicator helps to answer**
> To what extent are we financing our business through debts versus equity?

Why is this indicator important?

As discussed in the previous KPIs, companies can finance their operations either through investments from shareholders (equity) or by taking on debt. Understanding the proportion that is financed by debt as opposed to shareholders' equity is the debt-to-equity (D/E) ratio and a key indicator of the financial position of a company.

If a company has more debts than equity (sometimes also referred to as high leverage or gearing), it generally means that it has been aggressive in financing its growth with debt. Debt is not necessarily a bad thing because borrowing can finance growth. Taking on debt can increase the earnings beyond the level that would have been possible with just the shareholder capital. This means that as long as the company is able to increase earnings by a greater amount than the costs and interest payments for the debt, it is generating value.

However, overusing leverage can strangle a business and leave earnings subject to volatile interest expenses. Highly leveraged companies are particularly at risk during a recession or downturn. Investors often prefer a lower D/E ratio as their interests are better protected, with a reduced risk of not getting their money back in the event of liquidation. However, a low D/E ratio might indicate that a company is not leveraging its potential level of debt which, as discussed earlier, can increase its profits. It is the role of management to optimise the balance between debt and equity. Taking on the right level of debt can be the differentiator between a company that is struggling to survive and one that can respond flexibly to changing economic and market conditions.

Because different industries have different gearing levels, the debt-to-equity ratio is most useful in comparisons with similar companies in the same sector.

How do I measure it?

Data collection method

The D/E ratio is a simple calculation from readily available data off a company's balance sheet. It basically means dividing a company's total liabilities by its shareholders' equity.

Formula

The D/E ratio will generate a percentage score. If it is above 1 it means that funding by debt outweighs funding by equity.

$$\text{Debt-to-equity (D/E) ratio} = \frac{\text{Total liabilities}}{\text{Total equity}}$$

As with many of the financial KPIs, there are varying ways of calculating it. Sometimes, instead of total liabilities, only interest-bearing, long-term debt is taken into account in the calculation. Also, instead of using the book value (balance-sheet-based) figures for liabilities and equity, market-based values can be used if the company's debt and equity are publicly traded.

Frequency

The D/E ratio is usually calculated on an annual basis, but reported on a rolling quarterly basis.

Source of the data

The data for total liabilities and total equity can be taken from the firm's balance sheet or statement of financial position.

Cost/effort in collecting the data

Because the data are readily available, the effort of collecting the data is minimal.

Target setting/benchmarks

The level of debt-to-equity really depends on the industry and the circumstances. You can use online sites such as **http://ycharts.com** or **www.bizstats.com** to get listings of average debt-to-equity ratios by industry. Some experts argue that debt-to-equity ratios of greater than 0.75% should be avoided, as any higher leverage would leave a company too volatile and increase the likelihood of bankruptcy, but this is a very rough ball-park benchmark. Something around the 0.3% mark is usually considered a good debt-to-equity ratio.

Example

Let's look at an example (adapted from **www.investinganswers.com/term/debt-equity-ratio.htm**)

Company XYZ	
Short-term Debt	$5,000,000
Long-term Debt	$10,000,000
Total Debt	$15,000,000
Common Equity	$500,000
Preferred Equity	$250,000
Additional Paid in Capital	$6,000,000
Retained Earnings	$3,250,000
Total Shareholder's Equity	$10,000,000

Using the debt-to-equity formula and the information above, we can calculate that Company XYZ's debt-to-equity ratio is:

$$\frac{\$15,000,000}{\$10,000,000} = 1.5 \text{ times}$$

This means that for every dollar of Company XYZ owned by the shareholders, Company XYZ owes $1.50 to creditors.

Tips/warnings

It is important to note that there are many ways to calculate the debt-to-equity ratio, and therefore it is important to be clear about what types of debt and equity are being used when comparing debt-to-equity ratios.

Other issues to be aware of when using the debt-to-equity ratio have been summarised by the Motley Fool investing site:

> The D/E ratio has wrinkles similar to other equity-based ratios, including the possibility that a company can have a negative or distorted equity base. Consider Western Union (NYSE: WU), which has been loaded up with debt by former parent First Data (NYSE: FDC) to the point that it has negative equity. As a result, we can't calculate a D/E ratio. This was a deliberate capital decision by First Data and isn't unusual in spinoff situations. Western Union throws off so much cash from operations that it has sufficient funds to pay interest, pay down debt, buy back shares, and fund capital spending – but the D/E ratio can't guide us here.
>
> Some companies buy back so many shares that the stated shareholder's equity can be misleading. The originally issued shares show up on the balance sheet at par value (usually between $0.01 and $1 per share). However, when they're repurchased, they are put into the treasury – and subtracted from shareholders' equity – at the purchase price. Consider Anheuser-Busch (NYSE: BUD): it has debt of $8.2 billion and shareholders' equity of just $3.8 billion, for a staggering D/E ratio of 217%.
>
> A casual observer might take one look at this number and pass up the opportunity to invest. But the company's share buyback history shows a massive $15.3 billion in treasury shares and gives us the clue that the D/E ratio is distorted. Without those buybacks, the D/E drops to a more reasonable 43%.

References

www.investinganswers.com/term/debt-equity-ratio-358

www.investopedia.com/terms/d/debtequityratio.asp

http://beginnersinvest.about.com/cs/financialratio/g/debttoequity.htm

www.fool.com/investing/value/2007/06/20/using-the-debt-to-equity-ratio.aspx

Cash conversion cycle (CCC)

14

> **Strategic perspective**
> Financial perspective
>
> **Key performance question this indicator helps to answer**
> How well are we doing at maintaining a healthy cash position?

Why is this indicator important?

A main reason why companies get into difficulties is not necessarily a lack of sales but the company running out of money in the bank (cash) to pay for the day-to-day costs of the business. An old business saying is that 'cash is king'. With this recognition, a number of KPIs have been developed to assess a company's cash position, generally known as 'cash flow'. The cash conversion cycle (CCC) is such a measure.

The CCC metric assesses the length of time, in days, that it takes for an organisation to convert resource input into cash flow. It measures the amount of time each net input dollar is tied up in the production and sales process before it is converted into cash through sales to customers.

In essence the metric calculation captures three steps:

1 the amount of time needed to sell inventory;
2 the amount of time needed to collect receivables;

3 the length of time the company is afforded to pay its bills without incurring penalties.

Also known as 'cash cycle', in simple terms CCC measures the time between the outlay of cash and cash recovery (that is when the account is actually paid and not when a sale is made).

The longer it takes to convert the initial outlay back into cash in the bank, the more it will reduce, or squeeze, a company's cash availabilities. Conversely, a positive trend in the cash conversion cycle will add to a company's liquidity.

Generally speaking, the lower the CCC number in days the better for the organisation (although there are caveats – see the tips and warnings section on page 65). A shorter CCC means greater liquidity, which translates into less of a need to borrow, more opportunity to realise price discounts with cash purchases for raw materials and an increased capacity to fund the expansion of the business into new product lines and markets. CCC is similar to 'working capital ratio' (see the next KPI).

How do I measure it?

Data collection method

Data for the CCC KPI are collected through analysing sales records, inventory levels, payments outstanding/paid by customers (days sales outstanding) and payments outstanding/paid to suppliers (days payable outstanding).

Formula

Measured in days, CCC is calculated as:

$$CCC = DIO + DSO - DPO$$

Where:
- DIO represents days inventory outstanding
- DSO represents days sales outstanding
- DPO represents days payable outstanding.

Frequency

Organisations typically measure CCC on an annual basis but might report it quarterly on a rolling annual basis.

Source of the data

The data are drawn from inventory levels, sales records and accounting data.

Cost/effort in collecting the data

All organisations must collect data for payments made/received and should keep good records of inventory levels, so there is little extra cost/effort in creating this KPI over and above that already expended.

Target setting/benchmarks

There are organisations that collect CCC benchmark data, which are often arranged according to industry sector. Perhaps the most useful example is the annual North American and European survey by REL Consultancy, which shows industry performance against the DIO + DSO − DPO KPI.

Example Here we explain DIO/DSO and DPO and illustrate it through the fictitious company XYZ Corp.

DIO is computed by:

1. Dividing the cost of sales (income statement) by 365 to get a cost of sales per day figure;
2. Calculating the average inventory figure by adding the year's beginning (previous year-end amount) and ending inventory figure (both are in the balance sheet) and dividing by 2 to obtain an average amount of inventory for any given year; and
3. Dividing the average inventory figure by the cost of sales per day figure.

For XYZ Corp's FY 2005 (in $ millions), its DIO would be computed with these figures:

1. cost of sales per day   4,800 ÷ 365 = 2.2
2. average inventory 2005   620 + 700 = 1,320 ÷ 2 = 660
3. days inventory outstanding   660 ÷ 2.2 = 300

DIO gives a measure of the number of days it takes for the company's inventory to turn over, i.e. to be converted to sales, either as cash or as accounts receivable.

DSO is computed by:

1. Dividing net sales (income statement) by 365 to get a net sales per day figure;
2. Calculating the average accounts receivable figure by adding the year's beginning (previous year-end amount) and ending accounts receivable

amount (both figures are in the balance sheet) and dividing by 2 to obtain an average amount of accounts receivable for any given year; and

3. Dividing the average accounts receivable figure by the net sales per day figure.

For XYZ Corp's FY 2005 (in $ millions), its DSO would be computed with these figures:

1. net sales per day   3,500 ÷ 365 = 9.6
2. average accounts receivable   540 + 538 = 1,078 ÷ 2 = 539
3. days sales outstanding   539 ÷ 9.6 = 56.1

DSO gives a measure of the number of days it takes a company to collect on sales that go into accounts receivables (credit purchases).

DPO is computed by:

1. Dividing the cost of sales (income statement) by 365 to get a cost of sales per day figure;
2. Calculating the average accounts payable figure by adding the year's beginning (previous year-end amount) and ending accounts payable amount (both figures are in the balance sheet), and dividing by 2 to get an average accounts payable amount for any given year; and
3. Dividing the average accounts payable figure by the cost of sales per day figure.

For XYZ Corp's FY 2005 (in $ millions), its DPO would be computed with these figures:

1. cost of sales per day   800 ÷ 365 = 2.2
2. average accounts payable   140 + 136 = 276 ÷ 2 = 138
3. days payable outstanding   138 ÷ 2.0 = 69

DPO gives a measure of how long it takes the company to pay its obligations to suppliers.

CCC computed:

XYZ Corp's cash conversion cycle for FY 2005 would be computed with these numbers (rounded):

DIO   300 days
DSO + 56.1 days
DPO −69 days
CCC 287.1 days

FINANCIAL PERSPECTIVE

Tips/warnings

It should be noted that shortening the CCC number does carry some risks. While an organisation could potentially achieve a negative CCC by always collecting from customers before paying suppliers, a policy of strict collections and lax payments is not always advisable. For instance, it can lead to the firm gaining a reputation as difficult to work with, which can negatively impact the ability to attract quality suppliers and so damage customer service.

Also, the CCC KPI is not an end in itself. It should be used as the starting point for performance improvement interventions, such as reducing inventory levels (so introducing techniques such as lean or just-in-time production) and techniques to smooth the accounts receivable process (such as improved customer relationship management).

References

www.investopedia.com/terms/c/cashconversioncycle.asp

www.investopedia.com/university/ratios/liquidity-measurement/ratio4.asp

M. Theodore Farris II, Paul D. Hutchison and Ronald W. Hasty, Using cash-to-cash to benchmark service level performance, *Journal of Applied Business Research*, 21(2), 2005. http://journals.cluteonline.com/index.php/JABR/article/view/1494

REL Consultancy: www.relconsultancy.com

Working capital ratio   15

Strategic perspective
Financial perspective

Key performance question this indicator helps to answer
How well are we managing our cash flow?

Why is this indicator important?

We discussed the importance of cash flow in our previous KPI. The simple truth is that in order to build the business an organisation needs a healthy supply of cash. Without readily available cash an organisation will struggle to grow and will equally be challenged to fund day-to-day operational activities. To understand the cash position, organisational leaders will typically use the working capital ratio as another key cash-flow measure.

In essence, working capital (also referred to as current position) is a measure of current assets minus current liabilities and therefore measures how much in liquid assets a company has available to build and maintain its business. To make the numbers comparable between companies, we create the working capital ratio, which takes the current assets and divides them by the current liabilities to arrive at a ratio. Both the working capital and the ratio can be positive or negative, depending on how much debt the company is carrying. The ratio is positive when it is above 1 or negative when it is below 1.

The working capital ratio indicates whether a company has enough short-term assets to cover its short-term debt. In general, companies that have a lot of working capital and therefore a positive working capital ratio will be more successful since they can expand and improve their operations. Companies with negative working capital may lack the funds necessary for growth: such companies might be forced to borrow from the debt markets (which can be expensive), which over the longer term might further weaken the cash position and so put further pressure on an organisation's ability to grow or fund operations.

How do I measure it?

Data collection method

Collecting the data for the working capital ratio begins by determining current assets. Current assets are comprised of cash, marketable securities, accounts receivable and current inventory. Sum the total value of each of the above to arrive at the current assets.

The next step is to collect the data relating to current liabilities, which include accounts payable, accrued expenses, notes payable, short-term debt (such as bank loans and lines of credit) and the portion of long-term debt that is classified as current (that is, payable within 12 months). Sum all of these accounts to arrive at the current liabilities figure.

Formula

For the actual numeric value of your working capital, simply take the total of the current liabilities and subtract these from the current assets. The result will be the working capital:

Working capital = Current assets − Current liabilities

The working capital ratio is calculated by dividing the current assets by the current liabilities:

$$\text{Working capital ratio} = \frac{\text{Current assets}}{\text{Current liabilities}}$$

Frequency

Organisations typically measure their working capital once every quarter.

Source of the data

These data can be extracted from the accounting data and balance sheet.

Cost/effort in collecting the data

The cost for collecting this KPI is very low as all the data are readily available from the balance sheet.

Target setting/benchmarks

The benchmarks for working capital ratios are industry-specific. As a very rough ball-park benchmark, most believe that a ratio of between 1.2 and 2.0 is sufficient. For more detailed industry-specific data check out the working capital surveys by REL Consultancy, which has since the later 1990s been conducting a Working Capital Survey of 1,000 companies in both the US and Europe. The most recent year's survey results can be downloaded for free from the company website and include:

- key trends in working capital performance by company and industry (data from 2004 onwards);
- how an organisation's working capital performance compares with peers and top performers;
- metrics for measuring and managing working capital performance.

Example Consider the following example. In calculating current assets an organisation finds that it has $200,000 in cash, $100,000 in securities, $20,000 in accounts receivable and $60,000 in inventory.

On the current liabilities side, the company has $120,000 in accounts payable, $20,000 in accrued expenses and $40,000 in current debt.

The current assets are $200,000 + $10,000 + $20,000 + $60,000 or $380,000. The current liabilities are $120,000 + $20,000 + $40,000 or $180,000.

Take the current assets of $380,000 and subtract the current liabilities of $180,000 to arrive at the working capital of $200,000:

$$\$380,000 - \$180,000 = \$200,000$$

and a working capital ratio of:

$$\frac{\$380,000}{\$180,000} = 2.11$$

Tips/warnings

Working capital is often used as a barometer to measure an organisation's overall health and liquidity. As a result, it is a measure that is followed very closely by investors (and especially so as investors assess an organisation's ability to weather the severe global economic downturn). Being in a negative working capital position often makes an organisation unattractive to potential investors, so it can negatively impact the stock price and therefore damage shareholder value metrics.

All in all, working capital should always be at the forefront of senior executives' minds.

References

www.investorwords.com

Working Capital Newsletter: **www.relconsultancy.com**

Working Capital Survey: **www.relconsultancy.com**

www.investopedia.com/university/ratios/workingcapital.asp

Operating expense ratio (OER) 16

Strategic perspective
Financial perspective

Key performance question this indicator helps to answer
How well are we managing our operating expenses?

Why is this indicator important?

Companies incur ongoing costs of running their business including equipment maintenance costs, sales and advertising costs, research and development costs, licence costs, insurance premiums, legal fees, accounting expenses, rent, travel costs, electricity and water rates, IT support, etc. These costs are called operating expenses (OPEX) and encompass all the day-to-day expenses a company needs to pay to operate. This therefore means that the lower a company's operating expenses are, the more profitable it generally is.

Operating expenses are in contrast to the other major expense a company incurs, which is capital expenditure (CAPEX) and refers to any investment it makes in physical assets (for more information see CAPEX to sales ratio on page 75).

Looking at OPEX and creating a ratio which divides it by sales revenues provides companies an insight into how expensive it is to run their company. The resulting ratio is called operating expense ratio (OER) and provides the percentage of income that is spent on day-to-day operational expenses.

Especially when viewed over time, changes in the OER indicate whether the company can increase sales without increasing operating expenses proportionately. This in turn is an indicator of how scalable the business is. For example, if sales were to expand from year to year and the OER goes down, it would indicate that sales increased, and operating expense went down at an even faster rate. This would be a desirable position from a net income standpoint.

The OER is often viewed as a measurement of management efficiency because management typically have greater control over operating expenses than they do over revenue or capital expenses.

How do I measure it?

Data collection method

Data for the OER come directly from the financial statements and accounting systems.

Formula

$$OER = \left(\frac{OPEX \text{ in period } t}{Sales \text{ revenue in period } t}\right) \times 100$$

OPEX is the sum of all day-to-day expenses.

Frequency

Data for the OER are typically collected on a monthly or quarterly basis.

Source of the data

The data for the OER come directly from the income statement, where OPEX is the sum of a business's operating expenses for a period of time, such as a month or year.

Cost/effort in collecting the data

The costs for measuring the OER are relatively small when the OPEX information is readily available. However, if this is not the case and manual calculations for OPEX are required, the costs will go up significantly.

Target setting/benchmarks

There are no generally applicable benchmarks as the level of OPEX spending varies significantly by industry. For example, industries with high R&D costs such as pharmaceuticals will usually have higher operating costs.

Example Let's look at an example of how to calculate the operating expense ratio.

First, we need to establish the OPEX by identifying all expenses required for the on-going operation of the business. Administrative expenses and wages, maintenance costs, consumables, travel expenses, advertising costs, insurance, and other overheads such as rent on buildings and equipment are all operating expenses of a business. The OPEX for a specific period (e.g. one year) can be taken straight from the income statement and include all costs associated with the day-to-day running of the business (excluding capital expenditure).

If a company has the following expenses: research and development = $1,000, sales and marketing = $4,000, administrative expenses = $2,000, rent = $500, depreciation and amortisation = $150 for a given period and sales revenues of $40,000, then the calculations would be as follows:

$$OPEX = \$1{,}000 + \$4{,}000 + \$2{,}000 + \$500 + \$150 = \$7650$$

$$OER = \left(\frac{\$7650}{\$40{,}000}\right) \times 100 = 19.13\%$$

Tips/warnings

Remember that the OER is only useful as a comparative indicator for companies that operate in the same industry.

Also be aware that large-scale one-off expenses, such as a large R&D project that bears the costs in the period for which OER is being calculated but would be expected to deliver returns (revenues) over the coming years, can screw OPEX and therefore the resulting ratio.

References

www.money-zine.com/Definitions/Investing-Dictionary

www.investinganswers.com/term/operating-expense-ratio-oer-2800

CAPEX to sales ratio   17

Strategic perspective
Financial perspective

Key performance question this indicator helps to answer
To what extent are we investing in our future compared to our competitors?

Why is this indicator important?

Companies acquire new or update existing physical equipment, property or other so-called fixed assets to create future benefits. Companies make investments in fixed assets to help them to maintain or increase the scope of their operations. These investments are called capital expenditure (or CAPEX) and can include anything from repairing a roof to building a brand-new production plant.

When you compare CAPEX to sales it gives a company a sense of how much it is investing for the future. It is also useful to compare CAPEX to sales ratios between competitors in the same sector. It is important to note that a lower ratio is not necessarily better. This is because firms need to invest in their physical assets to maintain or increase their competitiveness.

This KPI will be more important for companies in sectors such as manufacturing where capital investments are more important, compared to service industries where it tends to matter less.

How do I measure it?

Data collection method

Data for the CAPEX to sales ratio come directly from the financial statements and accounting systems.

Formula

$$\text{CAPEX to sales ratio} = \left(\frac{\text{CAPEX in period } t}{\text{Net sales in period } t} \right) \times 100$$

Frequency

As this is a long-term measure it probably doesn't make sense to measure it more frequently than quarterly or six-monthly.

Source of the data

The data for the KPI will come directly from the accounting system.

Cost/effort in collecting the data

The cost of measuring the CAPEX to sales ratio is relatively small when the CAPEX information is readily available. However, if this is not the case and manual calculations for CAPEX are required, the cost will go up significantly.

Target setting/benchmarks

The target of the CAPEX to sales ratio will depend on the sector or industry the company operates in. Some companies are very capital intensive while in others CAPEX is less important. Compare, for example, the computer games industry to the coal-mining industry. As a very rough rule of thumb, companies have used 15 per cent of their sales on CAPEX.

> **Example** The following example illustrates how you can calculate your CAPEX to sales ratio.
>
> First, we have to establish the CAPEX. The best and most accurate way to calculate CAPEX would be to gain full access to the financial system of an organisation and add up all the capital expenditure for a given period (e.g. costs for buildings, vehicles, machinery and equipment). However, a simpler way is to use the financial statement to extract this information in the following way:

a. Collect the financial statements for two consecutive periods (say 2011 and 2012). These will include the assets and the liabilities of a business.
b. Identify the change in total assets. Locate the total assets of the business for 2011 and for 2012 and then subtract the assets of 2012 from the assets in 2011. So if the total assets in 2011 were $20 million and the total assets for 2012 were $25 million, then the change in total assets would be = $25 million − $20 million = $5 million.
c. Identify the change in total liabilities. Locate the total liabilities of the business for 2011 and for 2012 and then subtract the liabilities of 2012 from the liabilities in 2011. So if the total liabilities in 2011 were $10 million and the total assets for 2012 were $12 million, then the change in total assets would be = $10 million − $12 million = $2 million.
d. Identify the CAPEX by subtracting the total change of liabilities from the total change of assets. In this case: CAPEX = $5 million − $2 million = $3 million.

Now that we have identified the CAPEX we simply divide it by the net sales, which were $200 million for 2012. Therefore the CAPEX the sales ratio is:

$$\text{CAPEX to sales ratio} = \left(\frac{\$3 \text{ million}}{\$200 \text{ million}}\right) \times 100 = 2\%$$

Tips/warnings

CAPEX to sales ratio is a crude KPI that only gives you a sensible insight into future investment if we assume that the investments made will actually be beneficial, i.e. the company is spending its money wisely in the right areas.

References

www.businessdictionary.com/definition/capital-expenditure-to-sales-ratio.html

www.studentinvestor.org/glossary.php

Price/earnings ratio (P/E ratio)

18

Strategic perspective
Financial perspective

Key performance question this indicator helps to answer
To what extent is the current share price attractive to investors?

Why is this indicator important?

Understanding how attractive your shares are to potential investors is useful. An assessment of relative share price attractiveness compared to the shares of rival companies provides managers with insights into the ease of attracting investment capital (i.e. current investor demand for a company share) as well as the attractiveness of potential takeover bids. If the share price is trading lower than it should, based on the earnings expected, a company will make an attractive takeover target.

The P/E ratio is the most popular metric of stock analysis and looks at the relationship between the stock price and the company's earnings.

It looks at historic performance and measures the price an investor is paying for $1 of the company's earnings. Alternatively, it could be expressed in the time it would take investors to earn back their initial investment in a company if this company keeps generating the same earnings that it did in the past year. A higher P/E ratio therefore means that investors are paying more for each unit of net income (or have to wait longer for their return), so the stock is more expensive compared to one with a lower P/E ratio.

How do I measure it?

Data collection method

The data for this KPI are taken from the accounts of a company and the current stock market valuation.

Formula

$$\text{P/E ratio} = \frac{\text{Current price per share}}{\text{Earnings per share}}$$

Or

$$\text{P/E ratio} = \frac{\text{Current market capitalisation}}{\text{Earnings for the company for the year}}$$

Frequency

The P/E ratio is usually measured on a quarterly or annual basis following the earnings report.

Source of the data

The data for the P/E ratio come directly from the accounting information and from the share price data.

Cost/effort in collecting the data

The P/E ratio is easily calculated. However, most share price information systems such as Yahoo! Finance, MSFT and even financial newspapers such as the FT will figure the P/E ratio.

Target setting/benchmarks

There is no generic target or benchmark for the P/E ratio because different industries have different P/E ranges that are considered normal. The average P/E ratio for S&P 500 companies is currently 23.26 (mean: 16.40, median: 15.78) with a minimum of 4.78 (1920) and a maximum of 44.20 (1999).

Example If Company A is reporting earnings per share of $2 and the stock is selling for $20 per share, then the P/E ratio is 10 ($20 per share divided by $2 earnings per share = 10 P/E).

Compare this to Company B with reported earnings of $5 per share, which gives it a P/E ratio of 4 ($20 per share divided by $5 earnings per share = 4 P/E).

Company A has a price to earnings ratio of 10, while Company B has a P/E ratio of 4. This means that Company B is much cheaper on a relative basis. For every share purchased, the investor is getting $5 of earnings as opposed to $2 in earnings from Company A.

Tips/warnings

The main problem with the P/E ratio is that it takes past earnings to come up with a current value. We all know that past performance is not necessarily a guarantee for future performance. This is why investors increasingly look at the forward P/E ratio (share price divided by the expected earnings for the next year). This is particularly useful when the previous year's profits were distorted by events such as a large asset sale, a write-down or when a company is emerging from a period of losses (since dividing a share price of £20, for example, by a 'current' EPS number of −£2 gives a meaningless result of −10).

Take a company that made a loss of $0.03 per share last year, so has no historic P/E ratio, but has a forward P/E ratio of 50, based on analysts' predictions for a return to profit this year.

Also, when looking at P/E ratios it is important to check the units of the ratio. Most reported P/E ratios are in years, meaning the number of years to get your money back assuming nothing changes. However, when dealing with a low or fractional P/E, it might be useful to talk about P/E in terms of the number of months.

Finally, in some cases it makes sense to separate out pre-tax P/E ratio and post-tax P/E ratio to take taxes into account.

References

http://stocks.about.com/od/evaluatingstocks/a/pe.htm

www.whatithinkabout.com/what-is-the-pe-ratio-and-what-the-price-earnings-ratio-means/

www.thefinanceowl.com/financial-ratios/pe-ratio/

www.fool.com/personal-finance/general/2006/07/12/meet-the-pe-ratio.aspx

www.stock-picks-focus.com/pe-ratio.html

[PART TWO]

Customer perspective

Net promoter score (NPS)

19

> **Strategic perspective**
> Customer perspective
>
> **Key performance question this indicator helps to answer**
> To what extent are our customers satisfied and loyal?

Why is this indicator important?

Understanding how satisfied and therefore how loyal your customers might be is important for any company to know because happy and returning customers are likely to grow future revenues and profits.

The problem is that most customer surveys are complex, expensive and hard to interpret. In response to this, the net promoter score (NPS) was developed as 'the one number you need to know' based on just one simple question: How likely is it that you would recommend [company X or product Y or service Z] to a friend or colleague?

The NPS is based on the fundamental premise that every company's customers can be divided into three groups:

- Promoters
- Passives
- Detractors.

This allows an organisation to track these groups and get a clear measure of their performance through its customers' eyes. Moreover, and of critical importance, empirical research has shown that there is a striking correlation between the customer's grouping and actual behaviour – repeat purchase and referral patterns – over time.

Further research mapped the growth rates of companies with high NPS scores and in comparison to their competitors. The results were striking. In most industries, this one simple statistic explained much of the variation in relative growth rates; that is, companies with a better ratio of Promoters to Detractors tend to grow more rapidly than competitors.

Developed by (and a registered trademark of) Fred Reichheld, Bain & Company and Satmetrix, the NPS is a straightforward metric that holds companies and employees accountable for how they treat customers. When combined with appropriate diagnostics and follow-up actions, it drives improvements in customer loyalty and enables profitable growth.

How do I measure it?

Data collection method

NPS is collected using a survey (mail-based, online or conducted by phone). The best NPS practitioners collect the measurement in two ways:

1. Execute a top-down NPS. Set up an anonymous survey and contact existing customers to ask the NPS question – rating the overall customer/company relationship. At the same time, ask questions about the scores they would give to your competitors. This will enable a simple and direct comparison of performance through the eyes of the customer.
2. Measure NPS around transactions that are most vital (transactional NPS). Measure at a key customer touchpoint for a measurement that offers feedback on operational performance at that key moment of truth.

Formula

Using a 0 to 10 scale, an organisation can calculate its NPS by taking the percentage of Promoters and subtracting the percentage of Detractors.

- Promoters (score 9–10) are loyal enthusiasts who will keep buying and refer others, fuelling growth.
- Passives (score 7–8) are satisfied but unenthusiastic customers who are vulnerable to competitive offerings.
- Detractors (score 0–6) are unhappy customers who can damage your brand and impede growth through negative word-of-mouth.

To calculate the NPS, take the percentage of customers who are Promoters (those who scored between 9 and 10) and subtract the percentage who are Detractors (those who scored between 0 and 6). See Figure 19.1.

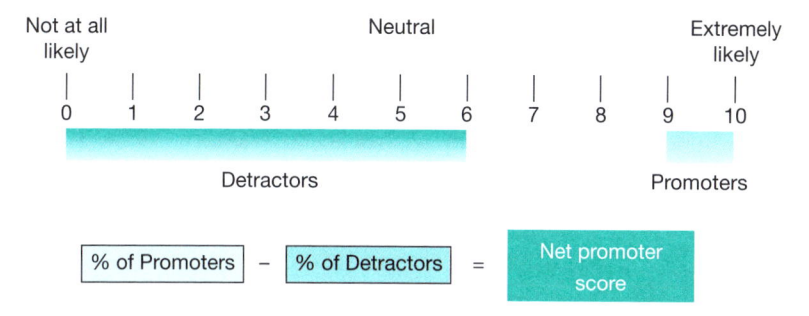

Figure 19.1

Frequency

Most companies don't collect customer data frequently enough. Instead of the 'big' annual customer survey, companies can use this simple one-question approach to collect data more frequently. A good idea is to collect data on NPS continuously from a subset of your customers or at least monthly (from e.g. 10% of customers). This way, you can get trends and avoid drawing conclusions on biased or outdated data.

Source of the data

The data for your NPS come from surveying your existing customers.

Cost/effort in collecting the data

The simple nature of this KPI makes it more cost efficient compared to more traditional customer satisfaction surveys. However, as with any customer satisfaction survey, costs can be significant. Costs are particularly high for hard copy and mail surveys. A way to reduce costs is to automate data collection.

Target setting/benchmarks

Here are some benchmarks from the NPS leader table compiled by Satmetrix:

Table 19.1 2011 Net Promoter Industry Reports for the US and the UK

NPS Leaders – US 2011		NPS Leaders – UK 2011	
Company	NPS	Company	NPS
USAA – Banking	87%	Apple – Computer Hardware	67%
Trader Joe's – Grocery	82%	First Direct – Banking	61%
Wegmans – Grocery	78%	LG – Television	39%

NPS Leaders – US 2011		NPS Leaders – UK 2011	
Company	NPS	Company	NPS
Costco – Dept Store and Wholesale	77%	Samsung – Television	35%
Apple – Computer Hardware	72%	Sony – Computer Hardware	30%

Source: Satmetrix

Example We can look as this simple calculation example. A company surveyed 1,000 customers with the question: 'How likely would you be to recommend the product from this company to a friend?' Respondents can then score their reply on a 0–10 scale (0 = Not at all likely, 5 = Neutral, 10 = Extremely likely. Here is a breakdown of the replies:

Score	Counts
0	1
1	2
2	0
3	0
4	2
5	5
6	10
7	110
8	170
9	400
10	300

The NPS is therefore:

NPS = (% of customers that are Promoters) − (% of customers that are Detractors)

$$\text{Promoters:} \left[\frac{(300+400)}{1,000}\right] \times 100 = 70\%$$

$$\text{Detractors:} \left[\frac{(1+2+0+0+2+5+10)}{1,000}\right] \times 100 = 2\%$$

NPS = 70% − 2% = 68%

CUSTOMER PERSPECTIVE

Tips/warnings

The NPS will give a nice, simple number; however, what it won't give you are the reasons why customers would or wouldn't recommend you or your products or services. A very powerful supplement to the single-question survey is a set of open questions along the following lines:

- What do you particularly like about this company/product?
- What or which areas could be improved?

This way, the company will not only get insight into how many customers are Promoters versus Detractors but also into the areas that need to be improved. Take this example from the Canada-based online retailer Zappos. The NPS survey is administered in two different situations: 1) after an order; 2) after a customer speaks with a customer loyalty representative.

Zappos online questions ask the NPS (on the 0–10 scale): 'How likely are you to recommend Zappos to a friend or a family member?'

However, to gain further information that would help them move their customers that are Detractors or Passive to Promoters status, they also ask the customer: 'If you had to name one thing that we could improve upon, what would that be?'

Moreover, following the interaction with the customer loyalty representative (and again on the 0–10 scale) the customer is asked: 'If you had your own company that was focused upon service, how likely would you be to hire this person to work for you?' Further questions ask 'Overall, would you describe the service you received from (insert name of customer loyalty representative) as good, bad, or fantastic?' and 'What exactly stood out as being good or bad about this service?'

As a point of warning, people highlight the fact that the NPS methodology lacks statistical integrity because grouping the responses into just three categories causes the error interval to multiply nine-fold. It might be that the NPS oversimplifies the scoring a little and companies might be better off looking at the actual breakdown of answers from the 10-point scale and their changes over time.

References

Net promoter is a customer loyalty metric developed by (and a registered trademark of) Fred Reichheld, Bain & Company, and Satmetrix.

Frederick F. Reichheld, The one number you need to grow, *Harvard Business Review*, December 2003.

Fred Reichheld, *The Ultimate Question: Driving Good Profits and True Growth*, Boston, MA: Harvard Business School Press, 2006.

www.netpromoter.com/

www.satmetrix.com

http://customermetrics411.com/other-metrics-net-promoter.html

Customer retention rate 20

> **Strategic perspective**
> Customer perspective
>
> **Key performance question this indicator helps to answer**
> To what extent are we keeping the customers we have acquired?

Why is this indicator important?

In order to keep making money, companies need customers who buy their products and services. Keeping the customers we already have is usually better and cheaper than trying to find and win new ones. First, attracting and converting leads to customers is expensive. It is generally cheaper to maintain an existing customer relationship than to create a new one from scratch. Second, once customers have made a decision to buy from you it is generally easier to re-sell, cross-sell and up-sell to them.

This is why most businesses aim to convert their first-time buyers into long-term profitable customers. In his book *The Loyalty Effect*, Fred Reichfeld makes the point that 'A 5% improvement in customer retention rates will yield between a 20 to 100% increase in profits across a wide range of industries.'

The customer retention rate is a powerful indicator of current customer performance as it demonstrates loyalty through real behaviours (customers have actually decided to come back or stay), instead of factors that might predict future loyalty such as the net promoter score and brand equity (customers might be more likely to re-purchase in the future but there is no guarantee). On the other hand, of course, current retention rates are no guarantee of future retention either, but as a rule of thumb it can be stated that customers who buy more frequently are more likely to continue to do so.

Customer retention is therefore a metric that allows you to understand what percentage of your existing customers remain customers or make a repeat purchase. If your retention rate is high, you can generally assume high customer satisfaction levels (unless the barriers to leaving are very high or the incentives you give your customers outweigh the bad service they might receive). If retention is low, you want to know not just the actual numbers but more importantly the reasons for dissatisfaction (especially relative to your competitors).

A final point to remember about retention is that you don't necessarily want to keep all the customers you have acquired. Reasons for this are that some might not be profitable or some might be more expensive to serve compared to others. This is why the customer retention rate needs to be understood in the context of other measures such as customer profitability and customer lifetime value.

A complementary measure of customer retention is the customer churn rate (or customer attrition), which measures the percentage of customers a business loses over a specified time-frame.

How do I measure it?

Data collection method

When companies have good and accurate customer data, data for your customer retention ratio come from your purchasing information, i.e. your general sales ledger or your CRM (customer relationship management) system. If no customer data are available, a survey could be used to estimate customer retention.

Formula

Retention rate measures the percentage of customers a company is able to retain over a specified period. The formula that is often provided in textbooks just divides the number of active customers at the end of the time period by the number of active customers at the start of the time period. The problem with this formula is that it not only measures retained customers but includes newly acquired customers and therefore is not really a measure of retention.

A better formula is:

$$\text{Customer retention rate (CRR)} = \frac{\text{Number of those customers that remained customers at the end of a period}}{\text{Number of customers at the beginning of a period}}$$

A slight variation on this formula and an even better measure of customer retention would be to divide the Number of customers at the beginning of a period that are at risk of leaving by the Number of those customers that remained customers at the end of a period.

Frequency

The frequency of measurement depends on the average lifespan, contract duration or average purchasing cycle. Monthly collection of the data usually makes sense in most industries.

Source of the data

These data can in most cases be extracted from the sales ledger or CRM system.

Cost/effort in collecting the data

The cost and effort involved in measuring retention rates depend very much on the quality and accuracy of your customer data. Banks, for example, who hold accurate data about customers, will find calculating retention very inexpensive. If you have no accurate data about your customers – e.g. a restaurant chain, for example – a survey might be necessary, which tends to bring the cost up significantly and the reliability down.

Target setting/benchmarks

In a typical company, customers are defecting at the rate of 10–30% per year. However, customer retention rate and churn rate targets need to be set in the context of your industry and against past performance, because retention rates vary widely between industries. While the retention rate in retail banking is still fairly high (but coming down as more young people are willing to switch), the retention rate in the mobile phone or internet service provider sector is generally low as customers are constantly looking for the best package deals. A recent study by J.D. Power and Associates of retention rates in the car industry found that Toyota (64.6%) leads the customer retention rankings, followed by Lexus (63.0%) and Honda (62.8%). Most commercial organisations will set customer retention targets as a key part of their (annual) marketing strategy development process.

Example One of my clients is a world-leading telecommunications company that wanted to understand customer retention as a key measure for its corporate dashboard. Using its CRM database it can calculate what percentage of the customers who are at risk are renewing their contracts.

Let's say that in December of a given year 200,000 mobile phone contracts are coming up for renewal and the company is able to review 130,000 of those. The customer retention ratio is:

$$\frac{130,000}{200,000} = 65\% \text{ (customer retention rate)}$$

This is giving them a very reliable picture of true retention and loyalty, as opposed to just measuring customer churn, which was hiding information such as customers who were counted as churn because they changed handset, changed phone number, moved from pay-as-you-go to pay-monthly contracts, or were disconnected by the company because they didn't pay the bills.

Companies without customer contracts or good customer records that allow them to identify customers might find measuring customer retention rates a little harder. Retailers might find it difficult to track customers (unless they are using a loyalty card) and therefore tend to track transactions rather than customers. The only way to track retention in that case is by surveying customers about their loyalty to specific retailers. Retail giant Wal-Mart does not identify its customers and therefore tracks only the number of transactions. The UK retailer Boots, on the other hand, now has an estimated 70% of sales revenue linked to its loyalty cards – which allows the company to get an understanding of retention rates based on past purchase history and basket estimations (how often you are predicted to come back and how much you are predicted to spend). Based on this they can determine whether you are returning or not.

Tips/warnings

There are a number of difficulties in measuring retention. The main one is identifying and counting customers correctly. In order to calculate customer retention rates correctly you need first to identify your customers and then count them correctly. For example, if you are a telecom company, do you count people with multiple contracts (phone, tablet, mobile, broadband) as one customer or multiple customers? How do you treat family contracts – as one customer or as multiple customers?

Another difficulty is measuring customer retention rates in industries where sales transactions are more sporadic and when they take place in non-defined intervals. A car company like Mercedes Benz might use research to come to the conclusion that we buy cars in intervals of, let's say, five years. If they are able to keep correct customer information they can then estimate customer retention. The difficulty again is identifying a returning customer (especially if this person has changed address, credit card, etc.).

Finally, remember that looking at customer retention in isolation is not good; you need also to look at measures such as customer profitability and customer satisfaction to get a more complete picture of customers.

References

Frederick F. Reichheld and Thomas Teal, *The Loyalty Effect: The Hidden Force behind Growth, Profits, and Lasting Value*, Boston, MA: Harvard Business Press, 2001.

Customer satisfaction index 21

> **Strategic perspective**
> Customer perspective
>
> **Key performance question this indicator helps to answer**
> How well are we satisfying our customers?

Why is this indicator important?

Customer satisfaction is perhaps the most popular of all non-financial KPIs. For a commercial organisation it is generally perceived as the most indicative non-financial measure of future financial performance, the belief being that the more satisfied the customer, the more likely they are to remain loyal/repurchase, which in turn leads to financial success. Put another way, measuring customer satisfaction provides an indication of how successful the organisation is at providing products and/or services to the marketplace.

Moreover, repeated research over several decades has shown that it is significantly more expensive to attract new customers than it is to retain existing ones. It is more financially beneficial, therefore, to ensure that current customers remain happy – that is, that they are satisfied.

Although lacking the financial motive or retention pressures, public sector organisations are also expected to keep customers (the consumers of services) happy. Unhappy consumers (who increasingly judge public sector service delivery against the highest standards of the private sector) vent their anger on elected officials, who then demand improvements from public officials (often through targets that are mandated, auditable and comparable with other public sector bodies).

Of the many benefits of measuring customer satisfaction, one of the most useful is that it provides executive leaders with insights into the gap between present product performance/service delivery and customer expectations. This enables the launching of interventions that improve customer-facing performance.

How do I measure it?

Data collection method

Both quantitative (objective) and qualitative (subjective) data collection tools are used to collect customer satisfaction data. Survey instruments are used extensively and in various ways. For instance, customers are often surveyed periodically to ascertain their overall satisfaction with a product/service (usually using a performance scale, such as from 1 – very dissatisfied to 5 – very satisfied). Also, customers are often surveyed directly after receiving a service to capture their satisfaction at the point of experience: a mix of performance scales, yes/no answers and even qualitative questions are used here.

Finally, many organisations conduct focus groups with customers to gain more qualitative (and typically richer) insights into customer satisfaction levels. A mixture of quantitative and qualitative approaches is generally recommended.

Formula

There are many ways to measure customer satisfaction. One useful approach is the creation of a customer satisfaction index (CSI). In essence, a CSI is simply an average of all attributes that are believed to contribute to customer satisfaction. Since different attributes can contribute differently to overall customer satisfaction, the individual attributes are often weighted. Within an index a single customer satisfaction score can be generated (and described according to very dissatisfied to very satisfied levels). The widely used American Customer Satisfaction Index (ACSI – see example on the next page) generates a single score based on measures of customer expectations, perceived quality, perceived value, customer complaints and customer loyalty.

Frequency

Given that there are many ways to measure customer satisfaction, it is often measured on an ongoing basis. Organisations might aggregate and report customer satisfaction scores on a quarterly basis with a commentary reflecting the qualitative data collected. Organisations might also run one annual survey (such as through the ACSI) which provides data that can be compared with other organisations.

Source of the data

Customer surveys/interviews.

Cost/effort in collecting the data

Large customer satisfaction surveys, especially when conducted by external bodies, can be expensive and are generally run once a year. Focus groups can also be expensive to set up and administer. But other approaches (such as the short surveys found in hotel rooms) are relatively inexpensive and provide valuable customer satisfaction data.

Target setting/benchmarks

There are many services available for benchmarking customer satisfaction, both within industry bodies and more globally. The ACSI (launched in 1994) benchmarks performance within many industries/sectors, such as automobiles, household appliances, hotels, airlines and telecommunications. Participating organisations can assess their score against their industry competitors as well as against organisations in other industries/sectors.

A UK Customer Satisfaction Index has been launched that rates and benchmarks performance within 13 sectors, including banks, the automotive sector and public services.

Example As an example of constructing a customer satisfaction index, consider the approach taken by the ACSI (the methodology is now used extensively by companies in the UK and elsewhere). ACSI uses two interrelated and complementary methods to measure and analyse customer satisfaction: customer interviewing and econometric modelling. Beginning with the interviewing, professional telephone interviewers collect data (in the form of survey responses) from randomly selected and screened customers of companies and organisations.

ACSI researchers put the data into a causal/structural equation model, which provides scores for measured latent variable components (such as customer expectations, overall quality, perceived value, etc.), and the relationships (or 'impacts') between these measured components. Most importantly, each measured company or organisation is given a customer satisfaction index score (an 'ACSI score') which reflects a weighted average of three satisfaction proxy questions (see next page). Each index score is on a 0–100 scale, and therefore a company can receive any score ranging from 0 to 100. In practice, scores have tended to range from the low 50s to the high 80s. While slight differences between questionnaires administered to respondents across industries and sectors do exist, the three satisfaction questions used to create the ACSI score for each company are identical. Coupled with the standardised 0–100 index scale, these methods permit comparisons between companies and organisations.

ACSI measures customer satisfaction annually for more than 200 companies in 43 industries and 10 economic sectors. Measurement is done on a rolling basis. During each quarter, data are collected for particular sectors and industries and used to replace data collected 12 months earlier. This data are then weighted by industry and sector to create a national ACSI score.

The ACSI score is derived from three questions, each rated on a different 1–10 scale. The latest phasing of the questions used by ACSI can be found on their website (www.theacsi.org).

An organisation can incorporate these or similar questions into its own customer satisfaction surveys for approximate comparisons to industry and corporate benchmarks.

Tips/warnings

Although few would argue that measuring customer satisfaction is a bad thing, there are watch-outs. First, organisations can (and have) gone out of business through being overly zealous about delivering exceptional customer satisfaction without paying enough attention to the cost of service delivery. The financial cost of delivering satisfaction must be factored into any equation.

Moreover, in today's fast-moving markets, customer satisfaction doesn't always tell the whole story of likely future customer loyalty and therefore financial results. In some markets a customer might be very satisfied with a product/service, which might be made obsolete by a new offering: the customer might be very satisfied with the offering but defects to the competition simply because the product/service is more appealing – especially true in technology sectors, for instance.

Organisations should also look to measure customer satisfaction, and using various techniques, on an ongoing basis so as to get a broader and more insightful view of customer behaviour and attitudes. A once-a-year survey is simply not enough because it won't give you trends and is much more likely to be influenced by things you can't necessarily control (such as a negative media report).

References

Bernard Marr and James Creelman: *More with Less: Maximizing Value in the Public Sector*, Basingstoke: Palgrave Macmillan, 2011.

American Customer Satisfaction Index. **www.theacsi.org**

UK Customer Satisfaction Index. **www.instituteofcustomerservice.com**

Customer profitability score

22

> **Strategic perspective**
> Customer perspective
>
> **Key performance question this indicator helps to answer**
> To what extent are we generating profits from our customers?

Why is this indicator important?

Satisfying or, more likely, 'delighting' customers has, in recent times, become nothing less than a corporate mantra, the belief being that it is by satisfying the needs of customers that organisations can make a profit and therefore grow and prosper.

Although the basic argument is fundamentally sound (organisations can only make money if their customers buy the supplying organisation's products or services), there is a caveat: not all customers are equal. Some customers contribute substantially to an organisation's profit line while others actually lead to the supplying organisation losing money – that is, the cost of delivering the product or service is more than the revenue generated from that transaction.

In their zeal to 'delight' customers, organisations run the serious risk of moving into a loss-making situation. Organisations offer, but do not recover the costs of delivering, additional product features and services to their customers.

This customer profitability 'inequality' has been known for several decades and verified by numerous studies. As one powerful example, a customer analysis of a

US-based insurance company found that 15–20% of customers generate 100% (or more) of profits. Further analysis found that the most profitable customers generate 130% of annual profits, the middle 55% of customers break even and the least profitable 5% of customers incur losses equal to 30% of annual profits (see working example on page 106).

Simply put, a measure of customer profitability ensures that an organisation does not lose sight of its ultimate objective: to make a profit from selling products or services.

How do I measure it?

Data collection method

Analysis of marketing and accounting data as well as the output from activity-based costing exercises.

Formula

Customer profitability is the difference between the revenues earned from and the costs associated with the customer relationship in a specified period. Put another way, customer profitability is the net dollar contribution made by individual customers to an organisation.

As customer profitability covers several time-frames, it is not in itself a single measure. There are four primary measurements of customer value:

- Historical value of a customer, which looks at the value earned from a customer relationship over an extended period of time, such as prior fiscal quarter, prior year or since the start of the relationship. It can be measured as a simple average of previous periods or can be time weighted, placing higher emphasis on recent periods. Averaging in this manner has the effect of smoothing reported results for a customer, lending consistency to the reported values.
- Current value of a customer, which looks to a shorter time-frame, often a month (in order to coincide with reporting cycles). Current value is often volatile, since cyclical factors in the relationship are often not reflected within a single month. Current value has the advantage of highlighting the effects of changes in the customer relationship when compared to previous period current values. It is most useful for quantifying the benefit of campaigns, new offers and pricing changes on customer value.
- Present value of a customer, which is a future-oriented measurement that typically considers the future revenue and cost streams of the customer's existing business. This measure is usually only extended to include the contractual lifetime of ongoing products or services. Present value is useful for ranking customers according to value and determining sales compensation rates, and is frequently used as a basis for modelling

the impact of decisions concerning price and service before they are implemented.

- Customer lifetime value, which is another future-oriented measurement. What distinguishes it from present value is a modelling component: lifetime value takes into account projected revenue and cost streams not only from the existing relationship but also from business that is expected to be done with the customer in the future (we will discuss customer lifetime value as a separate KPI in the next sub-chapter).

As part of their assessment of customer profitability, organisations will often also use time-based activity-based costing, which essentially measures the present total cost of providing services or products to a customer. This requires obtaining information on only two parameters: the cost per hour of each group of resources performing work, such as a customer support department, and the unit times spent on these resources by specific activities for products, services and customers. For example, if a customer support department has a cost of $70 per hour, and a particular transaction for a customer takes 24 minutes (0.4 hours), the cost of this transaction for this customer is $28. This can be readily scaled up to companies with hundreds of thousands of products and services and thousands of customers.

Frequency

When customer profitability is measured depends on the metric being assessed (see Formula section). Remember that there is no single measure of customer profitability as they relate to different time periods.

Source of the data

These data can be extracted from the accounting and marketing data, but also from time-based activity-based costing analyses.

Cost/effort in collecting the data

Measuring customer profitability is certainly important but it can be expensive, especially when an organisation is analysing the profitability of many customers. Many companies will use time-based activity-based costing to allocate appropriate costing. This requires training, resourcing and management and requires the costing staff to spend some time in the business.

Target setting/benchmarks

Companies should look to move loss-making or break-even customers up the profitability categories.

Example Here is an example of calculating customer profitability in a bank.

1. Establish the costs per customer: Using activity-based costing models the bank has established costs for different customer services or customer interactions. For example, mailing of statement = $1.00, calling the banks contact centre = $2.00, visiting the branch = $3.00.

   It then estimates the behaviours of customers and might even be able to put them into different categories. e.g. customers over 50 who are more likely to visit the branch. However, to keep this example simple we say that on average a customer receives a statement once a month, visits the branch once a month and phones the contact centre once every two months. This now means that it costs the bank on average (12 × $1.00) + (12 × $3.00) + (6 × $2.00) = $12 + $36 + $12 = $60 per year to do business with an average customer.

2. Establish profit per customer. In this example, the bank knows that on average it is able to generate a 3.5% profit on each dollar it can invest. So if customer A has a deposit of $1,500 and customer B has a deposit of $15,000, the customer profitability looks like this:

   Customer A:
   - generates a profit of $1,500 × 0.035 = $52.50
   - but overall is not profitable when subtracting the average costs per customers form the profits. In this case the customer profitability score is $52.50 − £60 = − $7.50 (a loss of $7.50)

   Customer B:
   - generates a profit of $15,000 × 0.035 = $525.00
   - and therefore a healthy profit. In this case the customer profitability score is $525.00 − $60.00 = − $465 (a profit of $465)

Tips/warnings

Organisations need to ensure that they look holistically at the information generated from customer profitability metrics. For example, customers that are presently unprofitable can have high customer lifetime values (and vice versa). Therefore, organisations should not be in a rush to cease trading with unprofitable customers.

A further warning is that in acquisitions organisations often focus heavily on the lifetime value profitability metric, without taking into account that there is usually high volatility in the purchasing behaviour of 'new' customers.

References

Robert S. Kaplan, A balanced scorecard approach to measure customer profitability, 8 August 2005, *Working Knowledge*, Harvard Business School, **http://hbswk.hbs.edu/item/4938.html**

Customer lifetime value

23

> **Strategic perspective**
> Customer perspective
>
> **Key performance question this indicator helps to answer**
> How well do we understand the financial value from our customer relationships?

Why is this indicator important?

Some of your customers might not be profitable in the beginning or might be expensive to acquire but could become more profitable as the relationship continues. Just think about banking as an example. Others might only become profitable after a certain length of time of being a customer (think of mobile phone contracts which initially subsidise handsets and recoup the money over time).

Customer lifetime value (CLV) is a measure that combines (1) the anticipated length of the relationship between the supplier and the customer with (2) the anticipated customer financial value. This creates a predicted measure of how profitable that customer will be. For example, if a customer was forecast to have a length of relationship of five years with an average spend of $1,000 per year, then their total value would be $5,000.

Essentially CLV is the net present value (NPV) of the cash flows attributed to the relationship with a customer. NPV is basically an indicator of how much value an investment or project adds to the firm. Companies that measure CLV typically place greater emphasis on customer service and long-term customer satisfaction rather than on maximising short-term sales.

Calculating CLV helps an organisation understand how much it can invest in retaining the customer so as to achieve positive return on investment. Such a metric is often used by investors as a way of assessing the present and future health of an enterprise (along with a range of other financial metrics that are covered in this book).

In theory, CLV has intuitive appeal because in theory it represents exactly how much each customer is worth in monetary terms, and therefore exactly how much a marketing department should be willing to spend to acquire each customer. Practically this is not always so straightforward (see Tips/warnings on page 110).

How do I measure it?

Data collection method

The data for CLV are derived from an analysis of marketing (cost of acquiring and retaining a customer) and sales (monies spent by the customer).

Formula

There are different formulas in use for measuring CLV. Most models to calculate CLV apply to the customer retention situation. These models make several simplifying assumptions and often involve the following inputs:

- Churn rate, the percentage of customers who end their relationship with a company in a given period. One minus the churn rate is the retention rate. Most models can be written using either churn rate or retention rate.
- Discount rate, the cost of capital used to discount future revenue from a customer.
- Contribution margin, marginal profit by unit sale.
- Retention cost, the amount of money a company has to spend in a given period to retain an existing customer. Retention costs include customer support, billing, promotional incentives, etc.
- Period, the unit of time into which a customer relationship is divided for analysis. A year is the most commonly used period. Customer lifetime value is a multi-period calculation, usually stretching 3–7 years into the future. In practice, analysis beyond this point is viewed as too speculative to be reliable. The number of periods used in the calculation is sometimes referred to as the model horizon.

Thus, one of the ways to calculate CLV, where the period is a year, is as follows (from **http://en.wikipedia.org/wiki/Customer_lifetime_value**):

$$CLV = GC \cdot \sum_{i=0}^{n} \frac{r^i}{(1+d)^i} - M \cdot \sum_{i=1}^{n} \frac{r^{i-1}}{(1+d)^{i-0.5}}$$

Where:

- GC is yearly gross contribution per customer,
- M is the (relevant) retention costs per customer per year (this formula assumes that the retention activities are paid for each mid-year and that they only affect those who were retained in the previous year),
- *n* is the horizon (in years),
- *r* is the yearly retention rate,
- *d* is the yearly discount rate.

Frequency

A year is the most commonly used period. Customer lifetime value is a multi-period calculation, usually stretching 3–7 years into the future.

Source of the data

Marketing and sales data. Firms need to collect individual-level data about all their customers on a large number of variables in order to compute CLV. Some key informational needs are demographic information, the amount of purchase, products purchased on each occasion, the number, time and type of marketing contacts.

Cost/effort in collecting the data

The cost and effort in collecting this data differ depending on the number of customers being assessed. For example, collection of transaction data for all the end consumers poses a great challenge for a business-to-consumer (B2C) organisation. The data collection can be very expensive because of the relatively large number of customers. In some cases, getting transaction data on all the customers is impossible because the firm is not in direct contact with the end consumers. This is true, for example, in the case of an FMCG (fast-moving consumer goods) manufacturer who sells through intermediary channels (e.g. supermarkets and shops).

When an organisation has only a small number of customers (most often found in business-to-business (B2B) relationships), the cost and effort in collecting the data are relatively small.

Target setting/benchmarks

Organisations can use the CLV of high-value customers as a target for future acquisitions and also as a guide to shaping offers, etc. that might migrate customers that are presently lower value to a higher-value position.

> **Example** Consider this as an example of how to measure an organisation's CLV:
>
> An organisation has 3,500 steady customers that remain with the organisation for an average of two years; for the past two years, the net profit was $1,000,000.
>
> The CLV can be calculated as:
>
> $$\frac{\$1,000,000}{3,500} = \$285$$
>
> What this means is that over an average customer lifespan of two years, each new customer that is acquired and kept is worth $285 in profits.
>
> The following example looks at a CLV analysis for best and average customers (thus recognising that not all acquired customers are of equal value; see Tips/warnings section).
>
> | | **Best customers** | **Average customers** |
> | --- | --- | --- |
> | Life expectancy | Three years | Two years |
> | Revenue year 1 | $300 | $150 |
> | Revenue year 2 | $300 | $150 |
> | Revenue year 3 | $300 | $0 |
> | **Lifetime revenue** | **$900** | **$300** |
> | Gross profit margin | 10% | 10% |
> | Lifetime gross profit | $90 | $30 |
> | Acquisition cost | $10 | $5 |
> | **Lifetime net profit** | **$80** | **$25** |

Tips/warnings

Practically, it is difficult to make an accurate calculation of lifetime value. The specific calculation depends on the nature of the customer relationship. Customer relationships are often divided into two categories. In contractual or retention situations, customers who do not renew are considered 'lost for good'. Magazine subscriptions and car insurance are examples of customer retention situations, in which the firm knows when the relationship is over. The other category is referred to as customer migration situations, in which a customer who does not buy (in a given period or from a given catalogue) is still considered a customer of the firm because he or she may very well buy at some point in the future.

Organisations can often mistakenly believe that all customers that are acquired are equal. This is not the case. Often the contributions from many customers are far less than the cost incurred by the firm to attract and retain them; they spend little and so are loss-making to the supplying firm (whereas others cost the same to attract but less to retain and are profitable). Therefore, it is worthwhile looking at specific segments (from high to low value) of customers based on CLV and developing strategies for each segment (moving lower-value customers to higher-value, profitable positions).

As a further consideration, note that CLV frameworks rely on gathering a customer's personal and behavioural information. There is growing concern among customers about the privacy of their information. Firms, while gathering and using customer-level information, should be aware of this and take steps to gain the confidence of customers.

References

Avinash Kaushik, Excellent Analytics Tips #17: Calculating Customer Lifetime Value, www.kaushik.net

Dr V. Kumer, Customer Lifetime Value: The Key to Profitability, www.drkumar.com

www.marketingsphere.com

Customer turnover rate 24

Strategic perspective
Customer perspective

Key performance question this indicator helps to answer
How well are we retaining customers?

Why is this indicator important?

Empirically based research has long since proven that the cost of acquiring a new customer is significantly higher than the cost of retaining an existing one. Therefore organisations typically expend great efforts on 'satisfying' their existing customers so to increase their likelihood of loyalty and, amongst other benefits, remove expensive replacement costs (see also the customer satisfaction index KPI (on page 97).

Customer turnover (also known as customer churn, customer defection or customer attrition) is a popular KPI used to track the loss of clients or customers.

Within many industries/sectors (such as financial services or telecommunications), measuring and minimising customer turnover has become a key focus of management because customers are extremely vulnerable to defection to competitors who might provide a 'slightly' better or more favourable product (in banking, for instance, it has been claimed that 'customer loyalty is dead'). Identifying and implementing initiatives that successfully 'win back' or retain vulnerable customers can have a significant impact on an organisation's bottom line, so tracking customer turnover rates – and what is being done to reduce them – should be an important focus area for organisational leaders.

How do I measure it?

Data collection method

For organisations with customers on contracts, the data can be collected though an analysis of which customers renew at the end of the contract period (mobile phones, for example) and those that do not. CRM and other business intelligence analytics tools can be used to collect data for organisations that have many customers (such as supermarkets).

To track the likelihood of customers defecting or ending the relationship, relatively simple surveys can be used to collect data on customer satisfaction/dissatisfaction. Customer focus groups can also be useful. More sophisticated business intelligence tools can be used to mine databases of customer information and analyse the factors that are associated with customer attrition, such as dissatisfaction with service or technical support, billing disputes or a disagreement over company policies. Such tools can provide some pointers to likely levels of customer defection and therefore turnover rates. The more dissatisfied the customer, the higher the likelihood of his or her defection to a competitor.

More sophisticated predictive analytics software uses churn prediction models that predict customer turnover by assessing their propensity of risk to churn. Since these models generate a small prioritised list of potential defectors, they are effective at focusing customer retention marketing programmes on the subset of the customer base that is most vulnerable to churn.

Formula

A simple way to calculate the customer turnover rate is to take the number of customers who end their relationship with the company over a given period and divide by the total number of customers at the end of the period.

$$\text{Customer turnover} = \frac{\text{Lost customers over period } t}{\text{Total number of customers at the end of period } t}$$

Frequency

Customer turnover rates will likely be assessed on a monthly or quarterly basis, depending on the sector or industry. Fast-moving sectors where customers are typically vulnerable (such as telecommunication services) will have a need to measure turnover rates more often than those in slower-moving markets.

Source of the data

For organisations whose relationship with customers is contract-based, turnover data are found in the number of contracts not renewed, which is usually available in the sales data. This makes it easy to identify defecting individuals. For other organisations, turnover rates might be more aggregate and found through surveying or other instruments that show buying patterns and/or customer behaviour.

Cost/effort in collecting the data

The effort in measuring customer turnover varies by industry depending on the number of customers and the relationship (clearly turnover is much easier to measure when there are a small number of contract-based customers). For organisations that market and deliver products/services 'one to many' the effort is greater, but the sophistication of CRM tools etc. means that it is not an onerous task. Measurement costs are relatively low.

Target setting/benchmarks

Many industry bodies hold benchmarking data and most consultancies or CRM vendors operating in this field will likely have industry/sector comparative figures.

Example Here is a simple example using the formula on the previous page:

On 1 November the organisation has 100 customers.

During the month the organisation gained 20 customers.

During the month the organisation lost 5 customers.

$$\text{End of November turnover rate} =$$
$$100 + 20 - 5 = 115 \text{ customers} = \frac{5}{115} = 4.34\%$$

Organisations that track customer turnover and act on analytics around why customers cease the relationship (and typically defect) often claim stunning financial results.

As one example from 2002 to 2004, Verizon Wireless grew its customer base from 29.4 million handsets in use to 43.8 million, reporting a total of $13.7 billion in operating earnings. But the real news was what happened to customer turnover during the same period. The company's monthly customer churn rate was reduced from 2.6% to 1.3%, increasing its customer equity by $13.9 billion. The company actually created more than twice as much value as was reflected in its financial statements. Forty per cent of the increase in the company's customer equity was attributable to the new customers it acquired during the period, but 60% was attributable to the increase in the value of all its customers due to the increased customer retention rate. In effect, Verizon Wireless created shareholder value every year from 2002 to 2004, amounting to about two-thirds of its actual value as a business at the beginning of 2002.

Tips/warnings

Given the much-publicised cost differential between acquiring new customers as opposed to retaining existing ones, organisations should put in place mechanisms for 'winning back' lapsed customers or for ensuring they keep those that are identified as 'vulnerable'. Many organisations have special departments for this purpose. But ultimately this will only prove successful if the organisation can deal with the reasons why the customer has ended (or is considering ending) the relationship.

Note too that it is important to make a distinction between voluntary turnover and involuntary turnover. Voluntary churn occurs due to a decision by the customer to switch to another company or service provider and so comprises factors that are within the organisation's control. Involuntary churn occurs due to circumstances such as relocation to a distant location or death. Although involuntary turnover numbers are nice to know, there is typically little that can be done to mitigate such attrition, so voluntary turnover should be the primary focus area, as these are the customers than might be 'won back', or at least insights into why they defected might lead to interventions to lessen the likelihood of it happening again. Also, in some cases there might be 'forced' churn, where a company decides to end the relationship with a customer (e.g. due to not paying bills on time).

A final watch-out is that in many industries it is difficult to assess accurately when customers have been 'lost'. They might just not have purchased for a while because of external circumstances – financial difficulties, etc.

References

Q&A with Don Peppers and Martha Rogers: Measuring Customer Value Can Be More Important than Measuring Revenue: **http://mthink.com/content/qa-don-peppers-and-martha-rogers-measuring-customer-value-can-be-more-important-measuring**

Customer engagement

25

> **Strategic perspective**
> Customer perspective
>
> **Key performance question this indicator helps to answer**
> To what extent are our customers engaged with our organisation?

Why is this indicator important?

This is the first of two KPIs in this book that consider customer engagement. Within the 'Marketing and sales perspective' section we describe how to assess how customers engage with an organisation through online vehicles (such as websites/discussion forums) – a burgeoning area of interest for senior managers and marketers alike as they struggle to make sense of how the internet has changed customer–supplier dynamics.

This KPI, however, looks at 'customer engagement' measurement more traditionally: that is, the strength of a customer's relationship with an organisation as assessed through the customer's overall perception of/experience with the organisation (through whichever customer – supplier touchpoints – online or offline).

Companies that are measuring 'customer engagement' are ultimately interested in building a loyal customer base that delivers superior financial returns. That said, conventional wisdom has it that satisfied customers = loyal customers = profit. So why measure engagement? Although we would strongly argue that satisfaction is an important KPI (see the customer satisfaction index KPI on page 97), research has found that it is not uncommon for a significant percentage of customers to defect to competitors even if they are satisfied with a supplier's products/services.

As early as the mid-1990s Xerox was finding that more than a quarter of 'satisfied' customers defected at the end of their contract. The company found that those that remained loyal were more likely to be 'very satisfied' and that this usually had something to do with how the customers perceived their relationship with Xerox – what today we would call 'engagement'.

More recently, the US-based Enterprise Rent-A-Car has moved away from relying on conventional measures of satisfaction to deploying an enterprise service quality metric that counts only those customers that are 'completely satisfied'. Internal research had shown that customers who are completely satisfied are three times more likely to return as a customer: analysis has found that these customers value the relationship with Enterprise Rent-A-Car and so can be described as 'engaged' (Marr, 2010).

And 'engaging' customers certainly delivers financial results to the supplier. The globally respected research firm Gallup has created a customer satisfaction metric that is based on just 11 questions. Based on the findings, Gallup categorises customer engagement according to four levels:

- Fully engaged customers: These are emotionally attached and rationally loyal and are an organisation's most valuable customers.
- Engaged customers: These are beginning to feel the stirrings of emotional engagement.
- Disengaged customers: These are emotionally and rationally neutral.
- Actively disengaged customers: These are emotionally detached and actively antagonistic.

Gallup's analysis across many industries serving both B2C and B2B customer sets (Gallup's most recent database, which covers a four-year time period, includes data collected from almost three million customers representing 47,000 workgroups in 16 major industries and 53 countries worldwide) reveals that customers who are fully engaged represent an average 23% premium in terms of share of wallet, profitability, revenue and relationship growth compared to the average customer. Actively disengaged customers, on the contrary, represent a 13% discount in those same measures. Organisations that have optimised engagement have outperformed their competitors by 26% in gross margin and 85% in sales growth. Their customers buy more, spend more, return more often and stay longer.

How do I measure it?

Data collection method

Data are collected through quantitative surveying tools. Customers might be asked to rate their experience of the supplier's service/product according to a Likert scale (for example from 1 – very dissatisfied to 5 – very satisfied) or by providing a simple yes/no answer. Room for more qualitative replies might also be provided to add further richness to the findings.

Formula

Although there are many ways to measure customer engagement, the Gallup approach is particularly noteworthy. Gallup's customer engagement ratio is a macro-level indicator of an organisation's health that allows executives to track the proportion of fully engaged to actively disengaged customers.

Gallup developed its metric over a number of years of talking with customers and analysing their behaviours and testing many metrics. A final list of eight emotional attachment questions and three rational loyalty questions consistently showed linkages to key business performance metrics. The final metric consists of 11 questions, which Gallup calls the CE[11].

The metric is the ratio of fully engaged customers for every actively disengaged customer. So a ratio of 5.4 to 1 means 5.4 actively engaged customers to 1 actively disengaged. Gallup can then place the organisation into the appropriate engagement category (see previous page) and describe likely financial consequences.

The CE[11] measurement survey is measuring a customer's rational assessment of a brand (questions 1–3) as well as their emotional attachment (questions 4–11), covering confidence, integrity, pride and passion.

Frequency

Usually measured and reported annually.

Source of the data

The data are drawn from the customer engagement surveys.

Cost/effort in collecting the data

When using an external firm to administer a customer engagement survey the cost might be fairly high (in line with any consulting engagement). If administered in-house the costs will be lower but the effort higher and the organisation will not have access to useful benchmarks.

Target setting/benchmarks

A customer engagement survey as administered by a company such as Gallup will typically have extensive databases of benchmarks of best practice performance from which the client organisation can identify and work towards their own targets against both industry comparators and the Gallup database as a whole. According to Gallup, in average organisations the ratio of fully engaged customers to actively disengaged customers is 0.8:1, while in world-class organisations the engagement ratio is 8:1.

Example

In 2009, Gallup studied a specific business category that illustrates the impact of customer engagement ratios on marketplace performance. It completed a multi-year study (2006 to 2008) that asked customers about their engagement with the restaurants they visit. The results revealed that restaurants with high engagement ratios clearly outpaced the overall industry in terms of growth.

In 2006, for example, one restaurant chain had an engagement ratio of 5.4 to 1; however, the ratio improved to 7.2 to 1 by 2008. Over that same timeframe, its overall sales in the United States grew by 30% and per-unit sales increased by 13%. In contrast, a competing chain had an engagement ratio of 0.63 to 1 in 2006 that declined to 0.46 to 1 in 2008, and its overall sales shrank by 2% over that period.

Tips/warnings

Although customer engagement is typically measured and reported annually, organisations might consider surveying customers more frequently (say 10% of customers 10 times per year) so as to get a picture of how engagement is progressing, especially in light of performance improvement interventions launched to drive up the engagement score. For many organisations a once-a-year metric might be insufficient for maintaining a competitive edge.

To gain a richer picture of relationships with customers, organisations should also ensure that they conduct qualitative assessments (through focus groups, etc.) to complement/validate the quantitative results.

Those organisations that deploy the Gallup customer engagement survey might consider using it alongside Gallup's employee engagement survey (see employee engagement KPI on page 269). Employees ultimately drive customer engagement and Gallup research has found that business units that score above its database median on both customer and employee engagement significantly outperform units that rank in the bottom half on both measures. Gallup calls this performance optimisation.

References

www.gallup.com/consulting/49/customer-engagement.aspx

Bernard Marr, *The Intelligent Company: Five Steps to Success with Evidence-based Management*. John Wiley, Chichester, 2010. **www.ap-institute.com**

Customer complaints   26

> **Strategic perspective**
> Customer perspective
>
> **Key performance question this indicator helps to answer**
> To what extent are we satisfying our customers?

Why is this indicator important?

Customers that complain are patently unhappy with some aspect of a product or service. Moreover, they can cause significant damage to an organisation's reputation and ability to attract new customers. A study by TARP Research as far back as 1999 uncovered the fact that on average an unhappy customer will tell 10 people about their experience. In turn, these 10 people will tell a further five people, meaning that a total of 60 people will have heard of this bad experience. TARP's findings have been supported by innumerable other research programmes over the past 20 or so years. As another example, a study conducted by the now defunct White House Office of Consumer Affairs in the United States found that each unhappy customer will share their grievance with at least nine other people, and that 13% of unhappy customers will tell 20 people or more. This is worrying in the light of other research that finds that 67% of people stated that the top source for making up their minds as to which product to buy is 'talking to friends, family and work colleagues'.

The White House research also found that satisfied customers tell only half as many people (five other people, on average) of their positive experience. An organisation therefore needs two satisfied customers for every one that is dissatisfied just to maintain the current status.

The challenge is that 95% of dissatisfied customers don't complain, they just stop buying. Of customers who do complain, between 54 and 70% will do business with the organisation again if their complaint is resolved. These figures go up to a staggering 95% if the customer feels that the complaint was resolved quickly.

But measuring customer complaints is more than a simple metric of dissatisfaction. It enables an organisation to put in place solutions to deal with the cause of the complaint (be that a product shortcoming or a customer service failure). Research finds that customers that complain and have that complaint resolved are likely to remain loyal. One company found that it recaptured a full 35% of its defectors just by contacting them and listening to them earnestly.

How do I measure it?

Data collection method

There are many ways to capture, and measure the level of, customer complaints. Customer satisfaction surveys are useful for capturing levels of dissatisfaction and should show why the customer is dissatisfied (by implication they have a complaint). Organisations should also leverage other opportunities, such as a hotel utilising the short customer feedback surveys that are placed in guest rooms, or an airline deploying 'video point' booths at an airport so that customers can air their views on arrival.

Larger organisations should also establish dedicated units for capturing customer complaints and, crucially, acting upon them, as part of a customer complaint management process.

Formula

There is no single formula for measuring customer complaints, but here are a few of the most popular. An organisation may wish to create a 'complaints index' comprising several of these metrics.

- Number of customer complaints, e.g. number of customer complaints over a period of time or number of customer complaints per number of million units sold or shipped or number of customer complaints divided by total number of orders.
- Time taken to resolve a customer complaint, e.g. average time taken to resolve customer complaints to the customer's satisfaction.
- Complaint response time, e.g. average time to respond to customer complaints.

- Complaint resolution costs, e.g. costs of resolving complaints per period as a percentage of sales.
- Call length, e.g. average total time online to satisfy a customer's enquiry/complaint/transaction.
- Employee empowerment and customer pacification, e.g. percentage of customers' complaints or claims that are satisfactorily closed out by frontline customer contact staff.
- Frequency of types of customer complaints, e.g. frequency of occurrence of complaint types such as delays, staff rudeness, breakages, quality, etc.
- Customer complaints resolution, e.g. percentage of customer complaints successfully resolved.

Frequency

Customer complaints data can be collected on an ongoing basis (such as through a dedicated unit) as well as infrequently (such as customer satisfaction surveys).

Source of the data

These data are extracted from customers (their actual experience) and are normally kept within the customer service or marketing departments.

Cost/effort in collecting the data

The costs and effort vary according to the data-capturing mechanism being deployed. Simple customer feedback surveys at point of experience are inexpensive and require little effort. Larger-scale surveys (especially when conducted by an external consultancy – and normally as part of a broader satisfaction/engagement survey) can be expensive but will require little input from the organisation (as the analysis should be done by the consultancy).

Setting up a customer services department (that will capture and act upon customer complaints) brings with it typical resource costs (people, equipment, etc.).

Target setting/benchmarks

Benchmark organisations such as the American Productivity and Quality Council (APQC) carry out ongoing studies into best practices in customer complaint management and most specialist consultancies will house relevant data.

Here are some general benchmarks (which will differ by industry):

- About 25% of customers are dissatisfied with their purchases.
- Of those 25%, only about 5% complain.

- The other 95% either feel that complaining is not worth the effort, or they do not know how or to whom to complain.
- Only half the people who complain feel that their problem has been resolved satisfactorily.

Example Consider the following example from a leading global airline. Since formalising a customer complaint process, the organisation's retention rate among those who complain to customer relations has more than doubled, while the customer services department's return on investment (the value of business saved plus increased loyalty and new business from referrals relative to the department's total costs) has risen by 200%.

In training its employees, the airline helped staff understand several key issues:

- If the company replies to a customer and claims that events did not happen as the customer suggested, then the customer perceives the company to be calling him or her a liar.
- If, after investigating, the company reports back to the customer that events indeed took place as the customer claimed, then the customer can become even more agitated, inferring that the company did not believe him or her at first.
- If the company relays information to the customer that he or she did not know, the customer may think that the company is trying to make excuses for poor service.

To deal with these issues, the airline's customer relations department developed a four-step process that it incorporated into all its technical and human systems:

1. Apologise and take up the problem. Customers do not care whose fault the problem was; they want an apology and they want someone to champion their cause.
2. Do it quickly. Aim to reply to the customer the same day, and if that is not possible, certainly within 72 hours. Research by the airline showed that 40–50% of customers who contacted it with complaints defected if it took company staff longer than five days to respond. A speedy reply demonstrates a sense of urgency; it shows that the company really cares about the customer's feelings and situation.
3. Assure the customer that the problem is being fixed. Customers can be retained if they are confident that the operational problem they encountered will truly be addressed.
4. Do it by phone. The airline found that customers with problems were delighted to have a customer relations person call them.

Tips/warnings

Nothing will agitate a customer more (and therefore increase their likelihood of defection) than making a complaint, but then finding that it is not acted upon. In creating a process for capturing complaints, organisations must ensure that the resolution phase is also well established and that employees have received the appropriate training to deal with the complaints and where possible resolve the problem.

Note too that most customers do not complain directly to the service/product provider and so the number of complaints captured will likely represent only the tip of the dissatisfaction iceberg. Organisations will need to consider the breadth of techniques used in capturing the customer experience to inculcate strategies for attracting and retaining customers (including social media – see KPI Social networking footprint / on page 169).

References

Business Performance Improvement Resource: **www.bbir.com**

TARP Research: **www.tarp.com**

Six Steps to Achieving Customer Service Excellence.
www.customerexpressions.com/cex/cexweb.nsf/6_Steps_to_Achieve_Customer_Service_Excellence.pdf

American Productivity and Quality Council **www.apqc.com**

Bernd Strauss and Wolfgang Siedel, *Complaint Management: The Heart of CRM*, 2004

Angelena Boden, *The Handling Complaints Pocket Book*, 2001

www.jvmarketing.co.nz/perspective/the+facts+you+need+to+know....html

[PART THREE]

Marketing and sales perspective

Market growth rate

27

> **Strategic perspective**
> Marketing and sales perspective
>
> **Key performance question this indicator helps to answer**
> To what extent are we operating in markets with future potential?

Why is this indicator important?

Understanding the size of the market in which a company is operating and the rate at which this market is shrinking or growing is a key indicator to assess future revenue growth potential.

A key role of the management team is that they identify future growth opportunities in existing and new markets. Therefore identifying these markets and evaluating their growth rate is a vital piece of performance data.

The size of the market is measured by the total number or value of units (goods or services) sold in that market during a specified time period (usually one year). The market growth rate is a simple ratio of taking the market size of this period (e.g. this year) and dividing it by the market size of the preceding period (e.g. last year). A market growth rate of below 1 indicates a shrinking market while a ratio of above 1 indicates a growing market.

How do I measure it?

Data collection method

Unless data are readily available for specified and well-defined markets through benchmarking databases or market research companies, obtaining accurate market size data can be tricky. There are different approaches companies could take to obtain an insight into the market size, including:

- Conducting a surveying of the providers (manufacturers, service providers, etc.). The danger here is that it may lead to problems of overstatement.
- Surveying the channel or distribution route. This might lead to problems of double counting and missing parts of the market.
- Surveys of customers and end users. These are generally the most expensive as they require a large amount of data.

Formula

$$\text{Market growth rate (\%)} = \frac{\text{Total sales in the market for this year}}{\text{Total sales in the market for last year}}$$

Where sales can be measured in monetary terms or in the number of units.

Frequency

Market growth rate is usually measured on an annual basis but it makes sense to report it quarterly on an annual-rolling basis.

Source of the data

The data for market size and market growth rates either come from existing and available market research data or have to be obtained through surveys.

Cost/effort in collecting the data

The cost and effort of collecting the data for the market growth rate can vary significantly. In some instances the data might be publicly available, in others companies have to pay market research firms for the information (which can be pricey) or companies might decide to do the research themselves, which will obviously drive up the costs significantly.

Target setting/benchmarks

It is impossible to provide a benchmark for market growth rates as they will vary significantly. Obviously, a fast-growing market is better than a shrinking one.

However, having said this, there are companies that specialise in shrinking markets (e.g. they enter markets that major players are leaving behind as growth potential disappears).

> **Example** Take these two examples:
>
> For market X the size in 2010 was $500m and in 2011 it was $750m. The market X has grown by $250m = $750m − $500m
>
> The market growth rate for market X is therefore:
> $$\frac{\$750m}{\$500m} = 1.5 \text{ (or plus 50\%)}$$
>
> For market Y the size in 2010 was $500m and in 2011 it was $400m. The market Y has shrunk by $100m = $500m − $400m
>
> The market growth rate for market Y is therefore:
> $$\frac{\$400m}{\$500m} = 0.8 \text{ (or minus 20\%)}$$

Tips/warnings

Many companies would also attempt to predict a market growth rate for the future year (or years) by taking into account trend data and market prediction.

It might also be useful for companies to understand the average basket size (i.e. how much each customer is buying or consuming in a given market). This can be achieved by obtaining the number of customers and dividing the market size by the total number of customers in that market.

References

David J. Reibstein, Neil T. Bendle, Paul W. Farris and Phillip E. Pfeifer, Marketing metrics: understanding market share and related metrics, in *Marketing Metrics: 50+ Metrics Every Executive Should Master*, Prentice Hall, 2006.

Relative market share   28

Strategic perspective
Marketing and sales perspective

Key performance question this indicator helps to answer
How well are we developing our market share in comparison to our competitors?

Why is this indicator important?

The relative market share metric essentially indexes a firm's or a brand's market share against that of its leading competitor and therefore gauges its true market strength and identifies opportunities for improvement. To explain, whereas 20% might be the dominant market share in many markets, it might be a distant number two or lower than others: hence the importance of the word 'relative'. There are no global benchmark figures for market share that cross industries and sectors – such a figure would simply not make sense.

Calculating relative market share (see Formula) enables managers to compare relative market positions across different product markets. As a measure, relative market share grew in popularity thanks to studies (in particular by the Boston Consulting Group – see next page) that suggested that major players in a market tend to be more profitable than their competitors (although there are those that fiercely oppose this assertion, see Tips/warnings on page 136).

Relative market share, it is argued, indicates likely cash generation because the higher the share, the more cash that will be generated. As a result of economies of scale (central to the Boston Consulting Group matrix – see below), it is assumed that these earnings will grow faster the higher the share.

The reason for choosing relative market share, rather than just profits, proponents argue, is that it carries more information than just cash flow. It shows where the brand is positioned against its main competitors, and indicates where it might be likely to go in the future. It can also show what type of marketing activities might be expected to be effective.

The relative market share metric was first developed in the 1960s but was further popularised by the Boston Consulting Group in its famous matrix of relative share and market growth.

In the Boston Consulting Group's growth-share matrix, one axis represents relative market share – a surrogate for competitive strength. The other represents market growth – a surrogate for potential (see previous KPI). Along each dimension, products are classified as high or low, placing them in one of four quadrants. In the traditional interpretation of this matrix, products with high relative market shares in growing markets are deemed stars, suggesting that they should be supported with vigorous investment. The cash for that investment may be generated by cash cows, products with high relative shares in low-growth markets. Question mark or problem child products may have potential for future growth but hold weak competitive positions. Finally, dogs have neither a strong competitive position nor growth potential.

		Market share	
		High	**Low**
Market growth rate	**High**	Stars	Question marks
	Low	Cash cows	Dogs

Source: Boston Consulting Group (**www.bcg.com**)

How do I measure it?

Data collection method

Analysis of annual reports or market research that is in the public domain. Bespoke analysis can also be carried out, if data are more problematic to attain.

Formula

$$\text{Relative market share (\%)} = \frac{\text{Organisation's market share}}{\text{Largest competitor's market share}}$$

As we can see, the exact measure is the brand's share relative to its largest competitor. Thus, if the brand had a share of 20%, and the largest competitor had the same, the ratio would be 1:1. If the largest competitor had a share of 60%, however, the ratio would be 1:3, implying that the organisation's brand was in a relatively weak position. If the largest competitor had a share of only 5%, the ratio would be 4:1, implying that the brand owned was in a relatively strong position, which might be reflected in profits and cash flows. If this technique is used in practice, this scale is logarithmic, not linear.

Frequency

Usually measured annually but perhaps more frequently in fast-moving markets.

Source of the data

The figures required to calculate the relative market share of a company can usually be sourced from annual reports or market research that has been carried out.

Cost/effort in collecting the data

Costs and effort for collecting market share can be very high, especially in those cases where no good-quality data are available and market research has to establish baseline data. Benchmark data are available in many industries but this can also be expensive. The lowest costs for collecting data are incurred when the data are readily available.

Target setting/benchmarks

Targets can be gleaned from existing market research. Benchmarks can be gleaned from articles etc. that explain how other organisations secured high relative market share positions.

Example Consider the following example concerning small urban cars. As a starting point for making the relative market share calculation, we describe the performance of the key players:

	Units sold (thousands)	Revenue (thousands of US dollars)	Market share
Zipper	25	375,000	40%
Twister	10	200,00	21.3%
A-One	7.5	187,500	20%
Bowlz	5	125,000	13.3%

	Units sold (thousands)	Revenue (thousands of US dollars)	Market share
Chien	2.5	50,000	5.3%
Market total	50	937,500	100%

In the market for small urban cars, managers at A-One wanted to know their firm's market share relative to its largest competitor. They did this by calculating it on the basis of revenues or unit sales.

In unit terms, A-One sells 7,500 cars per year. Zipper, the market leader, sells 25,000. A-One's relative market share in unit terms is thus 7,500/25,000 or 0.30. We arrive at the same number if we first calculate A-One's share (7,500/50,000 = 0.15) and Zipper's share (25,000/50,000 = 0.50) and then divide A-One's share by Zipper's share (0.15/0.50 = 0.30).

In revenue terms, A-One generates $187.5 million in car sales each year. Zipper, the market leader, generates $375 million. A-One's relative market share in revenue terms is thus $187.5m/$375m, or 0.5. Owing to its comparatively high average price per car, A-One's relative market share is greater in revenue than in unit terms.

Tips/warnings

While relative market share (and indeed market share) is an important metric, other measurements are needed to develop a complete picture. Units, revenues and margin must also be tracked in order to determine the ultimate value of an organisation's market share. There are many ways to measure share. The easiest is to rank revenue or measure absolute volume in units sold or gross sales generated. Volume measurements are a start but need to be further described by the value of an organisation's market share. Having 70% share of a market in which you are losing money is not a sustainable strategy. Indeed, the lack of a 'profit' dimension is a major criticism of the relative market share metric.

A useful way of depicting market share is over time and in comparison to market growth (see Figure 28.1). This provides the reader with a simple picture to understand whether their market share grows in line with the potential and growth of the overall market.

References

David J. Reibstein, Neil T. Bendle, Paul W. Farris, Phillip E. Pfeifer, Marketing metrics: understanding market share and related metrics, in *Marketing Metrics: 50+ Metrics Every Executive Should Master*, Prentice Hall, 2006.

Fast Company Staff, Why Market Share is the Most Important Metric, Fast Company, 8 August 2005.

Boston Consulting Group: **www.bcg.com**

Brand equity

29

Strategic perspective
Marketing and sales perspective

Key performance question this indicator helps to answer
To what extent is value driven by our brand?

Why is this indicator important?

A brand (at either corporate or product level) represents an enormously valuable piece of legal property, capable of influencing consumer behaviour and providing the security of sustained future revenues to their owner. The value directly or indirectly accrued by these various benefits is often called brand equity.

Brand equity is the value (positive and negative) that a brand adds to an organisation's products and services. Brand equity may ultimately manifest itself in several ways. Three of the most important ways are as the price premium (to consumers or the trade) that the brand commands, the long-term loyalty the brand evokes and the resultant market share gains. The communication company Saatchi & Saatchi Worldwide has coined the term 'love marks' to describe how consumers relate to 'great' brands. They 'love' the brand so stay loyal, pay a premium and become an unpaid ambassador for the company or product.

Increasingly seen as an important financial metric (or at least a proxy), brand equity has become a very important measure in the eyes of investors. The largest part of an organisation's market value is no longer in tangible assets (such as factories, plant, machinery) but in intangible assets such as reputation, trademarks, know-how and brand. If the brand is diminished in the eyes of the customer then there will be a commensurate fall in the overall value of the firm. Brand equity is not simply a nice to know KPI but one that has significant financial implications. Measuring brand equity enables an organisation to maintain, build and leverage that equity; that is, to help the organisation increase both the 'R' and 'A' in the brand's Return on Assets.

How do I measure it?

Brand equity data are collected through qualitative and quantitative measurement techniques.

Data collection method

Qualitative measures can help identify associations to a brand, its strength, favourability and uniqueness. Face-to-face interviews or focus groups are typically used here.

However, quantitative measures are desirable to provide a more solid ground for strategic and tactical recommendations. Quantitative brand-tracking studies are often used for this purpose. When setting up a brand-tracking study, brand managers should include measures of brand awareness, usage, attitudes and perceptions. Different aspects of awareness such as recall and recognition tell us how strong a brand is, but depending on how and when the purchase decision is made (e.g. at point of purchase or away from it) one may be more important than the other for different product categories.

Usage and customers' experience with different aspects of a product have an impact on perceptions about product performance, but often go beyond product attributes to encompass an overall attitude towards the brand and its maker. In the quest for sources of brand equity, product- and non-product-related associations and perceptions should be tracked. All these measurements will inform marketers about how to design marketing strategies and tactics that strengthen a brand's appeal and uniqueness and thus increase its equity.

Formula

The formula for measuring brand equity depends on the level at which the equity is being measured. Some measurement approaches are at the firm level, some at the product level and still others are at the consumer level.

Firm Level: Firm-level approaches measure the brand as a financial asset. In short, a calculation is made regarding how much the brand is worth as an intangible asset. For example, if you were to take the value of the firm, as derived by its market capitalisation, and then subtract tangible assets and 'measurable' intangible assets, the residual would be the brand equity. One high-profile firm-level approach is by the consulting firm Interbrand. To do its calculation, Interbrand estimates brand value on the basis of projected profits discounted to a present value. The discount rate is a subjective rate determined by Interbrand and Wall Street equity specialists and reflects the risk profile, market leadership, stability and global reach of the brand.

Product Level: The classic product-level brand measurement example is to compare the price of a no-name or private-label product to an 'equivalent' branded product. The difference in price, assuming all things equal, is due to the brand.

Consumer Level: This approach aims to map the mind of the consumer to find out what associations with the brand the consumer has. This approach seeks to measure the awareness (recall and recognition) and brand image (the overall associations that the brand has). Free-association tests and projective techniques are commonly used to uncover the tangible and intangible attributes, attitudes, and intentions about a brand. Brands with high levels of awareness and strong, favourable and unique associations are high-equity brands.

All of these calculations are, at best, approximations. A more complete understanding of the brand can occur if multiple measures are used.

Frequency

Brand perception is normally measured on an ongoing basis, especially within large organisations with multiple products.

Source of the data

Those that are being interviewed regarding their perceptions of the organisation's brand.

Cost/effort in collecting the data

The simple fact is that the larger and more complex the organisation, the higher the costs. Typically, external consultancies will be used extensively to carry out the interviews/analysis and report on the findings. This is not a cheap process, but given the importance of brand equity it is a price that most organisations are willing to pay.

Target setting/benchmarks

There are many consultancies that will help an organisation set brand equity targets over, say, a five-year period (as with any key performance indicator, it should be subjected to targets). Initiatives are launched to build areas such as brand awareness and brand promise around an overall brand vision.

The world's leading branding company, Interbrand, publishes an annual list of the world's top 100 corporate brands. For 2010, the top four were:

1. Coca-Cola: brand value (M) $70,452
2. IBM: $64,727

3 Microsoft: $60,895
4 Google: $43,557

Source: **www.interbrand.com**

Example Here is a good example of how not to build brand equity.

In the early 2000s in North America, the Ford Motor Company made a strategic decision to brand all new or redesigned cars with names starting with 'F'. This aligned with the previous tradition of naming all sport utility vehicles since the Ford Explorer with the letter 'E'. *The Toronto Star* quoted an analyst who warned that changing the name of the well-known Windstar to the Freestar would cause confusion and discard brand equity built up, while a marketing manager believed that a name change would highlight the new redesign. The ageing Taurus, which became one of the most significant cars in American auto history, would be abandoned in favour of three entirely new names, all starting with 'F': the Five Hundred, Freestar and Fusion. By 2007, the Freestar was discontinued without a replacement. The Five Hundred name was thrown out and Taurus was brought back for the next generation of that car in a surprise move by Alan Mulally. 'Five Hundred' was recognised by less than half the population, but an overwhelming majority was familiar with the 'Ford Taurus'.

Tips/warnings

Organisations, and marketers in particular, need to be careful that they do not get blinded by brand equity. Yes, the brand is critically important but this should not be at the expense of the quality (or functionality) of the product. Moreover, at the product level, keep in mind that no matter how powerful the brand it will provide little protection against a new competitor that enters the market with a product with functionality and characteristics that essentially make the 'high-brand' product obsolete.

References

www.brandingstrategyinsider.com

www.relevantinsights.com/brand-equity

www.interbrand.com/en/Default.aspx

Cost per lead 30

> **Strategic perspective**
> Marketing and sales perspective
>
> **Key performance question this indicator helps to answer**
> To what extent are the costs for generating new customers justified?

Why is this indicator important?

A key role of the marketing and sales function of a business is to create awareness and attract possible leads. However, many ways to attract new leads, such as buying marketing lists and following these up with direct mailing, cost money and businesses need to make sure the costs are justified. One popular KPI is cost per lead, which calculates how much has been invested in attracting potential customers (the body of prospects from which future customer revenue will be generated).

Cost per lead is a powerful leading indicator of likely future revenue streams. But perhaps more useful is the cost per qualified lead, which measures those leads that are 'sales ready', i.e. that satisfy all the criteria for conversion to an actual customer (the purpose of generating leads).

How do I measure it?

Data collection method

Cost per lead is measured through the capturing of 'names' that have some level of interest in the product/service (so might be captured electronically via e-mail or other online mechanisms or face-to-face at exhibitions, as two examples).

Formula

To track the average cost per lead, you need two pieces of information:

- the total amount of money spent on the marketing campaign;
- the total leads generated by that campaign.

Calculating the cost per lead is simply:

$$\text{Average cost per lead} = \frac{\text{Total money spent on marketing campaign}}{\text{Total leads generated}}$$

Frequency

Although the cost per lead metric can be measured directly after a marketing event, the cost per qualified metric will likely be collected several weeks/months after the event – after the marketing team has applied 'qualifying criteria' to leads generated.

Source of the data

The data can be found in the marketing department.

Cost/effort in collecting the data

There are no significant extra costs or effort in collecting these data over and above that expended by the marketing executives employed by the organisation. The costs and effort are captured in the marketing vehicles deployed to generate the leads – costs and effort are much higher for staged events than for e-mail campaigns.

Target setting/benchmarks

Although final costs vary widely depending on the cost of the solution being marketed, industry experts suggest that the following cost per lead metrics can be used to compare one organisation with another in the B2B sector:

E-mail: £10–£100

Paid search: £30–£100

Banner ads: £80–£100
Webinars: £60–£250
Telemarketing: £350–£1,250
Exhibitions: £350–£1,500

Example As an example of using the cost per lead measure for decision-making purposes, consider the following basic example. An organisation's marketing campaign A yielded an average cost per lead of $1, whereas marketing campaign B cost $0.25 per lead. If you only had $1 to spend on your next programme, you're much better off investing in campaign B (assuming the lead qualities of both programmes are comparable). That $1 spent would generate four leads in campaign B, versus only one lead in campaign A.

However, for a different perspective consider the following example of calculating the cost of a qualified lead.

Two different businesses are exhibiting at the same show, Exhibitor #1 sporting a nice 10×10 booth with two personnel and Exhibitor #2 displaying a 50×50 exhibit with a theatre presentation and 19 representatives. Both companies had the same goal: generating as many sales leads as they possibly could over the three-day event. Exhibitor #1 was offering a new iPad as a means to draw traffic, and Exhibitor #2 was giving away a t-shirt and a guitar autographed by a famous rock star – and they had a bar.

For the duration of the event, Exhibitor #1 captured 148 leads and Exhibitor #2 captured 1,110. While there is a huge disparity between the two in terms of the number of leads at the event, the difference in cost per qualified lead tells a different story.

Exhibitor #1 results:
  Total cost = $12,250
  Total sales-ready leads = 31
  Total incubation leads = 48
  Total trinket-seeker leads = 69
  Cost per qualified lead = $395.16

Exhibitor #2 results:
  Total cost = $76,000
  Total sales-ready leads = 71
  Total incubation leads = 295
  Total trinket-seeker leads = 62
  Cost per qualified lead = $1,070.42

Tips/warnings

To be useful, an organisation should calculate the cost per lead and cost per qualified lead metrics separately for each marketing channel utilised. For example, the cost per lead will be much higher for a trade show (which typically includes significant human and physical resource requirements) than for an e-mail campaign. Coming up with a single cost per lead/cost per qualified lead across all marketing channels might artificially skew the number high or low, depending on the marketing mix.

The statistics for high-response strategies, such as e-mail marketing and banner advertising, are dramatically lower because they produce higher numbers of 'mildly warm' leads which require qualification and further investment.

At the higher end of the cost per lead statistics, although telemarketing has a greater cost per lead, it provides highly qualified leads and in-depth background information about the prospect. The return on investment of exhibitions and events is higher than that of e-marketing strategies.

Finally, it should always be borne in mind that it is substantially more expensive to recruit a new customer (irrespective of the medium) than it is to retain an existing one. Therefore organisations should also expend effort on the latter (see the customer engagement and customer satisfaction index KPIs in the previous section).

References

www.aperandi.com/blog/cost-per-qualified-lead-turning-lead-into-gold-60

www.dontaskdontsell.com/blog/measuring-cost-per-lead-can-be-costly%E2%80%A6very-costly

www.emarket2.com/index.php?option=com_content&task=view&id=541&sectionid=5&Itemid=1385

Conversion rate   31

> **Strategic perspective**
> Marketing and sales perspective
>
> **Key performance question this indicator helps to answer**
> To what extent are we able to convert potential customers into actual customers?

Why is this indicator important?

The conversion rate basically looks at the success rate of turning leads or potential customers into actual customers. For example, once you have attracted visitors or potential customers (be this into your physical shop or to your website), your next challenge is to convert the visitors (or potential customers) into actual customers.

What constitutes a conversion can depend a little on your objectives. In a physical environment it might mean a visitor entering a shop and then purchasing a good or requesting a quote. In the online sphere a conversion could constitute the ordering of a product or it may refer to an online visitor making a phone call, signing up for membership, subscribing to a newsletter, downloading software, or other activity based on subtle or direct requests from marketers, advertisers and content creators.

Understanding the conversion rate will give companies an insight into how well their marketing and sales strategies and their operations are aligned. For example, if you attract 500 people into your shop or to your website and all of them leave without purchasing anything, then this is obviously cause for concern. It might mean that what you offer on your website or in your shop is not what the potential customer was expecting, the visitors couldn't easily find what they were after, it was too expensive, etc.

Conversion rate stands as an umbrella term for many different types of conversion rates that companies might want to measure to gain more specific insights, such as:

- Visitor sales conversion rates
- Lead generation conversion rates
- Click-through rates
- Tender or quote conversion rates

How do I measure it?

Data collection method

The data collection method will depend on whether the conversion rate is being calculated for physical shops or for websites. Online, free-to-use web analytics tools allow you to track conversion rates along the so-called conversion funnel – the path visitors take from the initial prompt to the targeted action (e.g. a purchase). In the physical world retailers often use simple counting mechanisms that count the number of people who entered the shop and compare this with the number of sales transactions. However, more sophisticated tools are now available that allow shops to track customers using camera technology and software that will automatically track and report conversion rates.

Formula

In its simplest form, the conversion rate is calculated by dividing the number of goal achievements by the number of visitors:

$$\text{Conversion rate} = \left(\frac{\text{Number of goal achievements}}{\text{Visitors}}\right) \times 100$$

The goal achievements can be broken down into the different steps of the conversion funnel (e.g. conversion from page view or ad view to visit – also called click-through rate (CTR); from click though to filled shopping basket; from shopping basket to order, etc.).

Frequency

Conversion rate is an indicator that is best monitored continuously.

Source of the data

The source of data will depend on the area of measurement. For websites, the data will come from an online tracking system or from web analytics tools. For shops and physical locations the data will come from the visitor counting and tracking system and the sales data.

Cost/effort in collecting the data

The costs for measuring conversion rates will depend on whether the conversion rate is calculated for websites or for physical shops and spaces. Online, the costs are minimal as analytics tools allow you to specify goals and track them automatically, providing you with the conversion rate.

In physical locations such as shops, shopping centres, airports etc., counting systems have to be installed, such as tracking cameras and software. This will push the costs of measuring conversion rates up considerably.

Target setting/benchmarks

Setting targets for conversion rates depends a lot on the products and the fact of whether it is online or physical. Frequently mentioned numbers for online conversion rates are between 2% and 3%. However, according to ClickZ, retailers such as Amazon or eBay have a conversion rate of around 10% and higher. In the physical world you would expect conversion rates to go up significantly.

Example Take an online retailer that is generating traffic from banner ads on Facebook. The company can get an insight into how many people visit the sites with the ad on and therefore get an idea of how many people see the ad – in this case 1 million.

The click-through rate (the rate of people who then click on the banner and get directed to the company's website) is 2%, meaning that 20,000 people have clicked on the ad:

$$\left(\frac{20{,}000}{1{,}000{,}000}\right) \times 100 = 2\%$$

Of those 20,000 visitors, 3,000 put goods into their shopping basket, a conversion rate of:

$$\left(\frac{3{,}000}{20{,}000}\right) \times 100 = 15\%$$

Of those 3,000 people who have goods in their shopping basket, 2,300 end up purchasing goods. For the shopping basket to sale stage there is a conversion rate of:

$$\left(\frac{2{,}300}{3{,}000}\right) \times 100 = 76\%$$

The company measures its overall conversion rate from the time people reach its website to making a sale, which is therefore:

$$\left(\frac{2{,}300}{20{,}000}\right) \times 100 = 11.5\%$$

Another example comes from a leading retailer that wanted to track conversion in its physical shop network in order to get some comparative conversion figures. It installed counting technology that uses cameras at the store entrance to count the number of customers entering and leaving each store. The retailer then uses sales data to track the number of sales transactions that have taken place:

Store	Number of visitors in period t	Number of sales transactions in period t	Conversion rate
London	10,000	4,800	48%
Paris	12,000	3,200	26%
New York	11,000	5,800	52%
Shanghai	15,000	7,600	50%

Tips/warnings

When calculating online conversion rates it is important to be aware of the fact that the web logs register many 'visitors' that are in fact not real visitors. For example, search engines use so-called robots (bots in short) or spiders to search the web. These and other factors mean that between 10% and 30% of traffic to your website is not caused by 'real visitors'. This is why it is important to count the number of 'unique visitors', data that most web analytics tools will give you, as opposed to raw traffic data.

References

www.vertster.com/conversion-rate/how-to-calculate-your-conversion-rate

www.countwise.com/index.php

www.clickz.com/clickz/column/1718099/the-average-conversion-rate-is-it-myth

www.kaushik.net/avinash/excellent-analytics-tip-8-measure-the-real-conversion-rate-opportunity-pie/

Search engine rankings (by keyword) and click-through rate

32

> **Strategic perspective**
> Marketing and sales perspective
>
> **Key performance question this indicator helps to answer**
> How well are we optimising our internet strategy?

Why is this indicator important?

Along with page views and bounce rates (see KPI on page 155), search engine rankings (by keyword) and click-through rate are among a number of metrics that are used in website traffic analytics for assessing the effectiveness of an organisation's internet strategy in attracting and gaining value from visitors.

Search engine rankings (by keyword) is simply a measure of website ranking based on relevant keywords. Unlike web directories, which are maintained by human editors, search engines operate algorithmically or are a mixture of algorithmic and human input.

The goal of achieving a high search engine ranking is to increase website visits. Simply put, the higher the ranking the greater the likelihood that a person browsing the web (a searcher) will visit your site (obviously they are more likely to look at a website that appears on the first page than at one that appears on page 9 or 10 – see Tips/warnings). This is called the click-through rate (CTR), which simply means the percentage of time that a searcher clicks on a website displayed in their search results versus a different site. CTRs are impacted significantly by the search engine ranking for a particular keyword. At present, the most dominant search engine worldwide is Google.

How do I measure it?

Data collection method

The online collection of rankings from search engines, such as Google.

Formula

A search engine ranking is simply a website's position on the search engine ranking.

Consider the following as an example of measuring a click-through rate. As reported in the book *The Small Business Owner's Handbook to Search Engine Optimization* (see References), a site that has earned a Google ranking of number one for a particular keyword produces a Google click-through rate of 42% versus the site that is ranked number 10, which produces a meagre 6.06% CTR.

Frequency

Search engine rankings and click-through rates can be measured on an ongoing basis but will be reported in line with the organisation's reporting cycles.

Source of the data

Search engine rankings.

Cost/effort in collecting the data

There are a number of software applications that enable a free (or very cheap) analysis of search engine rankings (see References). So there is little if any cost/effort in collecting the ranking data. However, the cost comes when the strategy is focused on search engine optimisation (the process of improving the visibility of a website or a web page in search engines). For this an external consultant is typically required.

Target setting/benchmarks

Organisations should aim for a high ranking on the most dominant search engine. According to Net Marketshare, in December 2010 Google's global market share was 84.65%, Yahoo was 6.69%, Baidu was 3.39%, Bing was 3.29% and others stood at 1.98%.

In the United States, Google held a 63.2% market share in May 2009, according to Nielsen NetRatings. In the People's Republic of China, Baidu held a 61.6% market share for web search in July 2009.

So the target (and benchmark) should be a high ranking on the search engine with the most dominant national position.

Example This example comes from **www.SEbook.com** (see References) for predicting an increase in online sales for each keyword. For example, say an organisation scored a Google website ranking of number one for a keyword that, according to the SEOBook.com Keyword Selector Tool (which provides a list of up to 15 of the most popular search queries for each word you enter), was searched on 100 times per day in Google. The site ranking number one would receive a Google CTR of approximately 40%. This would translate into 40 visits to the website each day (100 searches × 40% CTR = 40 visits), or 1,200 visits per month.

Now we will convert the 1,200 visits into dollars. For this we will assume that the website delivers the average 2–4% conversion rate (sales from visits). This means that the 1,200 visits should produce approximately 24 to 48 orders per month (1,200 unique visitors × 2–4% = 24 to 48). We will also assume that your average online order is approximately $50. Therefore, a single keyword with a Google website ranking of number one could drive between $1,200 and $2,400 of online sales for your business each month, or $14,400 to $28,800 annually.

Tips/warnings

It is important to remember how CTRs drop off precipitously after the number one position. This reinforces the need to keep your website ranked in Google's (for example) top 10 (first page of search results) for the keywords that matter to your business. Otherwise, a large percentage of your customers and prospects will not find your website if Google has you ranked beyond its first page of search results.

Also, it is important to position current search engine rankings and click-through rates as part of a wider search engine optimisation strategy.

References

http://seotrainingproducts.com/blog-life/google-website-ranking

Stephen Woessner, *The Small Business Owner's Handbook to Search Engine Optimization: Increase Your Google Rankings, Double Your Site Traffic ... in Just 15 Steps*, Atlantic, 2009.

Net Marketshare: **http://marketshare.hitslink.com/search-engine-market-share.aspx?qprid=4**

For free applications for search engine rankings see **www.gtms-inc.com/tip_websitemetricsguide.htm**

For search engine optimisation consultants see **www.seoconsultants.com/**

Page views and bounce rates

33

Strategic perspective
Marketing and sales perspective

Key performance question this indicator helps to answer
How effective is our internet strategy?

Why is this indicator important?

Page views and bounce rates are two of a number of metrics that are used in website traffic analytics for assessing the effectiveness of the pages of an organisation's website in attracting visitors and retaining them for the period of time required for them to meet the goals of the site owner – be that sales or information delivery, for example.

Page views is simply the total number of pages viewed on the site and so is a general measure of how extensively the site is used.

Average page views is one way of measuring visit quality. A high average number of page views suggests that visitors interact extensively with the website. A high average number of page views results from one or both of:

- appropriately targeted traffic (i.e. visitors who are interested in what the site offers);
- high-quality content presented effectively on the site.

Conversely, low average page views indicates that the traffic coming to the site has not been appropriately targeted to what the site offers or that the site does not deliver what was promised to the visitor.

Such information provides powerful insights into whether or not the site pages need to be redesigned or whether the marketing to potential visitors needs to be more targeted. Naturally, for organisations that promote content (such as news) a high average page view provides valuable data with which to sell page space to potential advertisers, for example, as it helps them determine expected revenues from their advertisements.

For the owner of the site this information can be useful to see if any change in the 'page' (such as the information or the way it is presented) results in more visits.

Bounce rates essentially represent the percentage of initial visitors to a site who 'bounce' away to a different site, rather than continue on to other pages within the same site. A visitor can bounce by: clicking on a link to a page on a different website, closing an open window or tab, typing a new URL, clicking the 'Back' button to leave the site or session timeout.

Bounce rates can be used to help determine the effectiveness or performance of an entry page (such as a home page). An entry page with a low bounce rate means that the page effectively causes visitors to view more pages and continue on deeper into the website. Bounce rate can be seen as a measure of visit quality in that a high bounce rate generally means that the site entrance page isn't relevant to the site visitors (but this isn't always the case – see Tips/warnings on page 158).

How do I measure it?

Data collection method

Analytics tracking software is used to collect the data.

Formula

$$\text{Page views} = \text{The total number of views on an internet page}$$

$$\text{Bounce rate} = \frac{\text{Total number of visits viewing only one page}}{\text{Total number of visits}}$$

Frequency

Measured on an ongoing basis, given the medium being analysed, and may be reported as frequently as required by the site owner.

Source of the data

Web analytics software.

Cost/effort in collecting the data

The page views and bounce rate can be collected for free using web analytics tools such as Google Analytics.

Target setting/benchmarks

Numerous industry and sector benchmark reports for website traffic analytics exist, and can be generally found through web searches or through industry consortiums. Consider the following, which is a benchmark industry report for US retail by Core Metrics and includes page views per session:

Metric	Feb-09	Mar-09	% Change (m/m)	Mar-08	% Change (y/y)
Page views per session[1]	11.69	11.39	−2.58%	12.78	−10.89%
Average time on site (in seconds)[2]	481.08	476.13	−1.03%	615.20	−22.61%
Average items/order[3]	5.21	5.82	11.74%	6.33	−8.09%
Average order value[4]	$138.26	$143.93	4.10%	$153.62	−6.31%
Shopping cart conversion rate[5]	34.39%	34.52%	0.38%	35.75%	−3.44%

Source: **www.coremetrics.com**

Regarding bounce rates, Google Analytics specialist Avinash Kaushik has stated: 'My own personal observation is that it is really hard to get a bounce rate under 20%, anything over 35% is cause for concern, 50% (above) is worrying.'

Consider this analysis of bounce rate by industry:

- Retail sites (driving well-targeted traffic) 20–40% bounce
- Simple landing pages (with one call to action such as 'add to cart') 70–90% bounce
- Portals (such as Yahoo!, MSN) 10–30% bounce
- Service sites (self-service and FAQ sites) 10–30% bounce
- Content website (with high search visibility) 40–60% bounce
- Lead generation (services for sales) 30–50% bounce

Example Yahoo! Inc. receives many millions of hits to its home page each hour. To test new assumptions (in this case that making a certain alteration to the home page will change behaviours of visitors) it randomly assigns one or two hundred thousand users to an experimental group and has several million other visitors as a control group. By doing so, it can quickly see whether or not the alterations to the home page lead to the assumed change in the behaviour of the customer (such as clicking through to other pages and so reducing bounce rates). This in turn allows Yahoo! to optimise its offerings to enhance revenues and profits. The results of these experiments can often be seen within minutes, and Yahoo! typically runs about 20 experiments at any given time. This way, the results of the analysis drive behaviours, cutting out lengthy discussions about website design best practices – which of course can be extremely subjective and biased (quote from *The Intelligent Company: Five Steps to Succeeding with Evidence-based Management* by Bernard Marr).

Tips/warnings

There are many ways to increase page views, such as natural link building, which is an important search engine optimisation technique that works most effectively when a highly trafficked site provides an outbound link to another website. The more quality links a website has, the better the chance it has of ranking well in the major search engines like Google, Yahoo! and MSN.

Tips to decrease bounce rates: provide relevant content, build a clear navigation path/menu, place search function prominently, get rid of pop-up ads, reduce external links (or have them open in a new window), improve the load-time of pages (the longer the load-time, the greater the bounce rate).

Keep in mind that the bounce rate measure needs to be interpreted relative to a website's objective. On an e-commerce site, where the sole aim may be to sell products online, the bounce rate is a primary concern and useful measurement. Information sources and sites which drive the customer to make contact via e-mail or phone may see much higher bounce rates. This may not be a bad thing as they are viewing only one page of the site (but contacting the company). Such companies are interested in page views and not bounce rate – an 80% bounce as rate might be perfectly acceptable.

References

www.coremetrics.com

Bounce Rate Demystified: **http://blog.kissmetrics.com/bounce-rate/?wide=1**

www.google.com/support/analytics/bin/answer.py?hl=en&answer=60127

Customer online engagement level

34

> **Strategic perspective**
> Marketing and sales perspective
>
> **Key performance question this indicator helps to answer**
> How well are we engaging our customers online?

Why is this indicator important?

Customer engagement (CE) refers to the engagement of customers with each other, a company or a specific brand, measured primarily by online interaction. The concept and practice of CE enables organisations to respond to the fundamental changes in customer behaviour that the internet has brought about.

CE considers several interrelated dimensions.

1 CE is a social phenomenon enabled by the wide adoption of online mechanisms.
2 The behaviour of customers that engage in online communities revolving, directly or indirectly, around product categories and other consumption topics. It details the process that leads to a customer's positive engagement with the company or offering, as well as the behaviours associated with different degrees of customer engagement.

3. Marketing practices that aim to create, stimulate or influence CE behaviour. Although CE marketing efforts must be consistent both online and offline, the internet is the basis of CE marketing.
4. Metrics that measure the effectiveness of the marketing practices which seek to create, stimulate or influence CE behaviour.

A customer's degree of engagement with a company lies on a continuum that represents the strength of his or her investment in that company. Positive experiences with the company strengthen that investment and move the customer down the line of engagement. CE expert Richard Sedley has defined CE as: 'Repeated interactions that strengthen the emotional, psychological or physical investment a customer has in a brand.'

CE is an important measure for organisational leaders (and marketers) to track because in today's fast-moving and highly competitive markets, the level of customer engagement is perhaps the most reliable leading indicator of customer loyalty and therefore financial success. Gallup has found that organisations that have optimised engagement have outperformed their competitors by 26% in gross margin and by 85% in sales growth. Their customers buy more, spend more, return more often, and stay longer. Recognising this fact, the online retailer Amazon recently re-branded into 'serving the world's largest engaged online community'.

Highly engaged customers:

- Are more loyal. Increasing the engagement of target customers increases the rate of customer retention.
- Are more likely to engage in free (for the company), credible (for their audience) word-of-mouth advertising. This can drive new customer acquisition and can have viral effects.
- Are less likely to complain to other current or potential customers, but will address the company directly instead.
- Regularly provide valuable recommendations for improving quality of offering.

How do I measure it?

Data collection method

Collecting data online revolves around quantitative analyses of customer 'engagement' with company websites (so will consider metrics such as page views and bounce rates as well as search engine rankings and click-through rates (see KPI on page 151) and a qualitative assessment of the content of the views of, and conversations between, current and potential customers on blogs, discussion forums, etc.

Formula

Being a new metric that aims to capture data from fast-evolving online sources (websites, communities, blogs, etc.), there is no single or generally accepted measure of customer engagement. As a work in progress, the World Federation of Advertisers has created a 'Blueprint for Consumer-centric Holistic Measurement', and the Association of National Advertisers, American Association of Advertising Agencies and the Advertising Research Foundation have put together the 'Engagement Steering Committee', to work on the customer engagement metric. Research firms such as Nielsen Media Research and Simmons Research are also all in the process of developing a CE definition and metric.

The following items have all been proposed as components of a CE metric:

Root metrics

- Duration of visit
- Frequency of visit (returning to the site directly – through a URL or bookmark – or indirectly)
- % repeat visits
- Recency of visit
- Depth of visit (% of site visited or number of pages viewed)
- Click-through rate
- Sales
- Lifetime value

Action metrics

- RSS feed subscriptions
- Bookmarks, tags, ratings
- Viewing of high-value or medium-value content (as valued from the organisation's point of view). 'Depth' of visit can be combined with this variable
- Enquiries
- Providing personal information
- Downloads
- Content re-syndication
- Customer reviews
- Comments: their quality is another indicator of the degree of engagement
- Ratio between posts and comments plus trackbacks

Frequency

CE can be measured on an ongoing basis but will probably be reported to the senior team on a quarterly basis.

Source of the data

Data relating to an organisation's websites as well as online communities.

Cost/effort in collecting the data

Collecting data on customers' relationship with an organisation's website and other online channels is relatively inexpensive as the medium is geared for such interaction. A qualitative analysis of how customers (current or potential) relate to the organisation (i.e. what they say about the company and/or its brand/s) is more expensive as it will require qualitative interpretation and may require specialist external consulting support.

Target setting/benchmarks

Being a new metric, CE benchmarks are still very much a work in progress. However, specialist consultants are creating their own benchmarks, as are relevant bodies.

Example Shevlin (2007) states that measuring engagement needs to be done in the context of a firm's strategy and its own theory of the customer – that is, the behaviours that the firm believes constitute an engaged customer. In one exercise Shevlin measured customer engagement of banks. He started with the following dimensions:

1. Product involvement. A customer who doesn't care about the product is likely to be less committed or emotionally attached to the firm providing the product.
2. Frequency of purchase. A customer who purchases more frequently may be more engaged than other customers.
3. Frequency of service interactions. Branding experts like to say that repeated, positive interactions lead to brand affinity. Shevlin states that this is correct to a certain extent, but ...
4. Types of interaction. ... not all types of interactions are created equal. Checking account balances is a very different type of interaction from a request to help choose between product or service options.
5. Online behaviour. Time spent on a site might be very important. But, like types of interaction, not all web pages are created equal.
6. Referral behaviour/intention. Customers that are likely to refer a firm to friends/family might be more engaged – a customer who actually does refer the firm, even more engaged.
7. Velocity. The rate of change in the indicators listed above may be a signal of engagement.

Shevlin segmented the respondents into four categories, based on their level of engagement and the breadth of their relationship with their banks (based on the number of products owned). The result: a metric that helped marketers address some strategic questions about their marketing and customer strategy (Figure 34.1).

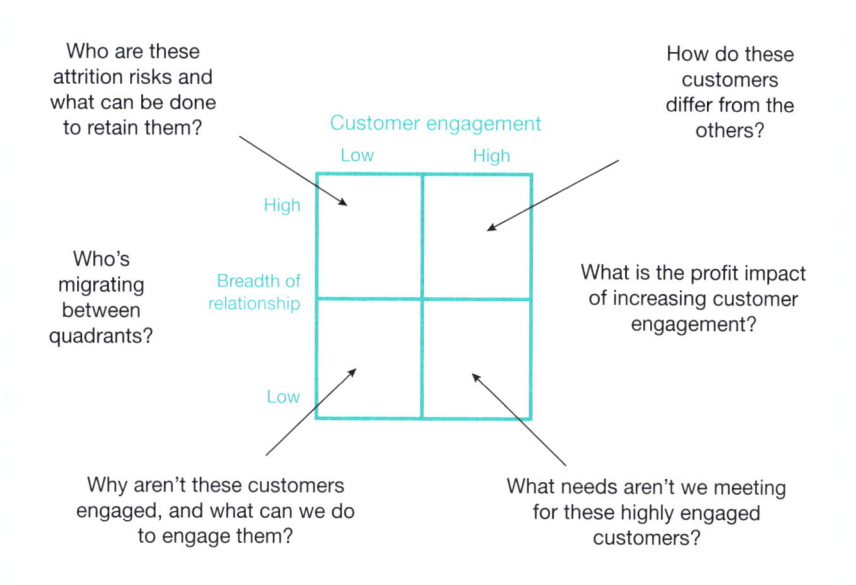

```
                        Customer engagement
                         Low           High
Who are these
attrition risks and              ↙
what can be done                           How do these
to retain them?    ┌──────┬──────┐         customers
                   │      │      │         differ from the
              High │      │      │         others?
                   │      │      │
Who's   Breadth of ├──────┼──────┤
migrating relation-│      │      │    What is the profit impact
between   ship     │      │      │    of increasing customer
quadrants?    Low  │      │      │    engagement?
                   └──────┴──────┘
                     ↑        ↑
Why aren't these customers        What needs aren't we meeting
engaged, and what can we do       for these highly engaged
to engage them?                   customers?
```

Tips/warnings

Customer engagement is more than just a metric to be collected; it is a core element of a broader relationship. As well as collecting data on how a customer relates to the organisation's online vehicles (websites, etc.) and what they say in discussion forums, it is important to begin a full, honest dialogue with customers. Suppliers no longer own the communication channels with their customers, so communication must be two-way.

References

www.gallup.com/consulting/49/customer-engagement.aspx

World Federation of Advertisers: **www.wfanet.org**

Nielsen Media Research: **www.nielsen-online.com**

R. Shevlin, *Customer Engagement Is Measurable*, Ron Shevlin's Marketing Whims, 2 October 2007, **http://marketingroi.wordpress.com/2007/10/02/customer-engagement-is-measurable/**

Online share of voice (OSOV)

35

Strategic perspective
Marketing and sales perspective

Key performance question this indicator helps to answer
To what extent and in what sentiment is our brand talked about compared to our competitors?

Why is this indicator important?

Most of us want to understand what others are saying about us, what is going round on the grapevine and whether what people are saying is positive or negative, especially as today's savvy consumers often trust 'word-of-mouth' more than traditional advertising. The beauty of the internet and particular social media platforms is that it allows us to do exactly that – listen in on the conversations people are having about us, our company, our brands and products etc. And what's more, there are free-to-use tools out there that track for us any user-generated content from across the online and social media universe.

This now enables companies to learn what people are saying and how their brands and products are being perceived and talked about. Tools such as Social Mention and Radian 6 are two of a growing number of solutions that allow companies to track not only what people are saying but also the sentiment of the mentions (i.e. positive, neutral, negative). Take the social media search and analysis platform Social Mention as an example: you simply type in your brand name (or product name etc.), press search, and you will get a dashboard with information including the number of mentions, strength score (the likelihood that your brand is being discussed in social media), the sentiment ratio (ratio of mentions that are generally positive to those that are generally negative), passion score (the likelihood that individuals talking about your brand will do so repeatedly) and other useful statistics, as well as a breakdown of the actual mentions.

While this in itself is very valuable information, collecting data for your own brand and that of competitors will allow you to calculate your share of voice. This will give you an insight into how your brand is talked about (in terms of both numbers and sentiment) relative to your competitors.

How do I measure it?

Data collection method

The raw data for your online share of voice KPI will come directly from online platforms such as Social Mention or Radian 6 and, once collected, you can use simple calculations or online widgets to calculate your share of voice.

Formula

To calculate your online share of voice you take the number of mentions your brand has relative to the sum of mentions that you and your competitors have:

$$\text{OSOV} = \frac{\text{Number of mentions for your brand}}{\text{Number of mentions for your brand and all your competitor brands}} \times 100.$$

For further refinements of this formula see the example on the next page.

Frequency

One of the advantages of the online platforms is that they allow you to create alerts for negative mentions, for example. This means that the measurement happens in predefined intervals every day. However, strategically you would only want to report this on a weekly or monthly basis – unless you are tracking the launch of a particular product, when you might want to measure and report more frequently.

Source of the data

Data will come directly from the online platforms.

Cost/effort in collecting the data

The costs for collecting data for OSOV are low because the hard work is done by the online platforms. The only costs required are to put the numbers into a little table or spreadsheet and calculate the relative share based on the individual numbers.

Some tools even include a widget to calculate OSOV, making it even simpler and cheaper.

Target setting/benchmarks

You would want a majority or at least a good share of the online voice compared to your key competitors. However, the target depends on the number of actual competitors. If there is only one other competitor then your target would be 50% or higher. If you are comparing yourself to 10 other competitors, then your target would be anything above 10%.

Example Let's look at the top fast-food burger chains as an example, using the Social Mention platform (**http://socialmention.com**). You simply type in the names of the brands you want to search for, e.g. McDonald's, Burger King, Wendy's and Hardees.

You can then note down the results for each competitor in a table like this (illustrative data only):

Organisation	Mentions			
	Positive	Neutral	Negative	Total
McDonald's	560	1,100	180	1,840
Burger King	350	770	40	1,160
Wendy's	99	203	27	329
Hardees	276	448	36	760
Total mentions	1,285	2,521	283	4,089

Total share of voice for McDonald's would be:

$$OSOV = \left(\frac{1840}{4089}\right) \times 100 = 45\%$$

However, some would argue that you only want to include the positive and neutral mentions and not the negative ones:

$$OSOV = \left[(\text{Positive mentions}) + \frac{(\text{Neutral mentions})}{(\text{Total mentions for all companies})}\right] \times 100$$

which would be in McDonald's case:

$$OSOV = \frac{(560 + 1100)}{4089} \times 100 = 40.5\%$$

Tips/warnings

The OSOV as outlined here will give you an idea about the actual numbers of mentions. In addition, it is useful to look at the average sentiment of the mentions. This can be calculated in the following way.

You can create a five-point scale with:

- positive = 5
- neutral = 3
- negative = 1

Now you can multiply each type of mention by the number in the above scale and divide it by the total number of mentions for this brand.

So for McDonald's we would take $\frac{(560 \times 5) + (1,100 \times 3) + (180 \times 1)}{1,840} = 3.41$.

You can now do this for each brand to get the comparative data.

References

www.clickz.com/clickz/column/2096125/tips-improving-online-share-voice

www.radian6.com/

www.socialmention.com/

Social networking footprint

36

> **Strategic perspective**
> Marketing and sales perspective
>
> **Key performance question this indicator helps to answer**
> How well are we using the internet to build our brand?

Why is this indicator important?

There is no doubt that social networking is transforming how people around the world connect and relate with each other.

According to The Nielsen Company, social networks and blogs are the most popular online category when ranked by average time spent in December, followed by online games and instant messaging. With 206.9 million unique visitors, Facebook was the No. 1 global social networking destination in December 2009 and 67% of global social media users visited the site during the month. Time on site for Facebook has also been on the rise, with global users spending nearly six hours per month on the site. Year-over-year growth in average time spent by US users, for both Facebook and Twitter, outpaced the overall growth for the category, increasing 200% and 368%, respectively. Among the top five US social networking sites, Twitter continued its reign as the fastest-growing in December 2009 in terms of unique visitors, increasing 579% year-over-year, from 2.7 million unique visitors in December 2008 to 18.1 million in December 2009. However, month-over-month, unique visitors decreased 5%.

Importantly, although social networking sites originally appealed to 'young' people (raised in a world where IT and internet literacy had become critically important – a skill equally as important as the traditional three Rs), the profile is changing rapidly. For example, in the January 2007–December 2008 time-span, the leading social networking site Facebook added almost twice as many 50–64-year-old visitors (+24 million) as it did under-18-year-old visitors (+7.3 million). Now more than a quarter of visitors are over 50.

Naturally, the concentration of potential customers within social networking sites presents mouth-watering business opportunities: for instance to market to/reach out to 'customers' wherever they are found throughout the world. As just one example, social networks lend themselves greatly to generating brand affinity. Consider the experience of Starbucks Coffee Company in the Example section. Such potential is available to most businesses – but there are not insignificant challenges (see Tips/warnings).

Those organisations that figure how to align their messaging with the thinking, mindsets and culture of social networking sites will reap huge benefits. This is one of the great opportunities facing organisations as we move deeper into the 21st-century knowledge-based globally connected economy.

How do I measure it?

Data collection method

Data are collected through sophisticated online tools (administered by the growing number of specialists in this area – such as those that focus on social media marketing) that measure and analyse how consumers interact with a brand on social networking sites.

Formula

A number of systems for measuring an organisation's social network footprint are entering the market, all with their own measurement methodology and assessment formula. As just one example (and this book is not recommending this approach over others) consider the Digital Footprint Index (DFI) launched by the US-based Zócalo Group. DFI, developed in conjunction with the Department of Marketing at DePaul University's Kellstadt Graduate School of Business, USA, is a multidimensional measurement methodology that sets out to enable marketers to do the following:

- Pinpoint where and how consumers engage and interact with the brand.
- Identify the social media channels consumers use to interact with the brand.
- Determine how well consumers understand and share the brand's message.
- Gauge the impact social media marketing efforts have on the growth of earned conversation.

- Understand how a brand compares to key competitors using social media.
- Track progress over time.

The DFI measures three dimensions of a brand's earned online presence:

- Height: the quantity of conversation and content about a brand across all social media channels, including blogs, forums, social networks, microblogs, picture-sharing sites, video-sharing sites, document-sharing sites and bookmarking sites.
- Width: the level of consumer engagement, interaction and sharing across all channels.
- Depth: the level of message saturation and sentiment or tone.

Frequency

The data can be collected on an ongoing basis but will likely be reported monthly within marketing functions and quarterly to management teams.

Source of the data

Analysis of the social media website data (Facebook, Twitter, LinkedIn etc).

Cost/effort in collecting the data

As the data for this metric will likely be collected and analysed by a specialised external consultant, the costs might be quite significant, especially as this is a new discipline. Costs will decrease as the discipline matures and competition increases.

Target setting/benchmarks

As social networking is relatively new and disciplines such as social media marketing are even more recent, how to set targets for social media footprint is still in its infancy, as is creating comparable benchmarks. But as social media marketing becomes more prevalent, both target setting and industry-specific benchmarking will become much easier due to the ease of collecting and analysing data.

Example The US-headquartered Starbucks Coffee Company is a pioneering organisation in realising and leveraging the brand and other benefits of social networking sites. As part of this, in March 2008 the organisation launched MyStarbucksIdea.com, which enables customers to share their ideas, engage in conversations and play a role in shaping Starbucks' future.

'My Starbucks Idea' allows users to submit suggestions to be voted on by Starbucks consumers, and the most popular suggestions are highlighted and reviewed. Starbucks then took it a step further and added an 'Ideas in Action' blog that gives updates to users on the status of the changes they suggested. Building the technology was the easy part; to ensure the success of this site, Starbucks set out to ensure that the departments impacted by the site had a representative who was responsible for being the liaison for each suggestion.

Starbucks has also created a Facebook site, which, as of the end of 2009, had over 5 million fans – it also has about 550,000 followers on Twitter. Starbucks joined Twitter to engage people in real time.

Starbucks also has its own YouTube channel, is active on LinkedIn and has launched a corporate responsibility social networking site called Shared Planet.

There is no doubt that Starbucks has figured out that leveraging social media can help it build its brand and drive customer engagement.

Tips/warnings

Although there are exciting opportunities in using social networks as a vehicle for targeting all demographic groups and therefore growing brand awareness and customer numbers, there are challenges that have to be overcome. For example, evidence shows that the current level of advertising activity on social networks isn't commensurate with the size – and highly engaged levels – of the audience. A key reason why advertising on social networks hasn't been as successful as more 'traditional' vehicles is because, thinking in terms of social networking sites being 'publishers', social networkers serve a dual role as both the suppliers and consumers of content. In the traditional model they simply consume the content supplied by the publisher. Therefore, members have a greater sense of 'ownership' around the personal content they provide and are less inclined to accept advertising. This is compounded by the fact that the content supplied by the social network members is also of a highly personal nature. This provides another 'Catch-22' situation for the social networks in that personal data are potentially one of their most valuable assets – highly attractive to advertisers – yet they provide a major obstacle in generating revenue. As the site becomes more attractive to advertisers it becomes less appealing to members, who see highly targeted advertisements as invading privacy.

A Nielsen Online survey in Australia showed that the challenge could be getting more difficult because consumers are actually growing less tolerant of advertising on social media. The study showed that in December 2008, 38% of Australians online considered advertising on social networking sites to be an intrusion, compared to 29% the year before. Also, those who didn't mind being served ads if they were relevant to their interests dropped slightly, from 51% to 47%.

Furthermore, those organisations (such as Starbucks) that set up their own social networking sites must be prepared to let go of much of the control that is traditionally expected of marketing vehicles. Such sites are not just a one-way flow of marketing messages, but an interactive, honest conversation – and the content of conversations is not always kind to the listener.

References

Global Faces and Networked Places, A Nielsen Report on Social Networking's New Global Footprint, **www.nielsen-online.com**

www.zocalogroup.com/

www.MyStarbucksIdea.com

Klout score 37

Strategic perspective
Marketing and sales perspective

Key performance question this indicator helps to answer
To what extent are we influential in the social media and online sphere?

Why is this indicator important?

Social media, and especially applications such as Facebook, Twitter and LinkedIn, are transforming the way customers, employees and any other stakeholders find, communicate and interact with companies. Most companies have by now realised that social media are a crucial element of any marketing strategy.

One of the big questions companies have is about the level of influence their social media activities really have. If you spend time tweeting on Twitter, building connections on LinkedIn and interacting with people on Facebook, does this help you to increase your 'influence'?

The Klout score is a measure that allows you to measure your overall online influence on a scale from zero to 100, taking into account over 35 variables on Facebook, Twitter and LinkedIn. The scoring was developed by a small start-up company but seems to be fast developing into a standard measure. The beauty of Klout is that it's free and you only need to register your Twitter, Facebook and LinkedIn accounts to get your score.

Companies are not only taking note of their own Klout score but also of the scores of their customers. For example, Facebook pages can now be personalised based on Klout score. Audi USA is one of the first brands to use the Klout App for its more than 3.5 million fans on Facebook. Each will receive a customised brand experience, tailored to them based on their Klout score.

How do I measure it?

Data collection method

Data will be automatically collected by the Klout application from the associated social media applications.

Formula

Klout uses over 35 variables on Facebook and Twitter to measure True Reach, Amplification Score and Network Score. The exact formula is not disclosed.

- True Reach is the size of the engaged audience and is based on those followers and friends who actively listen and react to messages.
- Amplification Score is the likelihood that messages will generate actions (retweets, @messages, likes and comments) and is on a scale of 1 to 100.
- Network Score indicates how influential the engaged audience is, and is also on a scale from 1 to 100.

Frequency

Once registered, measurement will take place continuously. Reporting on a monthly basis would make sense.

Source of the data

The data will be automatically collected from the social media apps.

Cost/effort in collecting the data

Because the service is free and the data are collected automatically, the costs for measuring your Klout score are basically zero.

Target setting/benchmarks

The range of the Klout score is between 0 and 100, zero being no influence and 100 the highest influence possible.

- Scores of below 20 indicate light users with very little influence.
- Scores of around 30 indicate regular users with moderate influence.
- Scores of 60 or over indicate that a user is very influential in the social media and online world.

Example At the last count my own Klout score was 68.

US President Barack Obama has a Klout score of 88, while presidential candidates trail behind, with former Minnesota Governor Tim Pawlenty at 66 and former Speaker of the House Newt Gingrich at 74.

Celebrity popstar Lady Gaga has a Klout score of 93, based on 40,550,141 fans on Facebook and 11,644,629 followers on Twitter.

Tips/warnings

The field of social media and online influence is new and very dynamic, with new players entering the social media landscape all the time. At the time of writing, the Klout score seems to be the key measurement tool for online influence.

References

http://corp.klout.com/kscore

www.brandchannel.com/home/post/Audi-Klout-Involver.aspx

http://corp.klout.com/blog/2011/06/a-beginners-guide-to-klout/

http://leedela.com/2011/05/23/presidential-contenders-whos-got-the-most-klout/

www.compukol.com/blog/what-is-a-klout-score-and-why-it-is-important/

[PART FOUR]

Operational processes and supply chain perspective

Six Sigma level

38

Strategic perspective
Operational processes and supply chain perspective

Key performance question this indicator helps to answer
How capable are our processes of delivering error-free work?

Why is this indicator important?

The Six Sigma metric (which was pioneered by Motorola in the late 1980s and later adopted very successfully by global giants such as General Electric and Honeywell as well as many other companies of various sizes) informs managers as to the stability and predictability of process results. The goal is that process defect or error rates will be no more than 3.4 per one million opportunities. As an analogy, consider a goalkeeper of a football team who plays 50 games in a season and who faces 50 shots from the opposing team in each game. If a defect is when the team scores, then a Six Sigma goalkeeper would concede one goal every 147 years!

It is important to stress that Six Sigma is both a measure and a performance improvement methodology. As a methodology Six Sigma represents a set of tools that enable continuous or preferably breakthrough performance. These tools are based on the DMAIC principles:

- Define customer requirements (internal or external); that is, their expectation of the process.

- Measure the current performance; what is the frequency of defects?
- Analyse the data collected and map to determine cause and effect and opportunities for improvement; why, when and where do the defects occur?
- Improve the target process by designing solutions to improve, fix or prevent problems.
- Control the improvements to keep the process on the new course; how can we ensure that the process stays fixed?

DMAIC implementation is through an in-house team of Six Sigma certified employees, known as Master Black Belts, Black Belts or Green Belts depending on their experience and levels of involvement.

In essence, the promise is that by reaching Six Sigma performance levels, customer dissatisfaction will decrease significantly and that, ultimately, superior and sustainable financial results will be achieved.

How do I measure it?

Data collection method

Data are collected from three primary sources: input, process and output.

- The input source is where the process is generated.
- Process data refer to tests of efficiency: the time requirements, cost, value, defects or errors, and labour spent on the process.
- Output is a measurement of efficiency.

Formula

A Six Sigma defect is defined as anything outside of customer specifications, while a Six Sigma opportunity is the total quantity of chances for a defect.

First we calculate defects per million opportunities (DPMO) and based on that a Sigma is decided from a predefined table (see Example).

$$DPMO = \frac{\text{Number of defects} \times 1{,}000{,}0000}{\text{Number of units} \times \text{Number of opportunities}}$$

The number of defects is the total number of defects found, the number of units is the number of units produced and the number of opportunities means the number of ways to generate defects.

Frequency

The Sigma calculation is measured at the start of the project (baseline), at the end of the improvement project and then periodically to ensure the 'control' principle of DMAIC.

Source of the data

From available or generated process data.

Cost/effort in collecting the data

Costs and effort for collecting Six Sigma data can be high unless data collection is automated and data are readily available. Manual data collection and analysis are warranted only for key processes in an organisation. For other processes where data are automatically collected, such as in automated manufacturing, the costs are significantly lower.

Target setting/benchmarks

The Six Sigma measure of 3.4 is in itself a benchmark target, so companies would aim for 3.4 or less.

Example Consider a food-ordering delivery project team that examined 50 deliveries and found the following:

Delivery is not on time (13).
Ordered food is not according to the order (3).
Food is not fresh (0).

So now DPMO will be as follows

$$\text{DPMO} = \frac{13 + 3 \times 1{,}000{,}000}{50 \times 3} = 106{,}666.7$$

According to the yield to Sigma conversion table (see below), 106,666.7 defects per million opportunities is equivalent to a Sigma level of between 2 and 3.

Table 38.1 Sample levels of Sigma performance according to the Sigma conversion table

Sigma level	DPMO	% Error
1	691,500	69.15
2	308,500	30.85
3	66,800	6.68

Sigma level	DPMO	% Error
4	6,200	0.62
5	230	0.00023
6	3.4	0.000034

Tips/warnings

A common criticism of Six Sigma is that the projects are typically implemented bottom-up. As a result, organisations spend a lot of effort on projects that look at tiny areas of their business. This way, they pick the lowest-hanging fruits but often miss the big opportunities. The biggest benefits from Six Sigma are secured when projects are related to the achievement of strategic goals. Six Sigma teams should focus on the most important strategically relevant projects and not just on those that deliver some financial gains.

Linked to the above, it is telling to note that although some of the organisations that became poster-boys for Six Sigma have indeed secured mouth-watering cost savings from their efforts, they have simultaneously been very poor performers on the stock market and have been recognised for their strategic failures. The argument has been that these organisations have been exclusively focused on using Six Sigma to identify cost-saving opportunities rather than as a tool to improve performance continuously against strategic goals: this is not how to get the best from Six Sigma projects.

References

Six Sigma Online: **www.sixsigmaonline.org**

Six Sigma.us: **www.6sigma.us**

Tutorials Point: **www.tutorialspoint.com/six_sigma/six_sigma_measure_phase.htm**

Pete Pande and Larry Holpp, *What is Six Sigma?* New York: McGraw-Hill, 2001.

Peter S. Pande, Robert P. Neuman and Roland R. Cavanagh, *The Six Sigma Way: How GE, Motorola, and Other Top Companies are Honing Their Performance*, New York: McGraw-Hill, 2000.

Bernard Marr, In defence of the nation and front-line troops, Raconteur on Lean and Six Sigma, *The Times* newspaper supplement, London, 8 June 2010.

Capacity utilisation rate (CUR)

39

Strategic perspective
Operational processes and supply chain perspective

Key performance question this indicator helps to answer
To what extent are we leveraging our full production/work potential?

Why is this indicator important?

When companies invest in production units (e.g. a machine or a factory) or in people and processes, they want to ensure that they get the intended benefit from this investment (i.e. produce products and deliver services for customers). Capacity is the ability to produce work or output in a given time-frame, e.g. a machine has the capacity to produce 40 widgets per hour and a factory has the capacity of 10,000 machine hours in each 40-hour week.

Capacity utilisation is a measure that provides insights into the extent to which a company actually uses its installed productive capacity. Thus, it refers to the relationship between actual output that 'is' being produced with the installed equipment and the potential output which 'could' be produced with it, if capacity was fully used.

Asset utilisation is a KPI that is most closely associated with manufacturing, but it can be equally used in the services sector where, for example, a team or a department can have a capacity to deliver outputs such as 3 projects per month or 15 consultations per day.

Low-capacity utilisation highlights slack and potential inefficiencies in the internal processes of an organisation and indicates areas for improvement. It also means that if a company is running at, let's say, 70% capacity utilisation rate, it has room to increase production up to 100% capacity utilisation rate without incurring costs of increasing capacity through, for example, buying new machines, building a new plant or hiring more people.

How do I measure it?

Data collection method

Data for the capacity (actual and potential) will be collected and estimated by hand (at least for the first time). Once the data for potential capacity are established, the calculation can be automated based on the actual capacity information that is available.

Formula

$$\text{Capacity utilisation rate} = \left(\frac{\text{Actual capacity in time period } t}{\text{Possible capacity in time period } t} \right) \times 100$$

Frequency

CUR is often measured daily or weekly, but depending on the unit of production that is being assessed, this can vary. For a single machine, for example, the CUR could be calculated hourly while for an entire factory or company the frequency would be weekly or monthly.

Source of the data

Data for the CUR KPI come from the manufacturing or internal processes system that tracks the amount of work or output that has been achieved in a given time period. The data for the possible level of capacity can be estimated based on machine data and the US Federal Reserve Board's definition for the FRB capacity utilisation index, which looks at the maximum level of production that a production unit could reasonably expect to attain under normal and realistic operating conditions.

Cost/effort in collecting the data

Unless automated through a software program that calculates the CUR score based on the actual production data, the costs for collecting data for this KPI can be quite high owing to the manual efforts required to collect and calculate the data.

Target setting/benchmarks

It is difficult to provide benchmarks here that are generic. A good starting point might be to look at the economy-wide CUR, which is around 80% in the US (according to the Federal Reserve) and marginally higher in Europe (at about 82%).

> **Example** Here is a simple calculation example for the CUR KPI:
>
> A production unit (say a plant or machine) can produce 10,000 units per day. The actual production is 8,500 units per day. The CUR is therefore:
>
> $$CUR = \left(\frac{8,500}{10,000}\right) \times 100$$
>
> $$CUR = 85\%$$

Tips/warnings

Capacity utilisation rates can also be used to determine the level at which unit costs will rise. Let's say, for example, that a company currently produces 10,000 units at a cost of $0.50 per unit and has a capacity utilisation score of 66%. This means that it could produce up to 15,000 units without raising the cost per unit.

Also, based on capacity information, a derivative indicator, the 'output gap percentage', can be used as a measure of actual output (AO) less potential output (PO) divided by potential output $\times$ 100.

$$\text{Output gap percentage} = \frac{(AO - PO)}{PO} \times 100$$

References

www.newyorkfed.org/research/quarterly_review/1976v1/v1n1article2.pdf

www.fabtime.com/files/MIMFINL.PDF

http://tutor2u.net/business/production/capacity_introduction.htm

Process waste level

40

Strategic perspective
Operational processes and supply chain perspective

Key performance question this indicator helps to answer
To what extent are our processes lean and effective?

Why is this indicator important?

Companies aim to have effective and lean processes in place that minimise or eliminate any waste that occurs. Under the principles of a 'lean enterprise' (or simply Lean), any expenditure of resources for any purpose other than the creation of value for the end customer is considered wasteful and therefore a target for improvement.

Waste is therefore any activity that does not add value. In Lean, two types of waste are differentiated: (a) waste that is necessary for the system to function and (b) waste that is unnecessary for the system to function. The latter is the focus for this KPI.

Taiichi Ohno, a pioneer of the Toyota Production System, identified seven types of waste (also known as the seven *mudas*):

- Transportation: the unnecessary movement of parts, materials or information between processes.
- Motion: as compared to transportation, motion refers to the unnecessary movement of the producer, worker or equipment.

- Inventory: any materials, work-in-progress (WIP) or finished goods that are in excess or do not have a value-added function.
- Waiting: any people, parts, systems or facilities idle, waiting for a work cycle to be completed.
- Over-production: producing more, sooner or faster quantities than the customer is demanding.
- Over-processing: any work that is being performed beyond what is required to satisfy the customer requirements.
- Defects: when the process results in anything that the customer would deem rejectable or unacceptable.

Getting data on the level of waste in the internal processes will enable companies to identify any problems and put improvements in place.

How do I measure it?

Data collection method

Data for the process waste level KPI will be collected manually by following and observing the processes. Individual measures will have to be designed for each waste type.

Formula

Measuring the waste depends on the metrics used for each waste type, but usually consists of simple counting or measuring. Sprick Stegall have identified the following metrics for each waste type:

Metrics to measure transportation waste:

- Steps associated with tube-travel diagrams
- Time and distance specimens spend in courier cars
- Distance your staff travels carrying reagents and supplies

Metrics to measure wasted motion:

- Travel distance associated with completing all process steps one time
- Spaghetti diagrams of your staff during peak operation times
- Walking distance to areas where materials, supplies and/or specimens are obtained

Metrics to measure the waste of inventory:

- Measure staff hours spent on ordering
- Measure staff time spent on rotating stock

- Measure the amount of consumables you have stored in the laboratory versus in the store room

Metrics to measure the waste of waiting:

- Telephone time spent waiting to relay critical results
- Length of time patients wait for outpatient phlebotomy
- Length of time technologists spend waiting for specimens

Metrics to measure over-production:

- Number of specimens delivered per hour
- Number of batches per shift
- Batch size passed between each process step

Metric to measure the waste of over-processing:

- Count the number of times specimens are sorted in specimen processing
- Count the number of times technologists sort specimens before placing them on an analyser
- Count the number of times specimens are sorted before being placed into storage

Metrics to measure defects passed downstream:

- Track defects passed downstream from process step to process step
- Count the number of corrected reports per day
- Count the number of specimens that required clean-up (re-spun, re-draw, re-label, etc.) prior to analysis per analyser.

Source: **www.sprickstegall.com/blog-the-laboratory-strategy-space/ bid/29843/8-Lean-Wastes-3-Optimal-Metrics-for-Each**

Frequency

Measuring process waste levels follows a Lean initiative in which specific key processes are identified and analysed. It is rare that these are then measured at regular intervals.

Source of the data

The data will come from manual counting and assessments of the processes.

Cost/effort in collecting the data

Measuring process waste levels requires a lot of effort owing to the manual nature of the data collection.

Target setting/benchmarks

It is not possible to provide meaningful benchmarks for this KPI because processes vary so significantly.

> **Example** An example comes from Portakabin, an international company that produces portable modular buildings for a worldwide market. The buildings are made in a factory and then put up where customers need them. Portakabin uses lean production methods and, as part of them, regularly conducts exercises to measure process waste levels. This allowed Portakabin to identify and cut out waste from the manufacturing system through clever module design, reuse of materials, changes in materials used and steel beams being pre-cut to precise length, as well as boards and floors being pre-sized, so no trimming is needed.

Tips/warnings

When measuring and reporting process waste levels it is less about the actual numbers and the reduction of them and more about identifying potential problems in the process design and finding ways of redesigning and improving the processes to eliminate waste altogether. The concept of measuring process waste is a measure of the Lean methodology which promotes the idea of continuous improvement and therefore continuous assessment of potential types of waste by everyone in every process.

References

www.dummies.com/how-to/content/types-and-forms-of-waste-in-lean.html#ixzz1RzvcKOpS

www.sprickstegall.com/blog-the-laboratory-strategy-space/bid/29843/8-Lean-Wastes-3-Optional-Metrics-for-Each

www.thetimes100.co.uk/studies/view-brief-study-lean-production-at-portakabin-35-358.php

Order fulfilment cycle time (OFCT)

41

Strategic perspective
Operational processes and supply chain perspective

Key performance question this indicator helps to answer
How efficient are our processes?

Why is this indicator important?

Order fulfillment cycle time (OFCT) is a continuous measurement defined as the amount of time from customer authorisation of a sales order to customer receipt of the product. This improvement concept applies equally well to manufacturing and service businesses.

OFCT (often known as customer order cycle time) is an important measure because it considers the performance of end-to-end business operations and therefore opens up significant improvement opportunities that are often missed in conventional efficiency programmes. For example, a manufacturing company might focus on reducing 'machine time'. However, machine time might represent just 5% of total OFCT, so efficiency gains will be minimal.

Driving improvements across the whole OFCT process is a powerful metric, as customers increasingly emphasise flawless delivery (that is, very short cycle times) and responsiveness to their changing needs in addition to price and quality.

Today, the customer largely dictates what products are manufactured and when. The customer says: 'I'll let you know what and how many I want, when I'm ready to buy, and then you ship it exactly as I want the product configured, and in a very short lead time'. In fact, in today's competitive environment flawless delivery and responsiveness can very often be the differentiator in getting new customers and keeping old ones.

As well as improving efficiency, the process re-engineering that is usually required to reduce cycle time can also lead to significant effectiveness improvements as the process becomes more responsive to internal and external customer needs.

How do I measure it?

Data collection method

Data are collected through an analysis of the end-to-end order fulfilment process, paying attention to the time to complete each step of each sub-step within the overall process.

Formula

OFCT is the average actual cycle time consistently achieved to fulfil customer orders. For each individual order, this cycle time starts from order receipt and ends with customer acceptance of the order.

OFCT = Source cycle time + Make cycle time + Delivery cycle time.

Frequency

Data can be collected (or recorded) whenever an order is made, and reporting timescales will depend on the order being tracked.

Source of the data

Data might be collected through electronic devices (such as within manufacturing) or from written records detailing the time the work step is received until the time completed.

Cost/effort in collecting the data

If few records are available then initial set-up of the data collection process might be costly, especially if the process has many sub-steps. Once in place, the cost/effort of maintaining the data collection process is typically relatively small – as it should be fully automated.

Target setting/benchmarks

Targets and benchmarks will depend on the OFCT process being tracked and improved. Also, each sub-process might be separately benchmarked, for instance inventory cycle times. Organisations such as the Supply Chain Council (which benchmark the order fulfilment cycle time) and the Hackett Group (which benchmark the end-to-end order–cash process) are useful sources of relevant benchmarking information (see References).

Example This example is abridged from a white paper from the management consultancy Satistar (see References).

An examination of an organisation's OFCT highlighted a major opportunity upstream from the core manufacturing process.

In three weeks, a detailed process design and detailed rollout plan was created, approved and kicked off that slashed cycle time from 18 days to just 4 hours without the addition of any labour or capital equipment. $400,000 in annual overtime costs were eliminated while allowing a one-time increase in working capital of $22 million and an inventory reduction of $11,500,000.

All of the significant cycle time improvements were generated through improving cycle times within the engineering, order entry, planning, scheduling … work in process and quality control steps. The results from this particular intervention are typical. The overwhelming contributors to cycle time are usually in the support activities (order entry, scheduling, logistics, engineering, quality control, etc.) that surround the manufacturing process, and this is the area where dramatic improvements are possible.

Tips/warnings

Measuring end-to-end processes comes with significant challenges as it crosses various functions (and therefore power bases). An end-to-end process manager should be appointed (with the authority to order any required improvements) and change management techniques should be deployed.

References

www.rmdonovan.com/cycle_time-reduction/

http://satistar.com/Whitepapers/Cycle%20Time%20Reduction.pdf

www.scelimited.com/orderfulfillmentcycletime.html

www.thehackettgroup.com

The Supply Council: **www.thesupply-chain.org**

Delivery in full, on time (DIFOT) rate

42

> **Strategic perspective**
> Operational processes and supply chain perspective
>
> **Key performance question this indicator helps to answer**
> To what extent are our customers getting what they want at the time they want it?

Why is this indicator important?

Delivery reliability is an important performance criterion that matters to customers and businesses alike. As consumers we all live ever-busier lives and expect to receive our orders in full at the time we specify. Not doing so can seriously impact customer satisfaction. However, delivering on time can be even more critical when supplying businesses that run just-in-time supply chains to minimise inventory levels or when we deliver to supermarkets that need to ensure their aisles are stocked.

On-time delivery metrics therefore provide an insight into the ability of a business to fulfil orders and meet customer expectations. More importantly, on-time delivery performance gives you an insight into the effectiveness and efficiency of your internal processes and your supply chain. If delivery reliability is too low, it can signal problems along the supply chain such as bottlenecks, inefficiencies in the production process or glitches in the performance of delivery partners.

Measuring whether the delivery has arrived at the customer on time and in full ensures that the entire supply chain is measured – not just part of it, e.g. measuring whether products have shipped in time. Products might leave your business promptly but get held up further down the supply chain. However, the customer will judge your performance not based on whether you have shipped the product on time but whether the product reached them on time and in full.

How do I measure it?

DIFOT is simply calculated as the number of units or shipments delivered in full and on time versus total orders shipped.

Data collection method

The easiest way to collect data for DIFOT is when you already have an order tracking system that allows you to track the order from order placement through to delivery to your customer. The difficulty might be the ability to track delivery right through to your customers (e.g. if you rely on third parties for parts of your supply chain). In this case you have two options: the easier is to rely on delivery information from your supply partner (most shipping companies allow you to track deliveries), or, if no system is in place to track delivery, you can measure the delivery to the point the shipment leaves your business and then use a survey tool to assess delivery to end users.

Formula

$$\text{DIFOT} = \frac{\text{Units or orders delivered in full, on time}}{\text{Total units or orders shipped}}$$

Frequency

The best way is to measure DIFOT continuously for every delivery you make. If data collection is automated, this is no problem.

Source of the data

The data can come from the order tracking system or in some cases be supplemented with customer surveys.

Cost/effort in collecting the data

The cost and effort involved in measuring DIFOT depend on whether an order tracking system is already in place. Most companies will have the ability to track order fulfilment as part of their accounting or quality monitoring systems. In this case, costs for extracting the data are minimal. However, should this not be the case and systems have to be put in place especially, then the initial set-up costs can be high. Also, having to conduct a survey will add significant costs to your data collection.

Target setting/benchmarks

A rough target or benchmark is that no company should let their DIFOT rate slip below 95%. However, this benchmark can easily go much higher (to 98% or 99%) in specific industries where delivery reliability is critical.

Example Let's look at an online grocery business as an example. Here customers place orders for their weekly groceries and select a time window for the home delivery of their groceries. In this sector it is very important not to let people wait for their shopping and to ensure that everything customers have ordered is delivered. When the originally ordered product is not available it has to be replaced with a similar suitable product that the customer will be happy with. If not, the customer can reject the replacement and the order will be deemed incomplete.

The data are collected from the company ERP (Enterprise Resource Planning) system which tracks orders coming in. Every delivery van also has a mobile device that tracks deliveries and on which customers sign when they receive their order. The device is also used to mark rejected items, which are then refunded to the customer.

Here is how they measure it:

Say 1,000 orders are placed in a given week, 980 orders are delivered on time (within the customer-specified time window), 20 were outside this window and arrived late, 550 orders were delivered with replacements and 50 of these were rejected. Three of those that were rejected were also late arrivals.

$$\text{On-time delivery: } \frac{980}{1,000} = 0.98 = 98\%$$

$$\text{In-full delivery: } \frac{950}{1,000} = 0.95 = 95\%$$

$$\text{DIFOT: } 1,000 - \frac{[50 + 20 - 3]}{1,000} = 0.933 = 93.3\%$$

They therefore identify the orders that were late and those that were not complete, add them up and take away any double counts. Then they divide this by the total number of orders to identify the percentage of orders delivered in full and on time.

Tips/warnings

DIFOT measurement can be difficult if there is no internal or automated delivery tracking system in place that ensures easy and accurate data collection. In that case companies have to rely on their customers to provide the data, which can sometimes be difficult.

References

www.leanmanufacture.net/kpi/ontimedelivery.aspx

Patrik Ertler, *Supply Performance Measurement in der Praxis,* VDM Verlag Dr. Müller, 2010

Inventory shrinkage rate (ISR) 43

Strategic perspective
Operational processes and supply chain perspective

Key performance question this indicator helps to answer
To what extent are we losing inventory along our internal processes?

Why is this indicator important?

Inventory shrinkage refers to the loss of products between the point where a product is produced or purchased and the point where it is sold. Losing inventory will push up costs for the producer and reduce profit margins for them and any retailer, which in turn are likely to be passed on and inflate prices for the consumer.

There are different reasons for inventory shrinkage, such as breakages, administrative errors, misplacement of goods, perishable goods not sold in time, etc. However, what is distressing is that the vast majority of shrinkage is assigned to theft. It is, in fact, estimated that about 44% of shrinkage is due to employee theft and another 35% to shoplifting.

Understanding the level of inventory shrinkage will help companies pinpoint to what extent inventory loss occurs, which in turn will help them to address the problem by adopting known good practices such as improved security, packaging or monitoring.

How do I measure it?

Data collection method

Data for the ISR will be collected by counting the level of inventory the company should have (according to its records of purchase or production) compared to the level of inventory it actually holds.

Formula

$$ISR = \frac{(IV1 - IV2)}{IV1}$$

Where:

IV1 is the inventory you should have according to your records

IV2 is the actual inventory you have

Inventory can be measured either in actual stock-keeping units (SKUs) or in financial terms using average selling prices.

Frequency

In most instances the inventory shrinkage is calculated on a six-monthly basis or aligned to the inventory stock-taking frequency. If automated systems are in place the frequency can be increased to e.g. monthly measurement.

Source of the data

The data for the ISR come from the inventory management system, manufacturing data, purchasing data and stock-taking information as well as sales and shipping data.

Cost/effort in collecting the data

Costs for measuring inventory shrinkage are moderate depending on the level of data already available. Most businesses will have an automated inventory system that allows them to understand the level of inventory they should have. Sales data or stock-taking data will provide the actual inventory, which often requires some manual counting. Manual counting will always push up costs but in many businesses the stock-taking process is a routine process already and not something that will have to be put in place specifically for this KPI.

Target setting/benchmarks

The target should be to eliminate or at least minimise shrinkage. As a benchmark we can look at the total shrink percentage of the retail industry in the United States, which was 1.52% of sales in 2008 according to the University of Florida's National Retail Security Survey. According to the 2010 worldwide shrinkage survey of the retail industry, the rates vary from 0.72% in the liquor and off-licence sector to 1.81% in the DIY, hardware and building materials sector.

Example Let's look at a whisky manufacturer that produces single malt whisky. One reason for shrinkage is that during the ageing process in wooden casks some of the whisky in each barrel evaporates through the oak. The distilleries refer to this portion as the 'angels' share', which increases the longer the whisky ages. For a 20-year-old whisky this can be 40% of the volume. This company produces a 10-year-old whisky which loses about 6% during maturation. In addition, spillage during bottling etc. results in a further 1% shrinkage. The overall shrinkage rate for the manufacturing process is therefore 7%.

Let's look at their retail shops now and assume they put 2,000 bottles into the shop (their book inventory). They then sell 1,000 bottles in a month and re-stock 1,000 bottles in the same period. So the inventory should be 2,000 bottles at the end of the period. However, the stock count reveals that only 1926 bottles are in the shop, giving an inventory shrinkage rate of

$$\frac{(2{,}000 - 1{,}926)}{2{,}000} = 3.7\%.$$

Overall shrinkage for this company would be 10.7%.

Tips/warnings

ISR as outlined here looks within the company; however, research has found that there is significant shrinkage along supply chains. It would therefore make sense to measure shrinkage across supply chains to understand where shrinkage is most likely to take place and come up with solutions that go across the entire supply chain to benefit all parties.

References

www.detay.com/UPLOAD/brosurler/Barometre_210.pdf

Paul Chapman and Simon Templar, 'Methods for measuring shrinkage', *Security Journal*, 19(4), 2006, 228–240

Project schedule variance (PSV)

44

> **Strategic perspective**
> Operational processes and supply chain perspective
>
> **Key performance question this indicator helps to answer**
> To what extent are our projects delivered on schedule?

Why is this indicator important?

Most strategic or change initiatives in companies are delivered in projects. Projects are temporary concerted efforts to achieve specific goals or objectives. Projects usually have a defined beginning and end as well as a defined budget. In fact, projects encompass every initiative in a business that is not 'business as usual' (or operations), which is the permanent functional work to produce products or services.

Projects therefore make up a large part of what companies do, which makes it important that project performance is being monitored and reported. Keeping an eye on project performance will enable companies to assess current performance levels, provide input into future goal setting and help anticipate any potential performance deviation. There are three key questions that help companies understand project performance:

1. Is the project on schedule?
2. Is the project on budget?
3. Is the project delivering the specified outcomes?

Understanding performance against schedule, budget and performance enables companies to plan and budget appropriately.

Here we will look first at the project variance against schedule, which provides information on whether projects are delivered within the timeline they were scheduled for. Also, when projects run over schedule they tend to overrun on costs too. Take, for example, the new Wembley stadium in London, which opened in 2007. It was originally scheduled to open in 2003. Or the Sydney Opera House, which was scheduled to open in 1963 at a cost of $7 million and actually opened in 1973 at a cost of $102 million.

PSV is a simple comparison of the planned or scheduled project time and the actual time taken to complete the project. If PSV is zero then the project was completed on scheduled time, if the variance is negative it shows an overrun and if the variance is positive it highlights completion ahead of the planned completion date.

How do I measure it?

Data collection method

The data collection method for PSV is a simple comparison of the scheduled project completion time and the actual completion time.

Formula

PSV = SCT − ACT

Where ACT is the actual completion time

And SCT is the scheduled completion time

ACT and SCT are measured in time intervals such as days or weeks.

For overall PSV (a number of different projects taken together) you can simply add the individual project variances together for an actual number or calculate a straight or weighted average variance score.

Frequency

The measurement frequency for project schedule variance is usually monthly but could be monitored more frequently for important short-term projects.

Source of the data

The data for this KPI will usually come from a project management software application or, if this is not available, from manual records.

Cost/effort in collecting the data

If a project management tool is in place and being used to track project performance then the effort to calculate project schedule variance is negligible. However, if manual data collection and calculations are required then costs will go up.

Target setting/benchmarks

If your planning is reliable then project completions should be close to the scheduled completion date. The target for PSV should therefore be anything close to zero. Negative numbers will indicate an overrun, which usually has cost implications, and positive numbers might indicate weak planning, when projects are completed long before their scheduled completion dates.

Example Let's look at this example, where a division is running three key projects:

	SCT	ACT
Project A	72 days	85 days
Project B	30 days	33 days
Project C	15 days	12 days

PSV Project A = 72 − 85 = −13
PSV Project B = 30 − 33 = −3
PSV Project C = 15 − 12 = 3
PSV Department = (−13) + (−3) + (3) = −13

Tips/warnings

Instead of calculating the variance between the scheduled time and the actual completion time of a project, some companies prefer to calculate the Project Schedule Performance Index (PSPI) which puts the actual time in relation to the scheduled time = SCT / ACT. This means that if PSPI is less than 1, the project is behind schedule. If PSPI is greater than 1, the project is ahead of schedule.

Furthermore, it is important to look at project performance KPIs not in isolation but in the context of the other two project parameters (budget and quality).

References

http://management.energy.gov/documents/performance_measures_final.pdf

www.ajdesigner.com/phpearnedvalue/schedule_variance_equation.php

Project cost variance (PCV)

45

> **Strategic perspective**
> Operational processes and supply chain perspective
>
> **Key performance question this indicator helps to answer**
> To what extent are our projects delivered on budget?

Why is this indicator important?

According to the Standish Group, 70% of projects are over budget and 52% of all projects finish at almost 200% of their initial budget. There are many famous examples, such as the Concorde supersonic aeroplane, which cost 12 times more than scheduled, the Channel Tunnel between the UK and France had a construction cost overrun of 80% and one of the most famous budget overruns happened at Boston's 'Big Dig' tunnel construction project which was 275% ($11 billion) over budget. The project was originally priced at $2.8 billion. *The Boston Globe* estimated that the project will ultimately cost $22 billion, including interest, and that it will not be paid off until 2038.

No company can afford significant cost overruns. What's more, overruns can have not only severe financial consequences but also reputational or legal consequences. For example, the software giant Oracle has recently been sued for an alleged $20 million budget overrun of one of their software implementation projects.

While the previous KPI looked at whether the project was on time, we now look at the budget. Here we will look at the project cost against schedule, which provides information on whether projects are delivered within the planned costs.

PCV is a simple comparison of the planned or scheduled project costs and the actual costs to complete the project. If PCV is zero then the project was completed on budget, if the variance is negative it shows a cost overrun and if the variance is positive it highlights completion below the planned costs.

How do I measure it?

Data collection method

The data collection method for PCV is a simple comparison of the scheduled project costs and the actual completion costs.

Formula

$$PCV = SPC - APC$$

Where SPC is the scheduled project costs

And APC is the actual project costs

For overall PCV (a number of different projects taken together) you can simply add the individual project variances together for an actual number or calculate a straight or weighted average variance score.

Frequency

The measurement frequency for PCV is usually monthly but could be monitored more frequently for important short-term projects.

Source of the data

The data for this KPI will usually come from a project management software application or the financial planning applications, if it is not available from manual records.

Cost/effort in collecting the data

If the project costing is available in a system then the effort to calculate project schedule variance is negligible. However, if manual data collection and calculations are required then costs will go up.

Target setting/benchmarks

Actual project costs should be close to the scheduled project costs. The target for PCV should therefore be anything close to zero. Negative numbers will indicate a cost overrun, and positive numbers might indicate weak planning when projects are completed within or below planned costs.

Example Let's look at this example, where a division is running three key projects:

	SPC (in $)	APC (in $)
Project A	500,000	600,000
Project B	250,000	270,000
Project C	75,000	70,000

PCV Project A = 500,000 − 600,000 = −100,000

PCV Project B = 250,000 − 270,000 = −20,000

PCV Project C = 75,000 − 70,000 = 5,000

PCV Department = (−100,000) + (−20,000) + (5000) = −115,000

Tips/warnings

For longer projects it might make sense to break the costs down into milestones along the project to ensure that insights are gained as the project continues, to avoid any surprises at the very end.

Instead of calculating the variance between the scheduled costs and the actual costs of a project, some companies prefer to calculate the Project Cost Performance Index (PCPI), which puts the actual costs in relation to the scheduled costs = $\frac{SPC}{APC}$. This means that if PCPI is less than 1, the project is over budget. If PCPI is greater than 1, the project is below budget.

Furthermore, it is important to look at project performance KPIs not in isolation but in the context of the other two project parameters (time and quality).

References

http://management.energy.gov/documents/performance_measures_final.pdf

www.ajdesigner.com/phpearnedvalue/schedule_variance_equation.php

Earned value (EV) metric 46

Strategic perspective
Operational processes and supply chain perspective

Key performance question this indicator helps to answer
To what extent are our projects making the desired progress?

Why is this indicator important?

With the previous two KPIs (PSV and PCV) we looked at the performance level after project completion. Especially for bigger and longer projects it is useful to monitor actual progress to date to get an understanding of where we are compared to where we should be.

To this end the earned value (EV) metric has been developed. EV is a project tracking measure that looks at the cost of work in progress and allows companies to understand how much work has been completed compared to how much was expected to be completed at a given point.

The user guide for Microsoft Project 2003 defines earned value as: 'A method for measuring project performance. It indicates how much of the budget should have been spent, in view of the amount of work done so far and the baseline cost for the task, assignment, or resources.' EV basically tracks the percentage of the total project budget actually completed at any given point in time.

In addition to assessing progress to date, EV allows companies to project what the likely costs of the complete project will be, assuming that performance levels remain as they have been to date.

How do I measure it?

Data collection method

Data for the EV metric will be collected from the project management system and requires data for project plan, actual work and work-completed value.

Formula

EV = % complete × BCWP

Where BCWP is the budgeted cost of work performed = the total budgeted costs for labour and resources for the project.

Performance level $= \left(\dfrac{ACWC}{EV}\right) \times 100$

Where ACWC is the actual cost of work scheduled or the total amount in labour and resources that has been spent on the project to date.

Frequency

The frequency for collecting EV data depends a little on the project type; however, as a rule of thumb, weekly (or for longer projects monthly) assessments would make sense.

Source of the data

The data for this KPI will usually come from a project management software application or any project records.

Cost/effort in collecting the data

The costs for measuring EV can be quite high because of the amount of effort that has to go into updating the records. If the records are updated automatically and sophisticated project management software tools are in place and being used, costs will come down significantly.

Target setting/benchmarks

The benchmarks and targets for this KPI will come from the project plan and the calculations – they will be unique to every project.

Example

The following example[1] shows how EV can be calculated and used:

The total cost of Project A was estimated at £600. So far, the ACWP (the cost of the work done on it) is £200, but it's only 20% complete.

The earned cost is £600 × 20% = £120.

The performance ratio is $\frac{120}{200} = 0.6$.

Using these values, the predicted forecast = $\frac{£400 \text{ [remaining cost]}}{0.6}$ + £200 = £866.67, which is worse than planned and will mean the project is over budget.

Project B was estimated to cost £800. The ACWP is £400 and the task is 70% complete.

The earned hours are £800 × 70% = £560 hours

The performance ratio is $\frac{560}{400} = 1.4$

The predicted forecast is $\frac{£400}{1.4}$ + £400 = £685.71, which is less than the estimate.

[1] Based on example provided by Linda Russell: **http://abirdseyeview.wordpress.com/2008/05/08/earned-value/**

Tips/warnings

EV is easily misinterpreted, especially given the rhetoric surrounding this indicator claiming it to be an objective quantitative measure of project performance. It is very important to understand that the EV metric hinges on how project progress is reported.

As with so many KPIs, it is important not just to see the final number of the EV metric but to use the metric as a tool to identify and rectify potential problems in project delivery.

Take the above two EV scores as an example. The data would indicate that project B is doing really well compared to project A. However, one needs to take into account the earned hours and the time performance. For example, the company might have used a more experienced (and hence more expensive) resource in order to reduce the amount of effort needed to complete the task, which could in fact be ahead of schedule. On the other hand, if the task is under budget, lower-value resources may have been allocated, and they may be underperforming.

As EV relies on good reporting and evaluations, it is important to be aware of some possible unwanted behaviours which could quickly skew the data and show better EV scores:

- Schedule projects for longer than actually anticipated, e.g. schedule six-month project time when only three months are needed.
- Putting the easiest tasks at the beginning of the project and the hardest tasks at the end can keep a project EV score looking good for a long time.
- Exaggerate the task completion percentages.
- Etc.

References

www.projectsmart.co.uk/what-is-earned-value.html

www.innovel.net/?p=55

www.acq.osd.mil/pm/

http://abirdseyeview.wordpress.com/2008/05/08/earned-value/

www.cioinsight.com/c/a/Past-Opinions/How-to-Lie-with-Earned-Value/

Innovation pipeline strength (IPS)

47

Strategic perspective
Operational processes and supply chain perspective

Key performance question this indicator helps to answer
To what extent have we got a strong innovation pipeline?

Why is this indicator important?

Innovation is a critical success factor in any industry. As product and service lifetime cycles tend to become shorter and shorter, companies have to ensure that the next new product or service offering is being developed. The number and potential of any new product or service offering in development (called the innovation pipeline) is important for any business or organisation, be it a large pharmaceutical company that requires a strong product pipeline to replace existing drugs that might reach the end of their patent protection period or hospitals that need to look for new and innovative ways of offering their services.

A study by McKinsey suggests that a large percentage of companies, even those that rely heavily on innovation, don't measure their innovation performance or potential. If measures are used they tend to be very crude KPIs such as the % of revenue spent on Research and Development (R&D). Here it is important to remind ourselves that R&D and innovation are means to an end and not ends in their own right.

The strength of the innovation pipeline can be assessed by estimating the revenue-generating potential for the products or services in development as well as the potential of completing the innovation and taking it to market.

By measuring the innovation pipeline strength, companies will gain an understanding about the future potential of their company and an insight into the potential return on their R&D investments.

How do I measure it?

Data collection method

The strength of the innovation pipeline can be measured by looking at the key innovation projects and estimating the potential future revenue generated by them.

Formula

$$IPS = \text{Sum (Innovation project} \times \text{Future revenue potential)}$$

The innovation pipeline strength is less of a defined measure because assessment of the future potential will depend on the product or industry. Some companies specify the period for which the return is expected (e.g. 6, 12 or 24 months after launch) and add a likelihood score to indicate that any innovation project might end up in commercial failure.

Frequency

IPS is usually measured on a quarterly basis but the frequency can be increased or decreased if the innovation cycles are longer or shorter.

Source of the data

Data for the IPS come from an internal analysis and estimations.

Cost/effort in collecting the data

The costs for measuring IPS can be substantial, based on the fact that reviews of the innovation projects are necessary and estimations about potential future revenues need to be made.

Target setting/benchmarks

There are no generally applicable benchmarks available. Within industries it is sometimes possible to find innovation pipeline assessments (e.g. pharmaceutical companies) which can be used to set some targets.

Example Take this example where a company is working on two new product innovations (product A and product B) and one service innovation (service X).

- With product A the company is entering a completely new market but is expecting to gain revenues of $500,000 in the first year, and $750,000 in year 2.
- Product B will replace an existing product that is currently generating revenues of $250,000. The company estimates that revenues will increase to $300,000 because the new product with its new features is expected to attract some customers from the competition, meaning an additional revenue of $50,000 per year.
- Service X is a new service offering around existing products and is expected to generate $60,000 in revenues for the first year and the same for the second year.
- With all the innovations in development the company is cautious and includes both a best- and worst-case scenario to indicate that facts such as entering a new market could cause product A to fail and the competition might come in with an even more innovative product or service to compete with product B or service X. See the table below for the expected revenues for each innovation as well as the best- and worst-case predictions:

Innovation	Expected revenues 12m	24m	Best-case revenues 12m	24m	Worst-case revenues 12m	24m
Product A	500K	750K	750K	1m	100K	100K
Product B	50K	50K	100K	100K	0	0
Service X	60K	60K	80K	80K	0	0

The individual innovation strengths are therefore:

- Product A over 12 months = 500k (+250k, − 400k)
- Product B over 12 months = 50k (+50k, − 50k)
- Service X over 12 months = 60k (+20k, − 60k)
- Product A over 24 months: 500k + 750k = 1,250k (+500k, − 1,050,000)
- Product B over 24 months: 50k + 50k = 100k (+100k, − 100k)
- Service X over 24 months: 60k + 60k = 120k (+40k, − 120k)

Overall IPS (12 month) = 500k + 50k + 60k = 610k (+320k, − 510k)

Overall IPS (24 month) = 1,470k = 610k (+640k, − 1,270k)

Tips/warnings

Because the IPS KPI is an estimation of future revenue generated by the innovations in development and because there are uncertainties and risks involved in the delivery of the revenues, it makes sense to report the pipeline strength in graphical format to show the estimated revenue as well as the best- and worst-case scenarios as funnels around it (Figure 47.1).

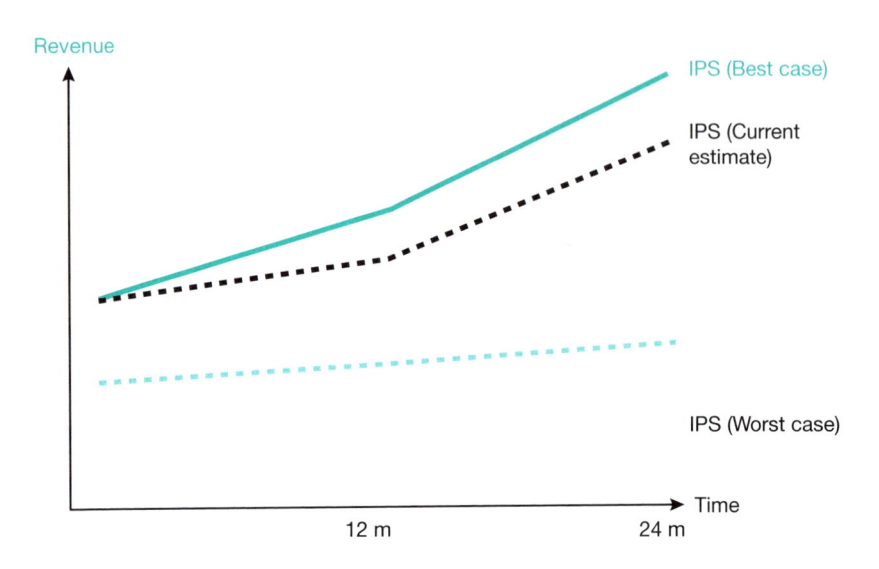

References

McKinsey Global Survey Results: Assessing innovation metrics, October 2008

Return on innovation investment (ROI²)

48

Strategic perspective
Operational processes and supply chain perspective

Key performance question this indicator helps to answer
To what extent are our investments in innovation generating a return?

Why is this indicator important?

Companies are spending on average 3.5% of their revenues on research, development and innovation activities. This can go much higher for manufacturing companies (around 7%) or high-tech or pharmaceutical companies (around 15%). While in accounting terms R&D spending is viewed as a sunk cost that has to be written off, companies see R&D as an investment in the future. They are hoping that their innovation pipeline (see previous KPI) is delivering future revenues.

Given the large expenses that companies pump into R&D and innovation, it is only fair to ask whether the investments are generating the expected revenues. Measuring the return on innovation allows companies to compare the investments in new products and services with the profits generated by the new products and services.

According to a Boston Consulting Groups (2010) report, fully 50% of managers are not happy with the return they are getting from their innovation process. Understanding the return on innovation provides companies with an insight into the effectiveness of innovation activities in your organisation.

According to Booz & Company partner Alexander Kandybin, the return on innovation investment (ROI^2) methodology also allows companies to compare innovation returns with returns from other types of investment, such as marketing, or returns from small projects versus large projects. It therefore makes comparison across innovation initiatives much easier, and that allows you to manage innovation returns very explicitly.

How do I measure it?

Data collection method

ROI^2 is calculated by comparing the profits of new product or service sales to the research, development and other direct expenditures.

Formula

Return on innovation investment can be calculated in several ways. The most common and useful way is:

ROI^2 = [(Net profit from new products and services) − (Innovation costs for these products and services)]/(Innovation costs for these products and services)

ROI^2 is most commonly used as a retrospective KPI taking into account actual costs versus actual profits. However, by using estimations of future revenues and projected costs, it is possible to estimate future ROI^2.

Frequency

ROI^2 can then be measured at the end of an innovation project or as a percentage return over a period of a year (most useful for longer-term projects), thus giving a calculation of how long it will take the organisation to cover its investment and then make a profit from that investment. If the rate of return is 33.3% in one year, it will take three years to recover the complete investment $\left(\frac{100\%}{33.3\%} = 3\right)$. If ROR is 50%, payback is two years; if 200%, six months.

Source of the data

The data for ROI^2 can usually be extracted from the accounting data and project data.

Cost/effort in collecting the data

The costs for calculating ROI^2 are moderate if all the information is readily available. The costs will go up significantly if future ROI^2 is measured, as this requires estimations (see also previous KPI: innovation pipeline strength).

Target setting/benchmarks

There are no generic benchmarks and targets available for ROI² because of the idiosyncratic nature of innovation projects, which can vary massively in scope and time frames.

Example As a simple ROI² calculation, if an innovation project costs $50,000 to implement, and you demonstrate $25,000 in net profits annually, then the calculation would appear as follows.

$$ROI^2 = \left(\frac{25{,}000}{50{,}000}\right) = 50\%$$

Tips/warnings

As with any return on investment KPI, it is worth keeping in mind that the calculation for return on investment, and therefore the definition, can be modified to suit the situation. It all depends on what the organisation (or part thereof) decides to include as returns and costs. The definition of the term in the broadest sense just attempts to measure the profitability of an investment and, as such, there is no one 'right' calculation.

Furthermore, care must be taken not to confuse annual and annualised returns. An annual rate of return is a single-period return, while an annualised rate of return is a multi-period, average return.

An annual rate of return is the return on an investment over a one-year period, such as 1 January through 31 December. An annualised rate of return is the return on an investment over a period other than one year (such as a month, or two years), multiplied or divided to give a comparable one-year return. For instance, a one-month ROI of 1% could be stated as an annualised rate of return of 12%. Or a two-year ROI of 10% could be stated as an annualised rate of return of 5%.

References

www.booz.com/global/home/what_we_think/reports_and_white_papers/article/47463070?pg=0

www.booz.com/media/file/ROI2_SMR_2009.pdf

The ROI Institute **www.roiinstitute.net**

Boston Consulting Group, *Innovation 2010 – a return to prominence and the emergence of a new world order*, 2010, **www.bcg.com/documents/file42620.pdf**

Time to market 49

> **Strategic perspective**
> Operational processes and supply chain perspective
>
> **Key performance question this indicator helps to answer**
> How quickly are we getting products/services to market?

Why is this indicator important?

Time to market can be defined as the time it takes from the conceptualisation of a product idea to the time it is ready to be distributed.

As a KPI, a faster time to market generally reflects a better integration of the design, manufacturing and management processes, as well as a more effective application of design and design management principles. This is translated into fewer product iterations, amendments and modifications.

This is an important KPI because as consumers become increasingly spoilt for choice and as product/service innovations proliferate (and from competitors located throughout the world), it is critical in most industries that organisations are offering customers a constant flow of new products/services – especially in industries where product life-cycle times are low (such as mobile telephony, for example). Indeed, a 2006 North American study by the Aberdeen Group found that time to market was the top-ranking product design and development (PD&D) KPI in the manufacturing sector, trumping other popular metrics such as new product success rate and percentage of revenue from new products (see Figure 49.1).

From a financial perspective, time to market allows for first to market (or prime mover) advantage, thus enabling an organisation to reap the lion's share of profits available from a new product innovation and thus higher profit margins (time to market laggards end up fighting over profit scraps). Through rapid time to market organisations also claim higher market penetration, which creates a positive environment for the sale of future services/products.

Figure 49.1 Top PD&D KPIs

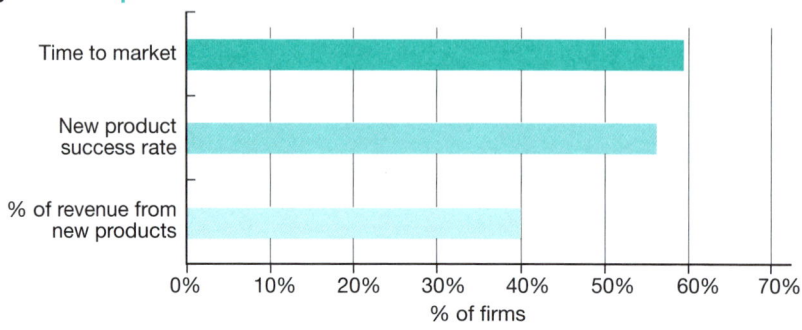

[Bar chart showing:
- Time to market: ~60% of firms
- New product success rate: ~55% of firms
- % of revenue from new products: ~40% of firms]

Source: Aberdeen Group

How do I measure it?

Data collection method

Data are collected from documents that start when a new product is first approved for design/development and continue until the product is actually available for purchase by the customer. Data therefore will need to be collected from both the new product development/research and marketing departments.

Formula

There are no standards for measuring time to market, and measured values can vary greatly. First, there is great variation in how different organisations define the start of the period. In some industries, automotive, for example, the development period starts when the product concept is approved. Others realise that little will happen until the project is staffed, which can take a long time after approval if developers are tied up on existing projects. Therefore, they consider the start point to be when the project is fully staffed. Next, definitions of the end of the time to market period also vary. Some people, who look at product development as engineering, say that the project is finished when engineering transfers it to manufacturing. Others define the conclusion as when they ship the first copy of the new product or when a customer buys it.

All that said, this book would argue that time to market can be simply measured as the time in days or months from the time the product is conceptualised to it being available to customers.

Frequency

Time to market is measured at the time the product is available. However, while in development, close attention is paid to the time the new product has already spent being developed (measured against target release data), as this has significant implications for development costs as well as ultimate financial benefits and market positioning.

Source of the data

Documents that start when a new product is first approved for design/development and continue until the product is actually available for purchase by the customer.

Cost/effort in collecting the data

Collecting the data for this KPI is neither costly nor time consuming, as the data should be readily available in the new product development/research and marketing departments of most organisations.

Target setting/benchmarks

Time to market targets or benchmarks are specific to particular industries or sectors and time-spans will differ significantly. For example, a study of time to market within Canadian manufacturers during 2002–2004 found that the average time to market for manufacturers was 13.7 months. However, depending on the nature of the product (complexity, seasonality, etc.), this KPI varies by manufacturing sectors. For instance, clothing and leather manufacturers, who face seasonal trends, bring their product to market 24% faster than manufacturers on average, while aerospace manufacturers, facing high product complexity, regulations and product quality requirements, take 35% longer on average than the manufacturing average. But targets and benchmarks should be readily available from industry bodies, etc.

Example The CEO of Company X calls a meeting to discuss identified needs for a new piece of software to support the requirements of their major customers. At the end of the meeting the green light for developing the product is given. This serves as the start date for the time to market calculation. A target for product launch (based on customers' expressed requirements and an understanding of internal capabilities) is set. Working groups are formed and milestone dates set for review of progress of the product development against the time-to-market target. The reason for any slippage is discussed at these reviews (gate reviews are held at major product milestone dates) and any remedial action ordered to contend with any delays. A culture of honesty and transparency is encouraged. The actual date that the product is available to the customer is the end date for the time to market calculation. In this case the time to market for the new product was seven months against an original target of nine months, which maximised profits and profit margins and ensured that competitive advantage was secured.

Tips/warnings

Although time to market is a critical KPI for profit and other considerations, organisations must ensure that they do not sacrifice product quality or appropriate testing in order to meet any time to market target. Product recalls, for example, can have a devastating impact on an organisation's short-term profits, but of greater concern will be the long-term damage to the reputation of the enterprise. Also, significant damage to financials and reputation might occur if the customer finds faults with the functionality of the product.

Moreover, organisations need to ensure that they agree a standard definition of how they calculate time to market: as examples, new product development and marketing must have the same definitions, as must different business units (especially important when used for internal/external comparison purposes).

To improve time to market without negatively impacting quality etc., an organisation will need to review its processes and where necessary remove developmental bottlenecks or bureaucracies. Quality metrics and techniques, process re-engineering and new product development best-practice frameworks will all be useful here.

Time to market is much more important in markets where products are outmoded quickly (such as those involved in information/communication technologies) than others.

References

Aberdeen Group, *The Mechatronics Systems Design Benchmark Report*

For information on product design and development see **www.ic.gc.ca/eic/site/dsib-dsib.nsf/eng/h_oq01750.html**

First pass yield (FPY)

50

> **Strategic perspective**
> Operational processes and supply chain perspective
>
> **Key performance question this indicator helps to answer**
> How efficient are our internal operational processes?

Why is this indicator important?

Companies aim to optimise their internal processes to reduce defect rates and minimise any rework. Defects or rework of any sort that are generated when products pass through the internal operational processes will decrease operational effectiveness and increase costs.

By measuring first pass yield (FPY) companies can see the percentage of items that are moving through a process without any problems such as requiring rework or scrapping of items, which would lower the output. FPY will give companies a good insight into the internal efficiency of their operational processes.

Most processes contain multiple steps with 'built-in' rework. Therefore, measuring input at the beginning versus output at the end of any operational process would not provide a true picture of efficiency. Instead, FYP aims to measure the yields of every step along the process, therefore detecting defects and rework steps that might otherwise stay hidden.

To this end, the process has to be broken down into segregated and independent steps. Once this has been achieved, a base measure has to be determined which allows an evaluation at each step of the process, e.g. the weight of a portion of pasta at every step through the food production process or a soft drink can without any dents in it.

FPY can be established for individual processes or for all operations simply by averaging together the individual FPYs to measure the entire production flow.

How do I measure it?

Data collection method

The data will be collected throughout the operation process, either automatically using sensors (e.g. in manufacturing) or manually using a set of samples. It is a simple count of the number of products that have passed a production step without any defect or rework needed, compared to the number of products that started this production step.

Formula

> FPY (process q step a) = (Number of units that complete process step a without defect or rework required / Number of units entering the process step a) × 100
>
> FPY (process q) = FPY (process step a) × FPY (process step a) × FPY (process step a) × ... × FPY (process step 'n')

Frequency

First pass yield is an internal process measure that, if automated, will be measured continuously. If manual data collection based on sampling is the only option, then appropriate time-frames have to be established.

Source of the data

The data will be collected directly from monitoring the operational process.

Cost/effort in collecting the data

For the automated version there are initial set-up costs and then maintenance costs for the measuring unit. The costs for collecting FPY are moderate unless automation is not an option and manual counting is required, which will push the costs up significantly.

Target setting/benchmarks

An FPY of 100% (or as close to it as possible) is desirable. For example, car manufacturers like Toyota are aiming for a Sigma rating of 5 or higher, which is the equivalent of 12 months' production with a yield of 100% (no defect or rework).

Example Take this example from an assembly plant. The assembly process of unit A (say an engine cable box) contains four discrete steps. After each step a quality inspection will remove the non-passes, which are either wrongly assembled, require rework or are scrapped. Using sensors, the number of units entering each step is automatically counted and the non-passes are counted by hand and later transferred to a system.

The data show that:

100 units enter step 1 and 95 pass the quality inspection.
95 units enter step 2, 92 pass the quality inspection.
92 units enter step 3, 88 pass the quality inspection.
88 units enter step 4, 88 pass the quality inspection.

FPY step 1 = $\left(\frac{95}{100}\right) \times 100 = 95\%$

FPY step 2 = $\left(\frac{92}{95}\right) \times 100 = 96.8\%$

FPY step 3 = $\left(\frac{88}{92}\right) \times 100 = 95.6\%$

FPY step 4 = $\left(\frac{88}{88}\right) \times 100 = 100\%$

For the entire process it would then be:

FPY (process) = FPY step 1 × FPY step 2 × FPY step 3 × FPY step 4

FPY (process) = 95% × 96.8% × 95.6% × 100% = 87.9%

As can be seen from this example, it doesn't take long for defect rates to stack up.

Tips/warnings

This method depends on good automatic monitoring or honest recording of defect rates. A lack of visibility can be a challenge, because most frontline workers want to do a good job and therefore might fix problems on the spot or help out their upstream co-workers. As a result, defects are not recorded, inflating the FPY rate.

References

www.cirris.com/testing/guidelines/first_pass_yield.html

Rework level 51

> **Strategic perspective**
> Operational processes and supply chain perspective
>
> **Key performance question this indicator helps to answer**
> How effectively are we driving waste out of our processes?

Why is this indicator important?

Much of today's obsession with the search for effective KPIs can be traced back to the emergence of Total Quality Management (TQM) in the 1980s, when manufacturers such as Xerox realised that Japanese competitors could sell goods at a lower price than it cost the manufacturers to make them. Investigations uncovered that this was largely the consequence of Japanese companies successfully applying the principles of TQM.

A key principle religiously applied was that quality should be built into the process of product manufacture and not inspected at the end of the assembly line. Amongst many benefits, ensuring that quality is built into the process could dramatically reduce manufacturing costs as there was no, or little, need to return goods from inspection to assembly for rework (or from customer to assembly, even more costly – see the example on pages 235–236).

For Western organisations keen to emulate the success of their Eastern competitors, the cost of rework became a key quality metric (defined as a product that fails the specification laid down by the company, but is capable of being altered in some way to exactly match the specification required). Western quality gurus such as Philip Crosby argued that the goal should be no rework – or zero defects. Crosby provided a methodology for moving towards zero defects in his seminal work *Quality is Free* (see References).

There are myriad reasons why organisations (both commercial and not-for-profit as the latter too has outputs that it ultimately delivers to the customer) should adopt a percentage of rework metric. As well as cost benefits, it establishes how effective the organisation is at delivering the specification that the customer wants without further correction, alteration or revision.

Moreover, inculcating 'in-process' inspection (key to driving down the cost of rework) identifies problems at the earliest opportunity and eliminates subsequent work being done to a product that already fails to meet specification. Also, as it shows whether employees are getting things 'right first time' the metric points to potential training or knowledge gaps.

How do I measure it?

Data collection method

Rework data can be collected in many ways and sophistication varies according to industry and sector. Many manufacturers will identify rework requirements (or out-of-spec product deviations) automatically whereas service companies might rely on inputs such as written reports of 'product' failure or variance.

Formula

Rework is a percentage of the products that are inspected that then require rework. If 100 products are inspected, with 4 reworked (and then passed), the measure recorded is a 4% rework rate.

Frequency

Frequency rates depend on the industry or sector and on the degree of customer pressure. Manufacturing companies might measure rework on at least a weekly basis, whereas monthly might suffice for a service company (although some might also do so weekly) and monthly or quarterly for a not-for-profit organisation.

Source of the data

The process that creates the product or the customer that consumes the product.

Cost/effort in collecting the data

Data collection costs might be fairly significant within manufacturers that purchase defect and rework tracking systems, but a return on investment calculation will likely prove it to be a wise investment. Cost and effort are fairly small in service or not-for-profit organisations.

Target setting/benchmarks

The target for rework should always be zero.

Example This fictional example (abridged) is from the performance measurement specialist Carpenter Group LLC (see References). It provides an overall cost of poor quality calculation (which includes a significant rework cost). This shows how the cost of rework can have much broader cost implications if the product gets to the customer before the need for rework is identified.

Strategically Fine Writing Instruments (SFWI) is a manufacturer of hand-crafted pens with 20 employees, mostly in the manufacturing department.

The retail price for a style pen is $89.95, wholesale price $42.25 and cost to produce $18.20, giving a profit of $24.05 per pen.

In February 2006 a major customer notified SFWI that they were returning the 4,000 pens purchased during the past three months that were still in their stock. Their complaint was that the pens were leaking. Also, this customer had already sold 2,500 pens of this style during the same three-month period. The shipping cost to return the pens was $35.85.

SFWI immediately quarantined all stock for thorough reinspection at a cost of $400. It was determined during the reinspection that the inside 'Cross-type' refills had a wall dimension within the design tolerance. The investigation also noted that a design change to the same wall dimension had been implemented in October 2005.

The thinner wall was cracking during installation or shipping, causing a slow leak to occur. SFWI concluded that all refills purchased after the dimension change were to be considered suspect and replaced. The appraisal cost of the 25,000 refills in stock and 8,000 completed pens was $2,500.

The registration records of individual writing instrument owners were downloaded from the database. This information was used to send recall notices to new pen owners regardless of their purchase location. Records indicated that 52,952 owners registered their purchase during the November 2005 through February 2006 period.

SFWI informed their 664 other retailers of this recall. The cost to create and send these notices was $2.17 per letter, including a postage-paid envelope to return any pens. The cost of the returns from the other retailers was $14,608.00. These retailers returned an additional 40,000 pens.

Rework time per unit was measured at 5 minutes per pen. The operators performing the rework make a loaded labour rate of $15/hr, making the per unit cost of the rework $1.25. The 8,000 completed pens needed to be reworked and the refills regarded as obsolete. Replacement refills cost SFWI $2.00 per refill.

Two pens per hour were tested taking 15 seconds per pen (126,664 total pens @12 per hour = 21,110 pens to be inspected at a cost of $0.125 per inspection). Additionally, the 25,000 refills in stock were scrapped.

SFWI needed to redesign the refills prior to conducting the rework and replacements. This new design cost $2,000.00 in engineering time. But owing to the urgency of the leaky pen issue, SFWI paid their supplier a $10,000 expedite fee to ensure the earliest delivery possible for the new refills.

Warranty costs for the pens returned from the retail customers were incurred. The wholesale cost was calculated to be the same $1.25 for labour, $2.00 for the refill plus an average of $1.00 per pen for a total of $4.25 per unit.

SFWI also incurred a one-time inbound shipping charge of $14,643.85 as a result of the wholesale customers returning their stock. The cost to initiate the recall was $2.17 per notice sent to the 52,952 individual owners plus the 664 other retail dealers. The customer who made the orginal complaint did not ask for replacement of their display case.

The total calculated cost of poor quality for the leaking pen problem was $603,558.57.

Tips/warnings

When identifying rework it is extremely important to prevent a 'blame culture' being created. If there is a witch-hunt for the culprit guilty of poor workmanship whenever problems are encountered, there will be a tendency to cover up or hide the problems.

The cost of rework metric must be supported by performance improvement interventions, most notably building inspection into the process.

References

Scrap and Rework. **www.D.Bowes.com**

Philip Crosby, *Quality is Free*, McGraw Hill, 1979

Carpenter Group LLC, **www.quality-improvement-matters.com/copq-calculate.html**

Quality index

52

Strategic perspective
Operational processes and supply chain perspective

Key performance question this indicator helps to answer
How is the organisation ensuring that it is delivering products/services that are fit for purpose?

Why is this indicator important?

The pursuit of 'quality' has been something of an obsession within many organisations across most industries and sectors since quality gurus such as W. Edwards Deming, Josef Juran and Philip Crosby introduced the principles of Total Quality Management (TQM) to Western firms struggling to compete with quality-savvy Eastern competitors (most notably from Japan).

However, the challenge is that there are many definitions of what the term 'quality' means in an organisational setting. For instance, it might mean perfect aesthetics for a furniture manufacturer, colour and texture for a paper manufacturer or ingredients and taste in a restaurant. In general, though, quality can be defined as 'the ability of a product or service to fully meet the customer's expectations, or fit for the intended use of the customer'. In this definition, quality is all about the customer and what is expected from the product or service and how it is delivered. TQM thought leaders such as Deming, Juran and Crosby all had the same goal – to achieve fit-for-use products and services. However, it is also important that products and services are provided at a cost that is acceptable to the supplier (to allow for a profit in commercial enterprise and to deliver within budget for a non-commercial organisation).

A quality index should therefore consist of a group of KPIs (perhaps between five and 10) that enable the supplying organisation to ensure that the customer-facing processes are operating at a level at which customer expectations are met (and, in many cases, exceeded) and are fit for intended use (often known as 'fit for purpose') at an acceptable cost to the supplier.

Given the cited industry/sector variances in understanding of the word 'quality' there is no single quality index template that can be applied within any organisation. However, example KPIs that will make up the index are:

- First Pass Yield (percentage of units produced which pass without rework in first pass).
- Predicted Quality, Defects Per Million Opportunities (the number of components that failed a quality inspection. As stated, it is expressed as a number per million parts. Alternatively, it may be expressed as a percentage of all like components).
- Order Delivery, Quality (quality of goods received or services delivered as per contract and/or PO).
- Cost of Quality (total cost of quality includes the price of non-conformance and the price of conformance).
- % customer complaints due to quality of services/products.
- Order Cycle Time (elapsed time from receipt of order to delivery of product).

How do I measure it?

Data collection method

The broad range of KPIs that might be included within a quality index means that various data collection methods will likely be employed. Data might be captured automatically within the manufacturing process (such as for first pass yield) or through various surveying tools (such as customer complaints due to quality of products or services). Other methods will be used as required.

Formula

A quality index will comprise a number of measures (perhaps between five and 10). Each measure will be weighted according to its importance (although some indexes will comprise KPIs of equal weighting). The final index score is the total points (expressed as a percentage), accounting for weightings. So if customer complaints due to quality of products or services has a 50% weighting score then its points account for half the overall score.

Frequency

The frequency of quality indexes varies according to industry and sector, with some manufacturing firms compiling indexes on a near real-time basis whereas quarterly might suffice for a non-commercial organisation.

Source of the data

Data can come from various sources, such as process performance reports generated by manufacturing (for defect-type data) or marketing/customer management (for complaints and other customer metrics).

Cost/effort in collecting the data

Initial costs might be high if data are presently not available or are in an inappropriate format. Moreover, it is not unusual for staff to be dedicated full time (or at least part time) to managing quality (and compiling an index will be within their remit), which has cost implications. But organisations should look to keeping such departments small and focused. These departments should also teach the business how to capture appropriate data, therefore making quality an everyday part of an employee's life.

Target setting/benchmarks

It is likely that there will be global or industry/sector-specific benchmarks for each KPI within the index. Industry/sector bodies or relevant benchmarking organisations should hold such information.

> **Example** Take a manufacturing organisation with a simple quality index as an example. It decided to use three indicators in its quality index, namely: first pass yield (see page 229), rework level (see page 233) and customer complaints (see page 121).
> For the index they decide to weight FPY with 50% and rework level and customer complaints with 25% each.
> For calculation examples of each individual KPI, see the relevant descriptions.

Tips/warnings

Organisations should be careful that they don't turn the creation and maintenance of a quality index into a 'tick box' exercise, but rather use the data findings for continuous improvement purposes. This is especially true when dedicated quality departments have responsibility for managing the index.

Moreover, a quality index is most powerful when the people/technology inputs into the index and customer/financial outcomes are also monitored and understood: this ensures that key internal processes are not viewed in isolation. The use of a strategic map and accompanying scorecard will be useful for this purpose.

References

www.leanmanufacture.net/quality.aspx

http://kpilibrary.com

The W. Edwards Deming Institute **www.deming.org/**

Juran Institute **www.juran.com**

Overall equipment effectiveness (OEE)

53

> **Strategic perspective**
> Operational processes and supply chain perspective
>
> **Key performance question this indicator helps to answer**
> To what extent is our operating equipment effective?

Why is this indicator important?

When a company invests in equipment and machines it wants to make sure that these are effective, i.e. producing the desired output. If not, then as a consequence it will reduce operating efficiency and profit margins.

Overall equipment effectiveness (OEE) is a composite KPI that measures output based on capacity, taking into account process availability, efficiency and quality. It rolls up a number of output losses into a single index which reduces complex production problems to a good and intuitive information source for overall production effectiveness.

Furthermore, the results of OEE are stated in a generic form which allows comparison between process units or businesses across different industries. It should not, however, be used as an absolute measure that provides this one magic number but instead is best used to identify scope for process performance improvement that can be analysed by looking not just at the top-line OEE level but also at the data for availability, performance and quality.

How do I measure it?

Data collection method

Data for the OEE KPI are collected either from the manufacturing system (when automated) or manually by hand.

Formula

OEE = Availability × Performance × Quality

- where availability takes into account downtime loss, and is calculated as:
  Availability = Operating time / Planned production time;
- where performance takes into account speed loss, and is calculated as:
  Performance = Ideal cycle time / (Operating time / Total pieces)

Ideal cycle time is the minimum cycle time that your process can be expected to achieve in optimal circumstances. It is sometimes called design cycle time, theoretical cycle time or nameplate capacity. Also, performance is capped at 100%, to ensure that if an error is made in specifying the ideal cycle time or ideal run rate the effect on OEE will be limited.

- Where quality takes into account quality loss, and is calculated as:
  Quality = Good pieces / Total pieces

Calculating OEE for an entire plant or business can be achieved by creating a straight or weighted average of the individual OEE levels.

Frequency

The OEE measurement frequency depends a little on the circumstances. For individual machines it could be produced on a weekly basis, whereas for larger processes or plants a monthly measurement cycle should be sufficient.

Source of the data

Data for OEE come from the internal operational processes and are either automatically collected or manually recorded.

Cost/effort in collecting the data

Measuring OEE manually and keeping paper-based records will cost a lot of money and effort. However, many manufacturing solution providers offer integrated automatic data collection solutions which reduce the costs and efforts of calculating OEE.

Target setting/benchmarks

World-class performance would be an OEE target of 90%. However, this could be seen as unachievable and unrealistic. A better way would be to base the target on the best actual data for availability, performance and quality taken from historic data on the machine or plant that is subject to the OEE metric. These then become realistic and achievable targets because we know that the machine or plant is capable of that level of OEE.

Example This worked example calculation is based on the table below, which contains hypothetical shift data. The source for this example is **www.oee.com**. Note that the same units of measurement (in this case minutes and pieces) are used consistently throughout the calculations.

Item	Data
Shift length	8 hours = 480 min
Short breaks	2 @ 15 min = 30 min
Meal break	1 @ 30 min = 30 min
Downtime	47 minutes
Ideal run rate	60 pieces per minute
Total pieces	19,271 pieces
Reject pieces	423 pieces

Planned production time = Shift length − Breaks
 = 480 − 60
 = 420 minutes

Operating time = Planned production time − Downtime
 = 420 − 47
 = 373 minutes

Good pieces = Total pieces − Reject pieces
 = 19,271 − 423
 = 18,848 pieces

$$\text{Availability} = \frac{\text{Operating time}}{\text{Planned production time}}$$

$$= \frac{373 \text{ minutes}}{420 \text{ minutes}}$$

$$= 0.8881 \text{ or } 88.81\%$$

$$\text{Performance} = \frac{(\text{Total pieces} / \text{Operating time})}{\text{Ideal run rate}}$$

$$= \frac{(19{,}271 \text{ pieces} / 373 \text{ minutes})}{60 \text{ pieces per minute}}$$

$$= 0.8611 \text{ or } 86.11\%$$

$$\text{Quality} = \frac{\text{Good pieces}}{\text{Total pieces}}$$

$$= \frac{18{,}848}{19{,}271 \text{ pieces}}$$

$$= 0.9780 \text{ or } 97.80\%$$

$$\text{OEE} = \text{Availability} \times \text{Performance} \times \text{Quality}$$

$$= 0.8881 \times 0.8611 \times 0.9780$$

$$= 0.7479 \text{ or } 74.79\%$$

Tips/warnings

As with any more complex or composite KPI, OEE data can be subject to misinterpretation if not understood and used properly. OEE is a measure that provides information that can be used for improvement of equipment effectiveness. This also means that OEE shouldn't be used as the basis to compare different machines, processes or plants, as this can be misleading. Also, if the focus is to improve OEE as an absolute number, this can drive unwanted behaviours where people simply manipulate the data to improve the final score (e.g. log a breakdown as planned maintenance).

The following example (source **www.oee.com**) illustrates that comparing two OEE numbers is not advisable:

	Shift 1	Shift 2
Availability	90.0%	95.0%
Performance	95.0%	95.0%
Quality	99.5%	96.0%
OEE	85.1%	86.6%

Source: **www.oee.com**

By just looking at the OEE data one would conclude that Shift 2 is performing better than Shift 1, since its OEE is higher. However, very few companies would want to trade a 5.0% increase in availability for a 3.5% decline in quality!

References

www.oee.com/index.html

www.mas-nw.co.uk/resources_local/manufacturing-measurements-kpis/measuring-oee-a-worked-example

http://world-class-manufacturing.com/OEE/oee-calculation.html

www.exor-rd.com/docs/vw121/5A55D3F673BC774EC1257481004B6C93/$file/The%20Complete%20Guide%20to%20Simple%20OEE.pdf

Process or machine downtime level

54

> **Strategic perspective**
> Operational processes and supply chain perspective
>
> **Key performance question this indicator helps to answer**
> To what extent are we operating our processes or machines effectively?

Why is this indicator important?

Any business wants to minimise non-productive time. If machines or processes are not available when they are needed, this reduces the output that can be generated and therefore reduces profits and margins for the business.

Downtime is any productive time in which a machine or process is not available due to circumstances such as faults or maintenance.

While machine downtime is traditionally associated with the manufacturing industry, process downtime is relevant to any industry. Take, for example, call centres that need to track the downtime of their help-desk processes or hospitals that want to monitor the non-availability of diagnostic equipment.

Understanding the level of downtime provides companies with an insight into how effective their internal operational processes are (be it equipment- or process-based).

How do I measure it?

Data collection method

Data for machine or process downtime will come either directly from the machine or process or from records.

Formula

Machine or process downtime level can be measured as a ratio:

Machine or process downtime level = $\left(\dfrac{TA\ t}{PPT\ t}\right) \times 100$

Where:

PPT t is the planned productive time that a process or machine should be available in a given time period t.

TA t is the actual productive time that a process or machine has been available in a given time period t.

Or it can be measured as an actual time level:

Machine or process downtime level = PPT − TA t

Frequency

Machine or process downtime is a measure that can, especially if monitoring is automated, be measured continuously and reported as an indicator if the downtime reaches a predefined threshold. Alternatively, monthly or quarterly reporting might be sufficient.

Source of the data

Data can be taken from the machine itself, as many machines track their own downtime automatically. If automated process monitoring is in place then the same applies to processes. In some cases manual record keeping might be required.

Cost/effort in collecting the data

Costs for measuring process or machine downtime are moderate, depending on the level of data already available. If machines and processes are automatically generating downtime data, the calculations are relatively simple. If manual record keeping is required, this will push up costs.

Target setting/benchmarks

The target for downtime level should be zero, with the aim of eliminating or at least minimising any unplanned interruptions to the production process – especially if a process or machine is not used around the clock and maintenance can be scheduled for non-productive times.

Example Let's look at a radiography department in a hospital, for example. The department has two CT (computed tomography) scanners for which it wants to measure downtime. The aim is to have at least one available 24 hours a day but both available during 'routine business hours' (between 9am and 5pm = 8 hours).

The hospital is measuring downtime as any time that one of the scanners is not available during routine business hours and critical downtime as any time when both CT scanners are not available.

Here is an example of a 24-hour time-frame:

CT scanner 1 was not available between 1pm and 3pm because of a fault and between 7pm and 10pm it was undergoing maintenance.

CT scanner 2 was not available between 7pm and 8pm because of a fault.

Downtime level for CT scanner 1 = $\left(\frac{2 \text{ hours}}{8 \text{ hours}}\right) \times 100$ = 25% or 2 hours

Downtime level for CT scanner 2 = 0%

Critical downtime = $\frac{1}{24}$ = 4.16% or 1 hour

Tips/warnings

When measuring machine downtime level it is useful to understand the cost implications, such as the direct labour costs that you are losing because the machine is not available but you still have to pay the costs for the people who are there to operate the machine.

References

www.downtimedb.com/calculator.asp

First contact resolution (FCR)

55

> **Strategic perspective**
> Operational processes and supply chain perspective
>
> **Key performance question this indicator helps to answer**
> How effectively are we resolving our customer queries at first contact?

Why is this indicator important?

Most companies run contact centres to interact and do business with their customers. For example, contact centres are used to handle customer questions or complaints, provide service advice or technical support and of course to do business with customers (e.g. make bookings, purchase goods, renew contracts, etc.). Customer contacts can be either live phone calls or e-mail interactions.

If you are resolving a customer problem at first contact it means that you are improving quality, reducing costs and improving customer satisfaction, all at the same time. If queries are not resolved it usually leaves irritated customers with unresolved issues and usually repeat calls, which have direct and indirect costs for your operations.

Let's face it, as a customer who contacts a company with an issue or query you want it to be resolved at first contact, or if further steps are required they had better be timely, transparent and aligned with expectations. Research has indicated that 34% of customers who didn't get their enquiry or problem resolved are likely to go to a competitor. Furthermore, the absence of first contact resolution has been found to account for a minimum of 30% of a call centre's operational cost.

How do I measure it?

Data collection method

There are different ways in which companies measure FCR. The simplest option is just to produce an approximation by comparing the number of queries with the number of calls. Such simple statistical analysis obviously has many limitations. Other companies use call logging, where call centre agents log whether the query has been resolved or not, or track queries through automated customer relationship management (CRM) systems. However, what really matters is what the customers think. Your internal system might show that the issue is resolved but if the customer disagrees then this is the reality you have to live with. To gather customer feedback on FCR, companies tend to use post-contact surveys or customer satisfaction surveys, which can take different formats such as: telephone keypad surveys that activate once the call has been completed, SMS or e-mail surveys that follow up on contacts, or mail-based customer satisfaction surveys.

For a more complete picture it makes sense to create a multi-source FCR measurement approach that uses both internal statistics and approximations as well as customer feedback and surveys. For instance:

- Customer satisfaction surveys can be used to determine overall FCR performance, by call type.
- Post-call surveys can deliver agent-level FCR performance.
- Internal call statistics can be used to calculate overall centre-level repeat-call performance.

Formula

Call statistics:

$$\text{FCR call statistics (A)} = \frac{\text{(Total number of queries)}}{\text{(Total number of calls)}} \times 100$$

Agent logs:

$$\text{FCR call statistics (B)} = \frac{\text{(Number of resolved incidents closed on the first contact)}}{\text{(Total number of incidents)}} \times 100$$

For the customer survey you simply take the responses that indicate first contact resolution and divide it by the total number of survey responses.

Frequency

The measurement of FCR should be continuous, e.g. following up every call that has been completed, logging each call, collecting statistics on all calls. The reporting frequency is usually weekly.

Source of the data

Depending on the methodology used, the data will come from the contact centre or CRM system used, the agent call logging system or the customer surveys.

Cost/effort in collecting the data

Using the statistical approximation method is the cheapest, as the data will be readily available from most call centre or CRM solutions. Logging calls will add costs as it takes some time to do this. The most expensive (but most insightful) is the customer survey method. Costs can be reduced by automating customer surveys.

Target setting/benchmarks

The target for contact centres should be to resolve all calls at first contact. However, this might not be realistic and global benchmarking studies show that best practice is at about 85% and higher.

Benchmarking data from different industries shows the following FCR rates:

Industry	Worst FCR	Average FCR	Best FCR
Car insurance claims	4%	19%	26%
Gas & electric utility collections	8%	39%	52%
Technical product support	41%	69%	97%
Bank customer service	74%	89%	98%
Consumer product information	82%	93%	99%

Example Take this consumer contact centre as an example.

The internal CRM system has logged that in month 11, the contact centre took 200,000 calls and handled 150,000 queries.

- Based on call statistics the FCR is $\frac{150}{200} \times 100 = 75\%$.
- The company is also using an agent call logging system which reports that 78% of calls have been resolved at first contact.
- The SMS and e-mail customer survey reports an FCR of 72%.

Tips/warnings

FCR is a key performance indicator for most businesses and generally the higher the FCR the better. But like any benchmark metric, FCR must be interpreted in context with other metrics, such as average speed to answer, average call length and abandon rates, before any definitive conclusions can be drawn about overall efficiency and effectiveness.

Focusing too much on FCR can distract from the fact that not all contacts are contacts that you want or contacts that are adding value to the company or the customer. Sometimes it is best to check whether calls are necessary or really add value or whether they should be avoided altogether or channelled to e.g. a self-service web portal. Offering the customer the ability to help themselves can in fact add to a positive customer experience.

We highlighted earlier that contact statistics and contact logging are proxy indicators and, as such, will not necessarily provide you with an accurate picture. Also, to avoid cheating (i.e. agents logging calls as resolved when they are not), regular audits and checks of the data are a good idea.

Finally, we said that customer opinions are the most important measure of FCR. However, the surveys need to be constructed in a way that provides useful feedback. For instance, if you are concerned with assessing FCR for billing concerns, it would make sense to contact the customer for resolution feedback after they have received the next bill rather than two days after they called the contact centre. They might think their issue has been resolved but don't really know for sure until they see the correction on the next bill. In fact, research indicates that while 67% of callers believe that the problem was resolved as measured by the real-time call surveys, an average of 20% of those callers do not have the problem resolved because of back-office process failures.

References

www.connectionsmagazine.com/papers/4/07.pdf

www.metricnet.com/metric_month.html

http://searchcrm.techtarget.com/definition/first-call-resolution

www.ascentgroup.com/research/sum_fcr.html

www.icmi.com/Resources/QueueTips/2005/March/Calculating-First-Call-Resolution

www.firstcontactresolution.com/

www.callcentres.com.au/first_call_resolution.htm

[PART FIVE]

Employee perspective

Human capital value added (HCVA)

56

> **Strategic perspective**
> Employee perspective
>
> **Key performance question this indicator helps to answer**
> To what extent are our employees adding value to the bottom line?

Why is this indicator important?

In many businesses, employees are not only the most important assets and key enablers of future success but often the biggest expense (or rather investment). It is therefore important to understand to what extent employees add value to the financial performance of the organisation. Employees are often a missing ingredient in accounting and finance (except as an expense) and with a little effort we can calculate the effects of people on financial performance.

Research finds that while most businesses have a range of HR indicators, less than half actively track the impact of employees on financial business performance. The reason I am given for not using such measures is often the argument that there are no agreed ways or valid ways of calculating this. Here I'd like to quote human capital guru Dr Jac Fitz-enz, who says: 'To contend that there is no valid and consistent way to do this is simply to admit one's ignorance.'

In the past, companies used over-simplified KPIs such as revenue per employee. If businesses are to understand the real profit impact of employees then we need to calculate human capital value added (HCVA). To get to the HCVA we take all non-employee-related expenses away from the revenue generated and divide this (adjusted profit figure) by the number of full-time employees. HCVA therefore gives us the profitability of the average employee.

How do I measure it?

Data collection method

The data for this can be easily extracted from the financial accounting systems or the financial statements.

Formula

The PWC Saratoga Institute suggests calculating HCVA by subtracting all corporate expenses except for pay and benefits from the revenue generated and dividing the adjusted profit by the average headcount.

$$HCVA = Revenue - \frac{(Total\ costs - Employment\ cost)}{FTE}$$

Where total costs are the difference between revenue and profit before taxes, employee costs are pay and benefits, and FTE is the average number of full-time employees.

Frequency

A quarterly calculation of HCVA is recommended.

Source of the data

The source of the data will be the financial accounting system.

Cost/effort in collecting the data

The costs for collecting and calculating this KPI are minimal as companies will already have all the financial information in their financial statements.

Target setting/benchmarks

As profitability per employee goes, the bigger the better really. It is impossible to provide a generic benchmark here and it is probably best to track this indicator over time with an aim of increasing the figure.

Example Let's look at a company with the following figures:

- Revenue is $100,000,000.
- Total costs are $80,000,000.
- Employee costs are $30,000,000 ($20,000,000 in pay and $10,000,000 in benefits).
- Number of employees is 650.

$$HCVA = Revenue - \frac{(Total\ costs - Employment\ cost)}{FTE}$$

$$HCVA = \frac{\$100,000,000 - (\$80,000,000 - \$30,000,000)}{650}$$

$$HCVA = \frac{50,000,000}{650}$$

$$HCVA = \$76,923.08$$

Tips/warnings

Just looking at the costs for full-time employees can sometimes slightly distort the picture as most businesses incur further employee-related expenses such as the cost for contingencies, absence and turnover. These can be added to the formula.

Also, some suggest[1] that the profit before tax figure is not a correct profit item as foreign exchange losses are included in it. The benchmark may be reasonable in developed countries where devaluation does not exist. Instead, you can calculate total cost as the difference between revenue and operating profit. The formula then will be:

$$HCVA = \frac{Revenue - (Revenue - Operating\ profit - Employment\ cost)}{FTE}$$

And to simplify the calculation:

$$HCVA = \frac{Operating\ profit + Employment\ cost}{FTE}$$

References

Jac Fitz-enz, *The ROI of Human Capital: Measuring the Economic Value of Employee Performance*, New York: AMACOM, 2009

www.pwc.com/saratoga

[1] http://humancapitalstrategy.blogspot.com/2009/09/measuring-employee-value-added.html

Nancy R. Lockwood, *Maximizing Human Capital: Demonstrating HR Value with Key Performance Indicators*, SHRM, 2006. **www.shrm.org/Research/Articles/Documents/0906RQuartpdf.pdf**

Leslie A Weatherly, *The Value of People: The Challenges and Opportunities of Human Capital Measurement and Reporting*, SHRM. **www.shrm.org/Research/Articles/Articles/Documents/0303measurement.pdf**

Revenue per employee (RPE)

57

> **Strategic perspective**
> Employee perspective
>
> **Key performance question this indicator helps to answer**
> How productive are our employees?

Why is this indicator important?

Employees are not only our most important assets but also usually our most expensive assets. Companies need to make sure that they are utilising their employees efficiently. In general, companies aim to deliver more revenue with fewer employees. This would demonstrate that a company is finding ways to squeeze more revenue out of each of its workers. Therefore, by putting revenues in relation to the number of employees you derive an important ratio of productivity.

Because labour needs vary widely between industries, the revenue per employee (RPE) KPI is most useful when compared with other similar companies in the same industry. Tracking the RPE ratio over time will provide managers with an insight into how well they are able to improve productivity per employee. Comparing RPE between companies allows investors and managers to understand the relative productivity of companies.

How do I measure it?

Data collection method

The data for the RPE KPI are easily collected from the financial statements of a company or the financial management system which will give you revenue data. The number of employees is usually readily available – it might need a little adjustment because you want to include full-time-equivalent employee numbers as part-time positions can inflate the employee numbers and skew the ratio.

Formula

RPE is calculated by dividing a firm's revenue by its total number of workers:

$$RPE = \frac{Revenue}{Number\ of\ employees}$$

Where number of employees are full-time equivalent.

Frequency

It makes sense to align the measurement of RPE with the calculation of revenue figures, with usually happens quarterly.

Source of the data

The data for this KPI come straight from the financial and HR systems.

Cost/effort in collecting the data

The costs for collecting RPE are minimal because all the data are readily available.

Target setting/benchmarks

Ideally, a company wants the highest possible RPE because the higher the number, the more efficiently the company uses its employees.

Even though there are no general rules about what constitutes a good level of RPE, there are some benchmarks available. To create benchmarks in your industry you can go to any business database and look up revenue numbers for companies (e.g. fact sheets for companies on **www.hoovers.com**). The employee numbers are often included, but if not they can usually be found on a company website.

Here are some RPE numbers for different companies:

Company	Revenue per employee
Starwood Hotels	$38,338
WalMart	$170,000
GE	$436,000
Microsoft	$646,000
Amazon	$925,894
Apple	$1,014,969
Murphy Oil Corp	$7,609,147

As benchmarks go, smaller companies usually average around $100,000 per employee while Fortune 500 companies average around $300,000 per employee.

Example Let's look at the Software & Service Industry and compare Google Inc. (GOOG) with Convergys Corp. (CVG), both listed in the S&P 500. Google with its 20,164 employees generates annual revenue per employee of $1,093,892 and annual profit per employee of $214,768. Convergys Corp. (CVG) with its 75,000 employees, on the other hand, is only able to generate annual revenue per employee of $36,855 and an annual profit per employee of −$1,344.

Tips/warnings

Taking the logic of this KPI slightly further, you could replace revenue with profits and employee numbers with payroll to create an even more meaningful internal indicator of Profit / Payroll ratio.

However, the problem is that the numbers for payroll are more difficult to obtain for your competitors.

Another popular variation of RPE is a salesperson performance ratio of sales per salesperson.

In *Working With Emotional Intelligence*, Daniel Goleman quotes a study of 44 Fortune 500 firms showing that the top 10% of salespeople had $6.7 million in sales compared to the average salesperson's $3 million. So, the best salespeople were over twice as effective.

References

www.investinganswers.com/term/revenue-employee-918

www.jbryanscott.com/2009/02/07/nasdaq-100-revenue-per-employee/

www.gazelles.com/columns/Revenue%20per%20Employee.pdf

www.cnbc.com/id/30888743/The_S_P_500_s_Leanest_Companies

Employee satisfaction index 58

> **Strategic perspective**
> Employee perspective
>
> **Key performance question this indicator helps to answer**
> To what extent are our employees happy in their jobs?

Why is this indicator important?

Along with customer satisfaction (see KPI on page 97), employee satisfaction is perhaps the oldest and most established of all non-financial indicators. Put simply, employee satisfaction is the terminology used to describe whether employees are happy and contented and fulfilling their desires and needs at work.

Few organisations do not measure employee satisfaction in some form, although an increasing number prefer the more sophisticated measure of employee engagement (see KPI on page 269). It has long been understood, and supported with convincing empirical evidence, that employee satisfaction is a powerful leading indicator of customer satisfaction, which is in itself a leading indicator of profit: indeed, the well-known service profit chain is essentially based on this employee–customer–financial causal linkage showing how happy employees deliver a better customer service, which in turn improves customer loyalty and financial performance.

There are innumerable case studies on organisations that have successfully deployed an employee satisfaction solution and there are equally large numbers of consultants offering such solutions. Moreover, the measure is typically found with an organisation's balanced scorecard (which captures both financial and non-financial goals and measures) or whatever performance management/measurement framework is being used.

How do I measure it?

Data collection method

Employee satisfaction (sometimes referred to as 'climate') surveys can be conducted by an external consultancy or research organisation or carried out by an in-house team, often from Human Resources.

Employee satisfaction is typically captured through some form of surveying instrument that guarantees anonymity – today usually online but sometimes still paper-based, telephone-based or face-to-face – with answers recorded using a Likert scale (from 1 = very dissatisfied to 5 = very satisfied, or 1 = strongly disagree to 5 = strongly agree, or some version thereof). Focus groups of employees are often used to provide a more qualitative assessment of employee opinion: these might be to support or elaborate on the findings from the survey or might be a spot employee satisfaction 'health check/temperature check', which serves as a quick checklist of how employees currently feel about the company and the work that they are doing.

Employee satisfaction surveys will normally cover the key areas impacting on the staff experience. These are likely to include areas such as:

- Leadership and direction
- Communications
- 'Local' line management
- Staff development opportunities
- Company working culture
- Facilities and environment
- Conditions of service

Formula

There are many ways to measure employee satisfaction, but a simple Likert-scale approach would look something like this:

1 Strongly disagree
2 Disagree
3 Undecided
4 Agree
5 Strongly agree

Then, add up the number of questions with answers against each response (1,2,3,4,5).
Identify total point of each response.
Identify total number of questions answered.

$$\text{Employee satisfaction index} = \left(\frac{\text{Total point}}{\text{Total question}}\right) \times 100.$$

Each particular question and score will be analysed and reported in the form of mean scores of satisfaction and the percentage of staff satisfied, examined across different classifications of staff, e.g. age, level of responsibility, department, location etc. Additional statistical analysis using correlations, regressions and Chaid analysis can be carried out to identify issues which are driving satisfaction and loyalty, and the relative impact of these issues on satisfaction.

Frequency

Employee satisfaction is normally captured through an annual survey. However, it might be more useful to administer the survey to 10% of the employee base 10 times a year as this will ensure that employee satisfaction scores remain current and show the effect of any interventions launched to remedy areas of employee discontent unearthed as part of the surveying process.

Source of the data

The employee base.

Cost/effort in collecting the data

Employee satisfaction surveys are reasonably cheap to administer, irrespective of whether they are conducted internally or externally, as they can be carried out online and the employee does not usually need to spend too long answering the questions. They also do not require significant effort to analyse.

Target setting/benchmarks

Most external bodies that offer employee satisfaction survey solutions will have performance benchmarks based on previous client scores – these are typically available universally (across all sectors or industries) or are sector/industry specific and even go down to function levels. An organisation should use an initial baseline score to set improvement targets year-on-year or period-on-period.

Example A leading North American financial services organisation had been running an employee satisfaction survey for about 10 years (up until early in the last decade). The survey was carried out every second year and consisted of about 90 questions. This gave an overall employee satisfaction score and feedback about the quality of leadership and management. 'However, we found that the survey was too long and that we were trying to hold managers accountable for everything on the survey when much of it was to do with cultural issues, for example, which may well have been outside the manager's direct control', says the HR Vice President.

Consequently, this survey was refashioned into two separate surveys. The first, called 'ViewPoint', captures employees' views of working in their own department, and asks for ratings on statements such as 'my department is a great place to work', 'my department provides high-quality service to its customers' and 'I have a good understanding of my current job responsibilities'. A 1–5 scale is used, again from strongly disagree to strongly agree. Importantly, departmental heads can be held responsible for these scores.

A second survey was designed that asked questions around 'engagement'. This focuses on areas such as the employee's willingness to recommend the organisation to other people as a company to work for and willingness to recommend the company's products to potential customers.

Tips/warnings

A measure of the success of an employee satisfaction survey is the percentage rate of employee involvement. The response is normally higher when the employee knows that their opinions count and can see action as a result of the survey. Simply put, the survey has to trigger remedial action when low satisfaction levels are found. If nothing happens, it is unlikely that employees will fill in the next survey. It is also critical that the anonymity of the employee is guaranteed, which is one reason why an external surveying body is often preferred to an in-house deployment.

For trending purposes, it is important to keep questions consistent over a multi-year period, although of course questions that are found to be poorly understood, ambiguous or that provide little information of value should be replaced.

As cited earlier, many organisations are moving more towards employee engagement surveys, believing that employee satisfaction itself does not provide a rich enough understanding of the employee's connection to the organisation. An employee might be 'satisfied' because the job is easy, well-paid, etc. They may not give discretionary effort in their day-to-day work.

References

Best Practices in Customer and Employee Satisfaction Management
www.benchmarkingreports.com

Derek R. Allen and Morris Wilburn, *Linking Customer and Employee Satisfaction to the Bottom Line*, ASQ Quality Press, Milwaukee, WI, 2002

For a list of books on employee satisfaction see **www.humanresources.hrvinet.com/employee-satisfaction-books/**

Employee engagement level   59

> **Strategic perspective**
> Employee perspective
>
> **Key performance question this indicator helps to answer**
> To what extent are our employees committed to delivering to the vision and mission of the organisation?

Why is this indicator important?

The level of employee engagement is one of the most important indicators of the likelihood of an organisation succeeding financially and delivering to its vision and mission statements.

Crucially, an employee engagement survey differs from the traditional employee satisfaction surveying instruments that have been used extensively by organisations for decades.

Indeed, engagement surveys emerged when leading organisations began to realise that 'satisfaction' does not tell the whole employee story. An employee might be 'satisfied' because he or she has an easy job, is not stretched (and doesn't want to be), is paid well and receives an excellent benefits package. This does not necessarily mean that he or she is committed to delivering to the vision/mission. The most dissatisfied employees might well be the ones that are performance-oriented and really want to do all that they can to deliver to the organisational vision and mission.

Employee engagement surveys emerged as a way not of measuring mere satisfaction (which will likely still be measured but as a subordinate measure to engagement) but as a mechanism for assessing the contribution of the employee to performance, productivity and ultimately sustainable financial results. Indeed, in a well-formulated engagement survey, satisfaction is not a focus area.

Yet for all the discussion around whether or not employees are engaged, a critical question is what tangible difference an 'engaged' employee makes to performance over one that is 'disengaged' (I explain the categories below in the Formula section). The research findings are compelling. The US-headquartered Gallup Organisation (which has what we can safely describe as the most mature and widely used of all the employee engagement surveys deployed today, although this is not to say that we necessarily recommend Gallup over the alternatives such as Towers Watson and Blessing White) estimates that fully 73% of North American employees are disengaged from the organisation for which they work (according to 2007 results, and we can expect similar findings from other geographical regions). This means that they either just turn up at work and go through the motions or, worse, do all they can to do as little as they can. Gallup estimates that this disengagement collectively costs the US economy up to $350 billion per year in lost productivity, including absence, illness and other problems.

The bottom line is that if employees are disengaged the organisation will almost certainly be haemorrhaging money, as well as losing key talent.

Moreover, research by the leading global HR consultancy Towers Watson found that companies with highly engaged employees generate more marketplace power than their competitors. Towers Watson analysed three years of employee data for 40 global companies. The firm separated these organisations into high-engagement and low-engagement categories according to their employee engagement survey scores. The data showed that over a period of 36 months those companies with a highly engaged employee population turned in significantly better financial performance (a 5.75% difference in operating margins and a 3.44% difference in net profit) than did low-engagement workplaces. In a separate analysis Towers Watson found that organisations that consistently show higher engagement levels than average organisations produced shareholder returns 9.3% higher than the returns for the S&P 500 Index from 2002 through 2006.

How do I measure it?

Data collection method

The data are derived from online employee surveys.

Formula

The most famous employee engagement survey is probably the one devised and deployed by the Gallup Organisation, although alternatives should be considered. Gallup's survey consists of just 12 questions. Gallup is interested in uncovering those behaviours or characteristics that will make a quantifiable difference to performance in the workplace.

Employees answer Gallup's questions, through straight yes/no responses in order to generate a score (**www.gallup.com**).

Based on the responses, organisations can see the percentage of employees that are actively engaged, engaged, disengaged or actively disengaged and from the Gallup analysis can get insights into the likely financial consequences.

Frequency

Normally done annually. However, in order to make data more actionable it is better practice to sample the workforce, so a subset of them is surveyed every month. This allows organisations to collect the full data set over a year. It means that individuals receive a survey only once a year but the organisation will have valid data available every month, which helps with spotting trends and overcoming bias.

Source of the data

The data are drawn from the employee engagement survey that is distributed to all employees.

Cost/effort in collecting the data

Costs and effort for collecting employee engagement levels can be very high. As with any survey-type data collection, the costs can be reduced by minimising the logistics and the administrative costs of collecting and analysing the data. Online tools and electronic data collection and analysis can bring costs down considerably.

Target setting/benchmarks

Employee engagement surveys are generally externally administered and therefore providers typically have extensive databases of benchmarks of best practice performance from which the client organisation can identify and work towards their own targets.

> **Example** The Toronto, Canada headquartered Scotiabank was a pioneer in using an employee engagement survey (at the turn of the century). Historically, the bank carried out an employee satisfaction survey that consisted of about 90 questions and provided an overall employee satisfaction score. However, on recognising the limitations, this survey was redesigned to capture measures of whether the employee is actively 'engaged' in working for the bank, rather than just passively satisfied.

> So the engagement survey focused on areas such as the employee's willingness to recommend the bank to other people as a company to work for and willingness to recommend Scotiabank products to potential customers. The employee engagement survey is focused on understanding what drives performance and measures commitment, loyalty, trust and those behavioural traits which inspire employees to perform to their ultimate capacity.

Tips/warnings

Employee engagement surveys should be short and focused, and the external provider should be able to demonstrate a link between high engagement scores and superior financial performance. It's also important to be able to drill down and see which parts of the organisation have large numbers of disengaged employees so that corrective actions can be launched. A single overall measure of engagement is not enough to drive performance forward. Also, the employee engagement survey should trigger behavioural change. If nothing changes as a result of the findings then it will only further demotivate a disengaged workforce.

References

www.gallup.com

www.towersperrin.com

www.blessingwhite.com

Marsh Makhijani and James Creelman, *Creating Engaged Employees: The Role of Employee Engagement Surveys*, OTI Indonesia, 2010. **www.otiinternational.com**

Staff advocacy score 60

> **Strategic perspective**
> Employee perspective
>
> **Key performance question this indicator helps to answer**
> To what extent are our employees advocates of our business?

Why is this indicator important?

Having employees that believe in your business is important as this shines through in the way they interact with customers and deliver operations. What's more, employees that are advocates of your business refer your company to their friends and family members, not only as potential customers but also as a potential employer.

Having your own employees on your side is critical in an era where personal views spread like wildfire through the social media and online universe. In a world where we compete for the best talent and where professionals connect through social media platforms such as LinkedIn, it becomes very apparent whether a business is a good employer or not.

Companies can basically look at their employees as 'internal customers' with their own wants and needs. Similarly to the idea of the customer KPI net promoter score (NPS) (see Customer perspective), a staff advocacy score can be derived just by asking one question: 'How likely is it that you would recommend this company as an employer to a friend?'

Understanding to what extent employees are advocates of the business they are working for is therefore an important indicator for understanding not only staff satisfaction and staff loyalty but the potential implications it has for your brand and the ability to attract new talent.

Based on responses to this single-question approach, organisations can group their employees into the following three categories:

- Advocates
- Passives
- Detractors

The staff advocacy index is therefore a simple and direct metric that holds companies accountable for how they treat their own employees.

How do I measure it?

Data collection method

The staff advocacy score is collected using a survey, which can be mail-based or conducted through the internet or phone.

Formula

Using a 0 to 10 scale, an organisation can calculate its staff advocacy score by taking the percentage of advocates and subtracting the percentage of detractors.

Advocates (score 9–10) are loyal and enthusiastic employees who will promote you as a potential employer.

Passives (score 7–8) are satisfied but unenthusiastic employees who are vulnerable to competitive offerings.

Detractors (score 0–6) are unhappy employees who can damage your brand and impede growth through negative word-of-mouth.

Staff advocacy score = (% of employees that are advocates) − (% of employees that are detractors)

Frequency

Most companies collect their staff advocacy data annually. However, it is much better to create smaller sets of surveys that look at a sample of employees (e.g. 10%). This way, data can be collected on e.g. a monthly basis to provide important trend information. It means that over a year a company will have surveyed everyone but on a monthly basis it gets data to identify trends throughout the year.

Source of the data

Data will come from surveys of your employees.

Costs/effort in collecting the data

The costs for collecting data for the staff advocacy score can be high, especially if an external surveying company is used to design, collect, analyse and report the data. However, measuring the staff advocacy score is a lot cheaper compared to more complex employee surveys, which are much more common practice.

Costs for the staff advocacy score also tend to spiral upwards for hard-copy surveys that have to be printed, distributed and manually transferred into IT systems for analysis. The more automated the data collection is, the cheaper it will become.

Target setting/benchmarks

There are few existing benchmarks for the staff advocacy score to go by, so the best bet is to look at some of the customer scores for the net promoter score. Here, good companies can score between 30% and 90%.

Example Let's take this example of a company that employs 1,000 people. The staff advocacy survey returned 976 responses with the following breakdown of scores:

Score	Counts
0	1
1	2
2	3
3	10
4	70
5	100
6	150
7	170
8	110
9	200
10	160

The staff advocacy index is therefore:

Staff advocacy score = (% of employees that are advocates) − (% of employees that are detractors)

Advocates: $\left[\frac{(160+200)}{976}\right] \times 100 = 36.8\%$

Detractors: $\left[\frac{(1+2+3+10+70+100+150)}{976}\right] \times 100 = 34.4\%$

Staff advocacy score = 36.8% − 34.4% = 2.4

Tips/warnings

The staff advocacy score will give a nice, simple number; however, it won't give you the reasons why employees are happy or unhappy. A very powerful supplement to the single-question survey is a set of open questions along the following lines:

- What do you particularly like about being employed here?
- What or which areas could be improved?

This way, the company will get insight not only into how many employees are advocates, neutrals or detractors but also into the areas that employees value or want to see improved.

References

www.netpromoter.com/

www.satmetrix.com (2008)

Fred Reicheld, *The Ultimate Question 2.0: How Net Promoter Companies Thrive in a Customer Driven World*, HBR Press, Boston, MA, 2010

www.mattberent.net/Netpromoter_-_AAPOR.pdf

Employee churn rate   61

> **Strategic perspective**
> Employee perspective
>
> **Key performance question this indicator helps to answer**
> How well are we retaining our staff?

Why is this indicator important?

Attracting, recruiting, training and developing talented staff takes time and costs money. This is why you want to make sure that once you have found and trained employees, you don't lose them too quickly.

Replacing employees is an expensive business. There is the cost of recruiting (in 2010 the US-based Society for Human Resource Management reported that it costs an average of $7,123 to hire an employee) as well as training costs and, even for the best educated or most professionally qualified staff, a cost associated with their getting up to speed with the way the company works and their becoming optimally productive in their new position There is also a sometimes sizeable, if hidden, cost associated with an employee leaving an organisation and taking with them a large amount of know-how that might, in some situations, take years to replace – if at all.

Not surprisingly, therefore, organisations have become focused on retaining employees rather than see them walk out the door.

Consequently, a measure of employee churn rate or employee turnover rate is used to gain an insight into how many of your employees your business is losing in a given time period in comparison to the overall number of employees.

How do I measure it?

Data collection method

Analysis of HR records.

Formula

Most organisations simply track their employee churn using this simple formula:

$$\frac{\text{Total number of leavers over period}}{\text{Average total number employed over period}} \times 100$$

The total figure includes all leavers, even people who left involuntarily due to dismissal, redundancy or retirement.

Frequency

Employee churn rates can be measured to any period. It is not uncommon for the data to be collected monthly and analysed by the HR team. However, it might be reported to the executive team annually as the figure can then be considered in the light of an understanding of wider economic, competitive and other influences that might influence the figure and explain any significant deviation from the previous year, such as changes to the economic landscape.

Source of the data

HR records.

Cost/effort in collecting the data

The costs and effort to calculate employee churn rate are low as the data should be readily available in most companies' human resources systems. If manual data collection is required (which should be rare), costs and efforts can increase quickly.

Target setting/benchmarks

It is impossible to set a meaningful employee turnover rate that can be compared across industries and sectors, as turnover rates vary considerably. Typically the highest rates are found in retailing, hotels, catering and leisure, call centres and among other lower-paid private sector services groups. Turnover levels also vary from region to region. The highest rates are found where unemployment is lowest and where it is unproblematic for people to secure desirable alternative employment. Furthermore, across the board, turnover rates fall sharply in an economic downturn.

That said, there are many organisations that can offer industry- or sector-specific data on employee turnover rates. The UK's Chartered Institute of Personnel and Development (CIPD) has an annual survey of employee turnover rates across industries and sectors (its 2010 survey found the overall turnover rate in the UK to be 13.5%), and in the US the Society for Human Resource Management holds such information. Such benchmark data provide valuable insights into how well other similar organisations are retaining their staff when faced with similar economic and other challenges.

Example Consider this example for a monthly turnover rate and how this aggregates up to an annual rate.

Starting with the formula for monthly turnover:

Five people leave in the month and the total number of employees is 250. This makes a monthly turnover rate of 2%.

$$\frac{5}{250} \times 100 = 2\%$$

The annual employee turnover is then calculated by adding up the monthly turnover figures or by recalculating it. In this example and for simplicity, if we assume that each month 5 people leave over the 12-month period, this gives us an annual employee turnover rate of 24%:

$$\left[\frac{(12 \times 5)}{250}\right] \times 100 = 24\%$$

Tips/warnings

Given the problems regarding the 'cost' of turnover cited at the beginning of this KPI description, organisations might want to consider the employee turnover rate alongside aligned metrics such as turnover cost (calculation of termination, new hire, vacancy and learning curve costs).

It might also be worth considering replacing the straightforward employee turnover rate calculation with one that reports on 'regretted' turnover: that is, a measure of those people who resigned whom the organisation would have liked to have kept. There will always be departing employees that the organisation is happy to lose.

A useful insight is that in high-turnover industries in particular, a great deal of employee turnover consists of people resigning or being dismissed in the first few months of employment. Even when people stay for a year or more, it is often the case that their decision to leave sooner rather than later is taken in the first weeks of employment. Poor recruitment and selection decisions, on the part of both the employee and the employer, are usually to blame, along with poorly designed or non-existent induction programmes.

Exit interviews, in which the departing employee is interviewed as to the reasons for their leaving, can be a useful way to begin to understand the drivers of high turnover so that appropriate interventions can be made.

References

Employee turnover and retention: CIPD factsheet, July 2010. **www.cipd.co.uk/subjects/hrpract/turnover/empturnretent.htm**

http://blogs.payscale.com/compensation/2009/12/costs-of-employee-turnover.html

Society For Human Resource Management: **www.shrm.org**

Average employee tenure

62

Strategic perspective
Employee perspective

Key performance question this indicator helps to answer
To what extent do our employees stay loyal to our company?

Why is this indicator important?

It is useful for companies to understand how long on average employees stay with their organisation. Long average employee tenure usually indicates that employees are more loyal and dedicated to the company. Long tenure will generally help to reduce recruitment and training costs.

Aggregate tenure KPIs can give an insight into the satisfaction of employees with their organisation. It can also be compared with average tenure for industry peers to assess the company's competitive standing. The average employee tenure metric can be calculated by total length of employment with the company or by length of employment in each position occupied by the employee.

How do I measure it?

Data collection method

The data for the average employee tenure KPI can be easily extracted from the HR system, which should include the start date for each employee and the time in the company.

Formula

$$\text{Average employee tenure} = \frac{\text{Sum of all tenures}}{\text{Number of full-time employees}}$$

$$\frac{\text{Average employee tenure by job role}}{\text{Job type}} = \frac{\text{Sum of all tenures in that particular role}}{\text{Number of full-time employees in that job role}}$$

Frequency

Average employee tenure should be measured on an annual or six-monthly basis.

Source of the data

The HR system.

Cost/effort in collecting the data

The costs and effort for generating this KPI are low if the HR system is used to calculate it. Alternatively, the data can be exported into a spreadsheet which can produce the data with little effort.

Target setting/benchmarks

Targets can be based on overall tenure figures. The latest figures (2010) from the US Bureau of Labor Statistics show that the median number of years that wage and salary workers stay with their current employer is 4.4. This tenure is 4.6 years for men (up from 4.2 in 2008) and 4.2 for women (up from 3.9 in 2008). The data also show that 29% of wage and salary workers aged 16 and over had 10 years or more of tenure with their current employer. However, there are industry differences and, for example, call centres and the hospitality industry traditionally have lower tenure rates than others.

Example As an example calculation, let's take a look at this engineering company, which employs 100 staff. The distribution of tenure follows the expected bell curve (Figure 62.1), with: 4 people who have been there 1 year; 11 people who have been there 2 years; 19 people who have been there 3 years; 40 people who have been there 4 years; 20 people who have been there 5 years; 4 people who have been there 6 years; 1 person who has been there 8 years; and 1 person who has been there 10 years.

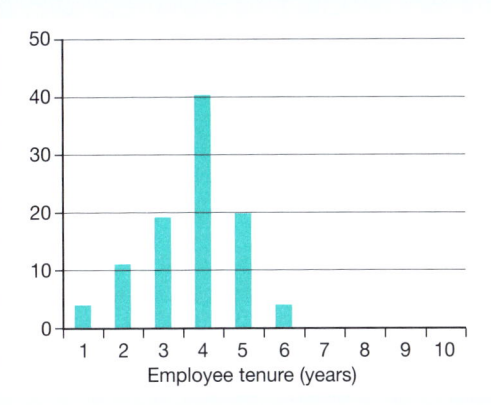

Average employee tenure is therefore calculated as

$$\frac{[(4\times1)+(11\times2)+(19\times3)+(40\times4)+(20\times5)+(4\times6)+(1\times8)+(1\times10)]}{100}$$

$$\text{Average employee tenure} = \frac{(4+22+57+160+100+24+8)}{100}$$

Average employee tenure = 3.85 years

Tips/warnings

Long average employee tenure can also indicate that employees might be too comfortable in their job and that maybe not enough fresh ideas and thinking are brought into the company. This is why employee tenure needs to be viewed together with employee churn to understand the situation in more detail.

Some employees return to the same employer after a spell at another company. In this case you have two options: either start the counting again or add the previous years the person has already spent with the company. Strategically, the latter makes sense.

References

www.cipd.co.uk/hr-resources/factsheets/employee-turnover-retention.aspx

www.cio.com/article/153600/Average_CIO_Tenure_Slips_But_Still_More_Than_Four_Years

Absenteeism Bradford factor

63

Strategic perspective
Employee perspective

Key performance question this indicator helps to answer
To what extent is unauthorised employee absenteeism a problem in our business?

Why is this indicator important?

When employees are absent from work it costs the business money and causes disruptions. In terms of costs it is not just the direct costs that matter but the indirect costs of absenteeism, such as the cost of replacing absent employees in critical positions and possible overtime payments to these replacement workers, as well as the effect the absenteeism has on workforce levels, medical aid costs, and group life and disability premiums. It is estimated that the indirect cost of absenteeism can easily be 200% or more of the direct cost of absenteeism. As a ball-park figure and depending on the industry, worker absenteeism totals an average of between 5% and 9% of annual profits.

Absenteeism is traditionally defined as an employee's unavailability for work. There are different types of absenteeism: legal (such as public holidays), authorised (such as approved holidays) and unauthorised. While legal and authorised absenteeism need to be managed and costed, it is unauthorised absence that causes the majority of problems. This is why most organisations strive to avoid unauthorised absenteeism and keep it to a minimum.

There are many reasons why people take time off work. The main reasons include personal illness, family issues and stress, as well as the attitude that people feel 'entitled to a day off'. Research finds that the level of disruption (and therefore costs to the business) is particularly high when employees take frequent, short and unauthorised or unplanned absences. This is where the Bradford factor comes in as a key performance indicator that is used to help identify staff whose sickness absenteeism needs reviewing in greater detail.

The Bradford calculation is believed to originate from the Bradford University of Management which developed the KPI as a way of highlighting the disproportionate level of disruption to an organisation's performance that can be caused by persistent short-term absence compared to single incidences of prolonged absence. The Bradford factor measures an employee's irregularity of attendance by combining measures of absence frequency and duration and is designed to highlight employees who take many short-term absences from work. It can be used to monitor trends in absence and generate 'trigger' points at which the absenteeism of individuals needs to be reviewed.

How do I measure it?

Formula

The Bradford factor score can be calculated by looking at unplanned absence over a period (often a year, but could be any time period) and counting the number of days absent and multiplying them by the squared number of absence episodes.

Bradford factor = $D_t \times E_t \times E_t$

D_t = Total number of days of unplanned absence

E_t = Total number of individual spells or episodes of absence

Frequency

In most cases it makes sense to calculate this Bradford factor annually (calendar year or rolling 12 months), but some companies might want to measure it quarterly or even monthly to identify issues in the short term and monitor progress against absenteeism reduction targets.

Source of the data

Most HR systems will track absenteeism and break it down into unplanned or unauthorised absenteeism. If this is not the case, sickness absenteeism can be used instead.

Cost/effort in collecting the data

The costs and effort of collecting the data depend on the level of available information. If the HR system contains a good record and categorisation of the absenteeism data then the costs of calculating the Bradford factor are small. The costs are reduced further if the HR system allows you to calculate the score automatically (which quite a few do). The costs will go up if manual data transfer and calculations are required.

Target setting/benchmarks

Targets are best set in industry comparisons or in relation to your historic performance. As an initial benchmark you might want to trigger reviews of individual absenteeism for the following Bradford factors:

Annually: Bradford factor of 80 or higher

Quarterly: Bradford factor of 27 or higher

Monthly: Bradford factor of 12 or higher.

Example Let's look at a number of example calculations:

If you get a person taking 10 one-day unplanned absences in a given period (say a quarter), then the Bradford factor would be: $1,000 = 10 \times 10 \times 10$.

If you get a person taking one 10-day unplanned absence in a given period, then the Bradford factor would be: $10 = 1 \times 1 \times 10$.

If you get a person taking five two-day absences in a given period, the Bradford factor would be: $250 = 5 \times 5 \times 10$.

If you get a person taking two five-day absences in a given period, the Bradford factor would be: $40 = 2 \times 2 \times 10$.

In May 2001, Her Majesty's Prison Service in the UK began using the Bradford factor (which they call an attendance score) to identify staff with high absenteeism due to short-term illness. They tied the factor to a sliding scale of management action:

- 51 points in 6 months leads to a verbal warning;
- 201 points to a written warning, and
- 401 points to a final warning.

This provides a clear framework for tackling persistent short-term absence, where a member of staff with an attendance score of 601 points in 12 months but with a final warning may be dismissed on the grounds of unsatisfactory attendance. This approach has had a significant effect in reducing short-term absence by an average of 0.4 days per person.

Tips/warnings

While the Bradford factor is a useful key performance indicator, there are often good reasons for employees taking unplanned leave. This means that taking the score as the only criterion is not recommended; instead, it should only be used as a trigger to prompt line managers to investigate an individual's absenteeism further.

There is another danger, as with so many indicators. If staff are made aware of the trigger points, the factor can be counter-productive because staff 'work up to their limits'.

References

www.cipd.co.uk/hr-resources/factsheets/absence-measurement-management.aspx

http://camsolutions.blogspot.com/2007/11/calculation-of-absenteeism-rates.html

Ministerial Task Force for Health, Safety and Productivity and the Cabinet Office, *Managing Sickness Absence in the Public Sector*, Department for Work and Pensions, London. **http://www.hse.gov.uk/gse/sickness.pdf**

www.teamseer.com/features/bradford-factor/

360-degree feedback score

64

Strategic perspective
Employee perspective

Key performance question this indicator helps to answer
How well are our people performing in the eyes of those who have a stake in their performance?

Why is this indicator important?

360-degree feedback provides an individual with a broad assessment of their performance based on the views of those who have a stake in their performance, such as supervisor/boss, reporting staff members, co-workers, customers, suppliers, etc. Most 360-degree feedback tools are also responded to by each individual in a self-assessment. How they assess themselves can be easily compared with those providing the feedback (or raters as they are often called), using a scoring method of, for example, 1–10. Therefore, feedback allows each individual to understand how his or her effectiveness as a leader, co-worker, staff member or supplier/customer is viewed by others. Such insight is often used for training and development purposes.

Results are also used by some organisations in making administrative decisions, such as pay or promotion, and are therefore more valuable than traditional top-down appraisal systems which are very subjective and often based solely on whether or not the supervisor likes the person being appraised. However, there is a great deal of controversy as to whether 360-degree feedback should be used exclusively for development purposes, or used for appraisal purposes as well.

How do I measure it?

Data collection method

Data are usually collected through an annual survey of those that are rating the performance of the individual employee being subjected to a 360-degree assessment. The questionnaires today are normally web-based (although paper-based and even face-to-face interviews can be used to collect data).

Formula

There is no single formula used within a 360-degree assessment, as there are many consultants in the field. That said, a 360-degree appraisal template typically contains the following column headings or fields, also shown in the template example on the next page:

- Key skill/capability type (e.g. communications, planning, reporting, creativity and problem solving, etc. – whatever the relevant key skills and capabilities are for the role in question).
- Skill component/element (e.g. 'active listening and understanding' [within a 'communications' key skill], or 'generates ideas/options' (within a 'creativity/problem solving' key skill]). The number of elements per key skill varies – for some key skills there could be just one element, for others there could be five or six.
- Question number (purely for reference and ease of analysis).
- Specific feedback question (relating to skill component, e.g. 'does the person take care to listen and understand properly when you/others are speaking to him/her?' [for the active listening skill]).
- Tick-box or grade box (typically using a Likert-scale rating of, for example, very poor to excellent and on a 1–5 or 1–10 scale. Note that providing clarification and definitions of a ratings system to participants and respondents is crucial, especially if analysing or comparing results within a group, when consistency of interpretation of scoring is important).

Consider this as a sample 360-degree feedback questionnaire.

Feedback form headings and instructions: appraisee name, date, feedback respondent name, position (if applicable) plus local instructions and guidelines for completion, etc.				
Key skill/ capability area	Skill/ capability element	Question number	Feedback question	Feedback score
		1		
		2		
		3		
		etc.		
		etc.		

See also the example on the following page.

Frequency

Usually measured annually.

Source of the data

Those 'raters' providing feedback on the individual's performance.

Cost/effort in collecting the data

Costs and effort of collecting 360-degree feedback scores can be very high as it will require significant time commitment for scoring, evaluation and feedback. There are few ways of bringing costs down other than simplifying data collection through the use of software and electronic data collection.

Target setting/benchmarks

It is possible to compare performance against others with the same or similar job profiles. An overall performance score can be given for an individual (the average of all scores) and the individual can compare this with others, with their past performance and for setting future targets.

Example This example can be found on the **www.360-degreefeedback.com** website. The following are extracts from the feedback reports for 'Steve Kane'.

The report began with a category summary, which included overall score (average, as well as from self, manager, peer and direct report) and then high-level results for the categories of 'leading change', 'results oriented' and 'team leadership', amongst others. A 1–10 rating score is used.

This was followed by open questions that consider Steve's strengths and priority improvement opportunities.

Then there are a number of questions that provide a score from each rater and that can be compared with the project average. Questions such as Steve's abilities in 'leading change', 'works toward team, departmental and organisational goals in addition to personal objectives', 'communicates respectfully during stressful times', and 'questions accepted practices and assumptions' are examples.

Tips/warnings

Since 360-degree feedback processes are usually anonymous, people receiving feedback have no recourse if they want to further understand the feedback. They have no one to ask for clarification of unclear comments or more information about particular ratings and their basis.

For this reason, developing 360-degree process coaches is important. Supervisors, HR staff, interested managers and others are taught to assist people to understand their feedback. They are trained to help people develop action plans based on the feedback.

Confidentiality is important to both the feedback recipient and the respondents. If the feedback recipient is not guaranteed that the results will remain confidential, they will tend to feel anxiety about the purpose of the process and the use of the data. If the respondents are not guaranteed that their names will not appear on the report or be linked to specific comments or ratings, then they may not provide accurate responses and be completely open. To ensure confidentiality:

- Select a neutral administrator (e.g. an external consultant or human resources representative).
- Print only one report per person.
- User-names and passwords should be required to access the survey and the response data should be encrypted.
- Ensure that online systems are encrypting the data and storing the results on a secure server.

There is a checklist of seven criteria used in constructing a good 360-degree survey (**www.360-degreefeedback.com**):

- Does the item utilise an ACTION VERB?
- Does the item describe an OBSERVABLE behaviour?
- Does the item describe ONLY ONE behaviour?
- Is the item described in CLEAR LANGUAGE?
- Is the item described as a POSITIVE, desired behaviour?
- Does the item describe an IMPORTANT behaviour?
- Does this item, taken together with all of the other items, SUFFICIENTLY DEFINE the category?

Finally, to ensure that people take an adequate time to consider each question and provide positive and constructive feedback, the survey should contain as few questions as possible. If survey items are carefully researched to ensure relevance, the number of questions should not exceed 50.

References

Susan M. Heathfield, *360 Degree Feedback: The Good, the Bad, and the Ugly*, **http://humanresources.about.com/od/360feedback/a/360feedback_3.htm**

www.businessballs.com

www.360-degreefeedback.com

Richard Lepsinger and Anntoinette D. Lucia, *The Art and Science of 360 Degree Feedback*, San Francisco, CA: Pfeiffer, 2009.

Salary competitiveness ratio (SCR)

65

Strategic perspective
Employee perspective

Key performance question this indicator helps to answer
To what extent are we offering a competitive salary to our employees?

Why is this indicator important?

Competition for the best talent is fierce in most markets and offering an attractive salary package is important in order to attract and retain talent. Just as businesses compete for customers to whom to sell their goods and services, they compete for the best talent.

Understanding how the salary your company pays compares to the pay competitors provide to their employees in similar positions in the same area or market gives you an insight into the competitiveness of your company as a potential employer and the level of temptation for existing employees to leave your company and take up better paid jobs elsewhere.

I completely acknowledge that pay is not the only element that matters – and many argue not the most important – but it is a good KPI to include. What companies want to ensure is that they offer a salary that is fair and competitive, but without paying too much. Comparing your salary rate with those offered by your competitors will provide these insights.

How do I measure it?

Data collection method

The way to collect data for this KPI is to gather data on competitor pay or industry average pay and compare this with your own salary levels.

Measuring the salary competitive ratio is easier in some industries and markets than others. Take supermarkets, hotels or call centres, for example, where job roles are well defined and salaries are based on either hourly rates or salaries. In these environments it is generally very easy to collect the salary rates from competitors and create the competitiveness ratio. If competitor pay levels are not obtainable it might be useful to conduct or pay for some market research to establish average pay levels for the industry.

Formula

When calculating the salary competitiveness ratio you compare the salary your company offers to the salary offered by competitors. You can select either one or a number of direct competitors or you can compare your salaries with the industry average.

$$\text{Salary competitiveness ratio (competitor)} = \frac{\text{Salary offered by your company}}{\text{Salary offered by your competitor}}$$

$$\text{Salary competitiveness ratio (industry)} = \frac{\text{Salary offered by your company}}{\text{Average salary offered in the industry or sector}}$$

Salary competitiveness can be calculated for specific job groups using the formula above or a composite ratio can be produced across all job groups by adding the ratios together.

In industries with hourly wages the salary can be replaced by the hourly rates.

Frequency

As salary levels in most industries are fairly stable, it probably makes sense to measure this KPI on an annual or six-monthly basis.

Source of the data

The data for the salary you are offering come from your own HR system or HR policy documents. The data for the salary offered by competitors or across the industry are a little harder to get and usually require some market research.

Cost/effort in collecting the data

The costs and effort of collecting the data depend on the level of available information about salaries in your industry. If your industry is open about salaries and if competitors publish their salaries then the effort is quite low. However, if market research is necessary then the costs of conducting this research have to be taken into account.

Target setting/benchmarks

The target for your salary competitiveness rate depends on your remuneration strategy (for more information see, for example, **www.salary.com/docs/resources/ salarycom_wp_competitive_pay_philosophy.pdf**).

A general rule of thumb for companies in competitive labour markets is that you want to offer equal or slightly higher pay than your competitors (but not too much), so a ratio of 1 or 1.1 is a good benchmark.

If your company is already very attractive (good brand, excellent non-financial benefits) then you might want to aim for equal or slightly lower than average pay, so a ratio of 0.9 or 1 is a possible benchmark.

Example A supermarket realised that recruitment for junior management positions for its stores was getting increasingly difficult. It realised that the talent pool was becoming smaller and it wanted to ensure that it offered competitive salaries (but not overpay unnecessarily). Simple research of job ads in the local paper gave it a good understanding of the salary levels of its competitors. The average salary among competitive positions was $25,000 per year. The company was currently offering $23,000 for that position.

The salary competitive ratio for this position was therefore:

$$SCR = \frac{23,000}{25,000}$$

$$SCR = 0.92$$

This was too low and the company decided to offer a new salary for this position of $26,000, which brought the ratio up to a more competitive 1.04.

Tips/warnings

In industries with a large proportion of commission payments and bonus payments it is advisable to include these in the calculation to ensure accuracy. Just using the base salary would provide a misleading picture of salary competitiveness.

References

www.salary.com/docs/.../salarycom_wp_competitive_pay_philosophy.pdf

http://humanresources.about.com/cs/compensation/a/aasalaryrange.htm

Time to hire   66

> **Strategic perspective**
> Employee perspective
>
> **Key performance question this indicator helps to answer**
> How well are we able to fill vacant positions in our business?

Why is this indicator important?

It is important for businesses to fill vacant posts. A failure to fill open jobs quickly will have a number of negative consequences, which include reduced efficiency (e.g. not enough staff to complete the work, existing workers having to cover the vacant job role), lost revenue (orders cannot be fulfilled, business does not run at full capacity) and costs (for e.g. hiring in temporary or agency staff).

By measuring the time it takes to hire employees, organisations will gain an insight into efficiency in filling employee vacancies from advertisement to offer, acceptance of position and start of work.

Traditionally, time to fill has been measured as an indicator of HR effectiveness and calculated as the elapsed time between the initial approval or posting of a vacant post and the final acceptance of a job offer from a qualified and approved candidate. However, as a strategic KPI we are less interested in the effectiveness of the HR process and more in the elapsed time between the initial approval or posting of a requisition and the actual day when the newly hired candidate begins work in the position.

How do I measure it?

Data collection method

If the HR system tracks the hiring process, the data can be captured and collected automatically. If not, manual tracking will be required. While the start date is usually available from the HR system, the day of posting of the vacancy is often not, and it needs to be captured.

Formula

The formula is the time taken from the initial posting of a vacancy to the time the new recruit starts.

> Time to hire = Elapsed time between time of posting and time to start

This time can then be averaged for specific job roles and across the entire company.

Frequency

Time to hire should be measured on a quarterly basis.

Source of the data

The HR system and manual capture.

Cost/effort in collecting the data

The costs and effort for generating this KPI can be relatively high if there is no automated system that will capture and track the hiring process.

Target setting/benchmarks

Time to hire rates vary by job role and industry. The benchmarks available for commercial companies range from about 20 to 80 days. In the US public sector it's 110 days as of October 2010 (dropped from a staggering 180 days). The US Office of Personnel Management would like to see hiring time reduced to at most 80 days.

> **Example** As an example calculation (taken from Creelman, 2001), take a company that posts a job on 5 January, the successful candidate accepts on 20 January and starts on 10 February. According to our formula, the time to hire is:

Time to hire = 36 days

Enterprise Rent-A-Car is a good example of a company that takes time to recruit very seriously. Enterprise is the largest car rental business in North America, with more than 7,000 offices in the United States and more than 900 in Canada, Puerto Rico, the UK, Germany and Ireland. In an effort to track and reduce time to hire, the company is pushing applications through its hiring website which is used to post vacancies and track progress.

A public sector example comes from the US government where President Barack Obama, in his 2010 executive directive, 'Improving the Federal Recruitment and Hiring Process', states: 'To deliver the quality services and results the American people expect and deserve, the Federal Government must recruit and hire highly qualified employees, and public service should be a career of choice for the most talented Americans. Yet the complexity and inefficiency of today's Federal hiring process deters many highly qualified individuals from seeking and obtaining jobs in the Federal Government.'

Tips/warnings

Time to hire will vary between industry and job roles. It therefore makes sense to report time to hire by similar job roles and not only as overall averages. If averages are used it's important to analyse and highlight variance and outliers that can skew average data.

References

www.ere.net/2004/08/11/understanding-time-to-hire-metrics-separating-time-to-fill-from-time-to-start/

www.bpir.com/recruitment-and-selection-bpir.com/menu-id-72/measuring-success.html

www.whitehouse.gov/the-press-office/presidential-memorandum-improving-federal-recruitment-and-hiring-process

James Creelman, *Building and Developing a HR Scorecard*, London: Business Intelligence, 2001.

Training return on investment

67

Strategic perspective
Employee perspective

Key performance question this indicator helps to answer
How effective is our training in driving business results?

Why is this indicator important?

'Training' is often perceived as a 'soft' measure and, as such, it is argued that it is difficult to quantify the 'hard' (especially financial) benefits to the enterprise. Unfortunately, many from a Human Resources background, or function, continually make this argument.

However, in recent years we have seen a growing library of best practices that do indeed trace how training expenditure impacts financial performance; put another way, it provides a measure of the return on investment (ROI) on the training dollar.

However, rather than being a 'new' metric, a measure of training effectiveness – the Kirkpatrick model – was first promoted and introduced into organisations as far back as the 1950s (and is still used by companies across the globe – see References). The five-step Human Resource ROI model (which primarily looks at training) described in this KPI, which was developed by Dr Jack Phillips of the ROI Institute, is essentially an extension of the four-step Kirkpatrick model.

Using an ROI assessment approach is one powerful way for HR to begin the process of talking to the business in the language of the business. HR's credibility can certainly be enhanced, because by showing the business impact of an HR intervention in such bottom-line terms, then HR can be said to be truly holding itself accountable for its actions. This will go some way to repositioning HR as an investment rather than a cost.

How do I measure it?

Data collection method

For the Jack Phillips ROI KPI, data are collected in several ways. Participants are surveyed to ascertain their satisfaction with the training programme immediately after the event, and questionnaires and surveys (of participants and their managers) are deployed several weeks later to assess behavioural or performance change. Later, data are collected from surveys/questionnaires to measure the training programme impact on areas such as output, quality, cost, time and customer satisfaction. Data are then collected to assess the benefit against costs (the ROI).

Formula

The five levels of the Phillips ROI model are as follows:

Level 1. Reaction and planned action

Level 2. Learning

Level 3. Application

Level 4. Business impact

Level 5. Return on investment

Level 1. Reaction and planned action
At this level, participants' reaction to and satisfaction with the training programme are measured. Also captured are the planned actions that the delegates intend to implement back in the workplace.

Level 2. Learning
This level is where an assessment is made on what participants believe they have learned in the programme (often through an end-of-class evaluation).

Level 3. Application
At Level 3, data are collected to determine if participants have implemented the HR programme successfully. This measures changes in on-the-job behaviour or actions as the programme is applied, implemented or utilised. Typically, questionnaire and survey instruments will be used to access this information.

Level 4. Business impact

At this level, the actual business results of the programme are identified and a monetary value applied to the behavioural/skills changes. Typical Level 4 measures include output, quality, cost, time and customer satisfaction.

However, even though the HR programme may produce a measurable business impact, there is still a concern that the costs for the HR programme may be too high.

Level 5. Return on investment

This is where the actual ROI is calculated. Essentially, the ROI calculation is identical to the ROI ratio for any other business investment, where the ROI is traditionally reported as earnings divided by investment. ROI is calculated as:

$$\frac{\text{Benefits} - \text{Costs}}{\text{Costs}}$$

The return on investment is calculated using benefits and costs. The benefit/cost ratio is the benefits of the HR programme or intervention divided by the costs:

$$BCR = \frac{\text{HR programme benefits}}{\text{HR programme costs}}$$

The return on investment uses the net benefits divided by costs. The net benefits are the programme benefits minus the costs. In formula form, the ROI becomes:

$$ROI\% = \frac{\text{Net HR programme benefits}}{\text{HR programme costs}} \times 100$$

The BCR and ROI present the same general information but with slightly different perspectives. An example illustrates the use of these formulas. An HR programme produced benefits of $581,000, with a cost of $229,000. Therefore the benefit/cost ratio would be:

$$BCR = \frac{\$581,000}{\$229,000} = 2.54 \text{ (or 2.5:1)}$$

As this calculation shows, for every $1 invested, $2.50 in benefits was returned. In this example, net benefits were $581,000 – $229,000 = $352,000. Thus the ROI would be:

$$ROI\% = \frac{\$352,000 \times 100}{\$229,000} = 154\%$$

This means that each $1 invested in the HR programme returned $1.50 in net benefits, after costs were covered.

Frequency

Applied to major training programmes.

Source of the data

The staff being trained and the HR department analysing the impact of the training.

Cost/effort in collecting the data

Collecting and analysing the data for this KPI can be expensive and time consuming. For this reason a full ROI calculation is usually applied to only a limited number of training programmes – typically those that are expensive and that are expected to be impactful (see Tips/warnings).

Target setting/benchmarks

HR process benchmarking organisations such as the Hackett Group will hold data on the cost of HR functions/processes such as training. Also, specialised HR ROI organisations, such as Kirkpatrick Partners and the ROI Institute, will be able to make benchmarking data available.

Example In the early 2000s the US-headquartered Nextel Communications applied a full ROI programme (which they labelled as a 'training scorecard') to high-impact training programmes. Here is an example of one programme.

Almost 400 managers/supervisors from throughout the organisation completed a five-hour training programme on performance management.

Data collection: Levels 1 and 2

The data for the Training Scorecard Level 1 (reaction and planned action) and Level 2 (learning) were collected through an end-of-class questionnaire. This included a self-assessment evaluation (rated from 1 = poor to 5 = excellent) against questions such as the following:

- What is your ability to apply each of the following skills back on the job?
- Coach employees on an ongoing basis to assure continuous process.

The Level 1 and 2 analyses for the performance management course showed that participants provided a 4+ rating against all key measures.

Level 3 (application) evaluation

Data for this evaluation were collected via a questionnaire distributed to course participants by e-mail, about 90 days following the date of the course. Crucially, it included questions that ask participants how much they attributed their performance improvement to the training received through the performance management class and how much to other factors.

Level 4 of the Training Scorecard looks at business impact. This is where data are converted into monetary values to give a comparison with programme costs. One participant was able to report savings of $16,200 per quarter, which, multiplied by four, gives an annual figure of $64,800. This was multiplied by a percentage of the savings attributable to the class (in this case 20%) and multiplied again by a confidence factor of 100%, which led to a final figure of $12,960 per year.

The analysis of the performance management course comprised all costs related to the course, which were calculated at $283,267.

The Level 5 ROI ratio was calculated as follows:

$$ROI = \frac{\$2{,}106{,}088 - \$283{,}267}{\$283{,}267}$$

The ROI is 643%.

Tips/warnings

Although almost all HR staff groups conduct evaluations to measure satisfaction, few actually conduct evaluations at the ROI level. Perhaps the best explanation for this is that ROI evaluation is often characterised as a difficult and expensive process (which is typically the case). For this reason, organisations should select only a few interventions for an ROI evaluation.

References

For more on the Kirkpatrick Model see **www.kirkpatrickpartners.com**

For more on Jack Phillips, see **www.roiinstitute.net**

Jack Phillips, *Return on Investment in Training and Performance Improvement Programs (Improving Human Performance)*, 2nd edn. Oxford: Butterworth-Heinemann, 2003.

Community for Human Resources Management **www.chrmglobal.com/Replies/531/1/Training-Effectiveness.html**

James D. Kirkpatrick and Wendy Kayser Kirkpatrick, *Training on Trial: How Workplace Learning Must Reinvent Itself to Remain Relevant*, West Babylon, NY: AMACOM, 2010. See **www.kirkpatrickpartners.com**

James Creelman, *Creating The HR Scorecard*, London: Business Intelligence UK, 2001

www.thehackettgroup.com

PART SIX

Corporate social responsibility perspective

Carbon footprint 68

Strategic perspective
Corporate social responsibility perspective

Key performance question this indicator helps to answer
How well do we safeguard the environment in the execution of our business operations?

Why is this indicator important?

Although still sometimes disputed, most people believe that climate change is one of (if not the) most serious and urgent challenges facing the world's global population and the natural environment. Many people accept that the greenhouse gas emissions (GHG) released into the atmosphere in still rapidly growing volumes are the primary reason for the quite dramatic and unpredictable changes to normal climate patterns that we are witnessing throughout the world.

All organisations have a role to play in global efforts to put a brake on further climate change. The most effective way is to measure its 'carbon footprint': that is, to quantify how much damage the organisation is doing to the environment by way of GHG emissions.

As well as the moral reasons for taking the measurement of carbon footprint seriously, organisational leaders must pay attention because of ever-increasing legislation and regulation as well as an ever-watchful and demanding societal base – for many organisations, not performing well against carbon-footprint-type measures can have devastating effects on reputation and consequentially on profits and share price.

How do I measure it?

Data collection method

Data are collected from various sources, such as emissions from plant/products or by the amount of time executives spend in aeroplanes.

Formula

A carbon footprint is the measure of the amount of greenhouse gases, measured in units of carbon dioxide, produced by human activities. A carbon footprint can be measured for an individual or an organisation, and is typically given in tons of CO_2-equivalent (CO_2-eq) per year. For example, the average North American generates about 20 tons of CO_2-eq each year.

An individual's or organisation's carbon footprint can be broken down into primary and secondary footprints. The primary footprint is the sum of direct emissions of greenhouse gases from the burning of fossil fuels for energy consumption and transportation. For example, more fuel-efficient cars have a smaller primary footprint, as do energy-efficient light bulbs in your home or office. Worldwide, 82% of anthropogenic greenhouse gas emissions are in the form of CO_2 from fossil fuel combustion.

The secondary footprint is the sum of indirect emissions of greenhouse gases during the life cycle of products used by an individual or organisation. For example, the greenhouse gases emitted during the production of plastic for water bottles, as well as the energy used to transport the water, contribute to the secondary carbon footprint. Products with more packaging will generally have a larger secondary footprint than products with a minimal amount of packaging.

Frequency

Organisations will likely do an annual assessment of their corporate carbon footprint, with product assessments also typically yearly but sometimes more frequent.

Source of the data

There are various data sources, such as data pertaining to plant and products as well as travel documentation.

Cost/effort in collecting the data

Given that assessing carbon footprint can be a lengthy process and involve specialised consultants, this can be an expensive metric to populate and can include not inconsiderable effort from business executives.

Target setting/benchmarks

Carbon footprint benchmarks are readily available for most industries/sectors. Approaching industry bodies would be a good way to identify benchmarks. Also, once a carbon footprint assessment has been done, consultants usually compare results with similar findings, which provide benchmarks for improvement. Of course, at national and international levels countries set targets for GHG emissions that can provide a steer to organisational leaders.

> **Example** The International Organisation for Standardisation (ISO) has developed a comprehensive, usable, international standard for carbon management under its 14000 environmental management family: the ISO 14064 series (see References).
>
> **Step 1: Setting organisational parameters and boundaries**
> An organisation may include one or more facilities, as simple as a single cubicle or as complicated as a conglomerate with several locations serving different functions scattered across the country.
>
> Each facility may include GHG sources (something that emits greenhouse gases), GHG sinks (something that removes GHGs from the atmosphere) or GHG reservoirs (places to capture and store GHGs). To get an accurate picture of an organisation's total carbon inventory, it will need to consolidate facilities based on financial and/or operational control, or on the portion of a shared facility. The total carbon footprint is the aggregate.
>
> The organisation must also determine the GHG emissions from operations, which may include:
>
> - Business travel
> - Energy consumed (but not generated) by your organisation
> - Outsourced activities or franchises
> - Physical facilities or processes you own or control
> - Production of purchased raw or primary materials
> - Transportation of goods

- Use and end-life phases of products and services
- Waste generated

Step 2: Measuring GHG activity

Once what needs to be measured has been determined, establish a base year, using either historical data or the first inventory year, so that you can monitor improvement over time.

Step 3: Choosing methodologies

Quantification methodologies help minimise uncertainty and provide accurate, consistent and reproducible results that allow you to track progress over time.

There are three main types of methodology: calculation, measurement and combination.

Calculation includes:

- GHG activity data multiplied by GHG emission or removal factors
- Use of models
- Facility-specific correlations
- Mass-balance approach

Measurement is the gathering of hard data, either continuously or periodically, and the combination methodology includes both calculation and measurement.

Step 4: Reporting

This is where results are shared with stakeholders. The best way is to publish the organisation's carbon inventory report on a respected, third-party registry.

If the plan is to publish with a registry that conforms to ISO 14064, you will need to ensure that the report includes:

- The reporting period
- Organisational boundaries and parameters
- Emissions in tons of CO_2-eq
- Removals in tons of CO_2-eq
- Disclosure of any GHG sources or sinks you did not include, and why
- The base year inventory
- A description of the methodologies used
- The results of the uncertainty assessment
- Statement of verification (this will be explained in Step 5: Verification)

Optional information that might be included:

- A description of organisational policies, strategies or programmes
- A description of organisational emission reduction activities and results
- Any purchased or developed GHG offsets
- Emission details for each facility
- An assessment of organisational performance against relevant internal or external benchmarks

Step 5: Verification
Obtain verification to get true value from your carbon footprint report – and to protect against any accusations of 'greenwash'. The principles and process mirror those used in financial audits. The goal is an independent, objective review of the data and many registries and programmes require third-party verification.

Tips/warnings

Completing a carbon footprint assessment is not enough. An organisation must use the findings to launch interventions that will reduce its carbon footprint, such as enhancing energy efficiency, mitigating carbon emissions by means of green energy and then compensating for remaining GHG emissions by investing in carbon offsets. (Instead of reducing its own emissions, a polluter can receive credit for supporting a project that either reduces emissions abroad or reduces emissions in an industry domestically that is not mandated to reduce emissions.)

Organisations should also ensure that their effort in this area is in line with the responsibilities of their industry/sector. It is not advisable for an organisation to expend a lot of time and effort on this if it is in an industry with low GHG emissions.

References

www.pe-international.com

www.green-business.ca

www.iso.org/iso/iso14064_ims2_06.pdf

Maggie L. Walser, Carbon footprint, The Encyclopedia of Earth, **www.eoearth.org/article/Carbon_footprint**

Water footprint 69

> **Strategic perspective**
> Corporate social responsibility perspective
>
> **Key performance question this indicator helps to answer**
> How well do we safeguard the environment in the execution of our business operations?

Why is this indicator important?

Fresh water is a scarce resource; its annual availability is limited and demand is growing. Good information about the water footprints of communities and businesses will help us to understand how we can achieve a more sustainable and equitable use of fresh water.

There are many spots in the world where serious water depletion or pollution takes place: rivers running dry, dropping lake and groundwater levels, and species endangered because of contaminated water. The water footprint helps to show the link that exists between our daily consumption of goods and the problems of water depletion and pollution that exist elsewhere, in the regions where our goods are produced. Nearly every product has a smaller or larger water footprint, which is of interest for both consumers that buy those products and businesses that produce, process, trade or sell those products at some stage of their supply chain.

The water footprint is an indicator of water use that looks at both direct and indirect water use of a consumer or producer.

A water footprint has three components:

- The green water footprint refers to consumption of green water resources (rainwater stored in the soil as moisture).
- The blue water footprint refers to consumption of blue water resources (surface and ground water).
- The grey water footprint refers to pollution and is defined as the volume of fresh water that is required to assimilate the pollutant load based on existing ambient water quality standards.

Reducing the water footprint can be part of the environmental strategy of a business, just like reducing the carbon footprint (see KPI on page 311). Second, many businesses actually face serious risks related to fresh-water shortage in their operations or supply chain. A third reason to do water footprint accounting and formulate measures to reduce the corporate water footprint is to anticipate regulatory control by governments. Finally, some businesses also see a corporate water footprint strategy as an instrument to reinforce the corporate image or to strengthen the brand name.

How do I measure it?

Data collection method

Data are collected though various qualitative and quantitative means to consider water used through the supply chain, within the plant or for other everyday operations.

Formula

The water footprint of an individual, community or business is defined as the total volume of fresh water that is used to produce the goods and services consumed by the individual or community or produced by the business.

The water footprint of a business, the 'corporate water footprint', is defined as the total volume of fresh water that is used directly or indirectly to run and support a business. It is the total volume of water use to be associated with the use of the business outputs. The water footprint of a business consists of two components: direct water use by the producer (for producing/manufacturing or for supporting activities) and indirect water use (in the producer's supply chain).

Frequency

Water footprint assessments will likely be on an ongoing basis, especially in large organisations that are heavy water users. The water footprint measure might be reported annually.

Source of the data

Water footprint data come from many sources. These will likely be operational and supply-chain data.

Cost/effort in collecting the data

Initially, assessing the water footprint might involve specialised consultants. This can be an expensive metric to populate and includes not inconsiderable effort from business executives. However, there are focused training courses, such as those delivered by the not-for-profit Water Footprint Network, that enable the building of expertise in in-house water experts.

Target setting/benchmarks

The World Business Council for Sustainable Development (WBCSD)'s Global Water Tool is a free and easy-to-use tool for companies and organisations to map their water use and assess risks relative to their global operations and supply chains. It compares a company's sites with validated water and sanitation data on a country and watershed basis. The tool also helps companies understand their water needs in relation to local conditions, such as water availability (current and projected), water scarcity, access to safe drinking-water sources and sanitation, as well as population and industrial growth.

Example The Coca-Cola company – a heavy consumer of water – has conducted many water footprint assessments, including for juice beverages.

Two orange juice products produced for the North American market were selected for the water footprint pilot study:

- Simply Orange (not from concentrate) in a 59 oz PET carafe
- Minute Maid Original (reconstituted from concentrate) in a 64 oz fibre-based-board gable-top carton

The calculations consider all water consumed in growing oranges and in processing and packaging the final orange juice products. The oranges for Simply Orange are grown in Florida and the state of São Paulo, Brazil. The oranges for Minute Maid Original are grown primarily in Florida and Costa Rica. The processing of oranges into juice or concentrate occurs in the regions where the oranges are grown. The percentage of oranges sourced from each region varies by year, and different sourcing scenarios were evaluated to reflect this variability. Both products are packaged in the United States at multiple locations.

Data were not available for water use associated with manufacturing of the packaging materials in the supply chain, so only operational water use was accounted for in the packaging plants.

Water footprints were calculated according to the accounting method outlined in the *Water Footprint Manual* (available from Water Footprint Network, see References) and based on available information. The manual has four steps:

1. Setting goals and scope
2. Water footprint accounting
3. Water footprint sustainability assessment
4. Water footprint response assessment

Public data were used for Brazil and to fill other data gaps where supplier data were not available. The water footprint associated with orange growing makes up approximately 99% of the total water footprint for both products, and the remainder is associated with processing and packaging the final orange juice products.

The results show that in terms of consumptive water use (green plus blue water), Florida has the largest water footprint.

Importantly, Florida has a significantly larger blue water footprint than Brazil and Costa Rica. This is because the calculated crop water requirements are substantially greater for Florida compared to Costa Rica and Brazil.

Tips/warnings

For most businesses the supply-chain water footprint is much larger than the operation footprint. Achieving improvements in the supply chain may be more difficult – because it is not under their direct control – but may be more effective. Businesses can reduce their supply-chain water footprint by making supply agreements which include standards requirements with their suppliers or by simply changing to another supplier.

References

Water Footprint Network: **www.waterfootprint.org**

Heather Gadonalex, *Sustainability 101: Water, The New Carbon. Measuring Your Water Footprint*, 30 June 2009. **www.triplepundit.com/2009/06/Sustainability-101-water-the-new-carbon-measuring-your-water-footprint/**

The Global Water Tool, World Business Council for Sustainable Development, **www.wbcsd.org/publications-and-tools.aspx**

Product Water Footprint Assessments, September 2010: **www.thecocacolacompany.com/presscenter/TCCC_TNC_WaterFootprintAssessments.pdf**

Energy consumption 70

> **Strategic perspective**
> Corporate social responsibility perspective
>
> **Key performance question this indicator helps to answer**
> To what extent are we reducing our energy consumption?

Why is this indicator important?

The worldwide consumption of energy is constantly increasing while the world's fossil resources (the main sources of energy) are becoming more limited, and as a consequence energy prices are rising. We can make the fair assumption that energy prices will continue to increase and that environmental protection will become an increasingly important issue (and possibly a competitive differentiator as consumers become more conscious of the environmental impact their consumption has).

As a business it therefore makes financial and ethical sense to invest in energy-saving projects and renewable energy solutions. What's more, many governments are now taking energy consumption seriously. For example, the UK government has recently passed legislation called the Carbon Reduction Commitment which means that businesses that consume more than 6,000 megawatt hours (MWh) a year must register for a carbon-trading system and identify their annual CO_2 carbon-reduction performance.

Tracking energy consumption provides companies with an insight into how much money they are saving and how much they are helping the environment. The easiest way to track energy consumption is by the amount of energy purchased.

How do I measure it?

Data collection method

Your energy supplier will provide your consumption and the cost of the energy you have purchased. You can simply use this information for your KPI.

Formula

Total amount of energy purchased in a given time period.

Frequency

Depending on your billing period, you can collect this data monthly or quarterly.

Source of the data

The data will come from your energy supplier.

Cost/effort in collecting the data

Because this data are provided by an external supplier there are no costs to you.

Target setting/benchmarks

It is impossible to provide a benchmark or target for energy consumption because energy usage varies enormously across industries and companies. The best way to set targets initially is to create an internal benchmark of your current consumption and then set a target of, say, 15–20% net reduction per year.

> **Example** Nestlé, which refers to itself as the world's leading nutrition, health and wellness company and owns brands such as Nescafé, Pure Life, KitKat, Häagen-Dazs, Purina, Smarties, Shreddies and Munch Bunch, has set itself a target of becoming the most energy-efficient food manufacturer. Since 2000, Nestlé has reduced its energy consumption by almost 3% while increasing its production volume by 73%. Nestlé seeks to achieve energy-efficiency improvements of at least 5% in each of its key product categories over the next

five years, and will continue to investigate the setting of energy consumption targets by product category.

Another company that is committed to reducing total energy use is mobile phone and communications giant Vodafone, which has adopted this as one of its strategic KPIs listed in its annual report.

Governments which have signed up to carbon reduction targets are keen to monitor and reduce energy consumption in public sector and government organisations. Take, for example, Nottingham Trent University which has energy consumption as one of its publicly reported KPIs:

Year	Energy consumption (KWh)	Percentage change
2005/06	65,916,243	N/A
2006/07	56,112,380	−14.87%
2007/08	59,387,350	−9.90%
2008/09	59,964,377	−9.03%
2009/10	60,937,420	−8.60%

Source: www.ntu.ac.uk/ecoweb/document_uploads/94617.pdf

Tips/warnings

As many executives still struggle to understand what a saving of 500,000 kilowatts means, it is useful to express the numbers in actual costs as well.

Many experts now advise that establishing the energy costs per unit of output (e.g. each product or service your business produces or offers) allows everyone to understand the proportion of costs linked to energy and therefore the implications of reducing energy consumption on profit margins and bottom-line performance.

References

www.energyadvantage.com/blog/2011/02/energy-expenditure-consumption-expressed-function-key-performance-indicators/

www.nestle.com/CSV/WaterAndEnvironmentalSustainability/ImprovingEnergyEfficiency/Pages/ImprovingEnergyEfficiency.aspx

http://datacenterjournal.com/index.php?option=com_k2&view=item&id=2352:energy-consumption-is-plaguing-the-data-center&Itemid=500

www.vodafone.com/content/annualreport/annual_report08/performance/corp_responsibility/kpis.html

www.ntu.ac.uk/ecoweb/document_uploads/94617.pdf

http://archive.defra.gov.uk/environment/business/reporting/pdf/envkpi-guidelines.pdf

Savings levels due to conservation and improvement efforts

71

> **Strategic perspective**
> Corporate social responsibility perspective
>
> **Key performance question this indicator helps to answer**
> To what extent are we actively reducing the environmental impact of our business?

Why is this indicator important?

Every business is aiming to cut costs and reduce the impact of its business activities on the environment. Collecting data on the savings generated by conservation and improvement projects will give businesses an insight into the effectiveness of these projects and programmes.

The best way this can be measured is by identifying a number of projects designed to reduce the environmental impact of your company and then tracking the savings levels generated by these projects in terms of reduction in greenhouse gas emissions, water usage and energy usage as well as actual cost savings.

Savings levels due to conservation and improvement efforts are very closely linked to the carbon footprint, water footprint and energy consumption KPIs discussed earlier.

How do I measure it?

Data collection method

The data for this KPI will in most cases have to be calculated manually. Based on the project definitions, savings targets will have been identified. These will then have to be tracked against the baseline consumption prior to the start of the project.

Formula

Total level of savings (in carbon emissions, water usage, energy usage or costs) generated from the conservation and improvement projects identified.

Frequency

Usually savings levels are tracked on a quarterly basis but the frequency depends a little on the project time-frames – for example, if all projects have a long project timeline such as one or two years then it might make sense to report only after that period or to break the project up into shorter milestones that can be reported against.

Source of the data

The source of the data will have to be manual input and calculations.

Cost/effort in collecting the data

Costs for collecting data for this KPI can be very high due to the sometimes complex and time-consuming nature of calculating saving levels.

Target setting/benchmarks

As projects differ enormously, it is not possible to provide meaningful benchmarks or targets for this KPI.

> **Example** We can take another look at global food giant Nestlé. To measure the level of savings generated through conservation and improvement efforts the company completed an energy-target-setting initiative in 2010, during which it identified more than 200 projects.

The annual savings of these projects include energy savings of about 1.3 million GJ and a reduction in CO_2 emissions of approximately 88,000 tonnes. In addition, water savings of 1.9 million m^3 were identified and the monetary savings totalled CHF 27 million.

Tips/warnings

One tip is to contrast the savings made with the costs of the projects to identify value-for-money projects. When generating a value-for-money analysis, however, it is important to take into account not just savings made to date but also project future savings.

References

www.nestle.com/CSV/WaterAndEnvironmentalSustainability/ImprovingEnergyEfficiency/Pages/ImprovingEnergyEfficiency.aspx

http://archive.defra.gov.uk/environment/business/reporting/pdf/envkpi-guidelines.pdf

Supply chain miles

72

Strategic perspective
Corporate social responsibility perspective

Key performance question this indicator helps to answer
To what extent are we minimising the environmental impact of our business?

Why is this indicator important?

In a globalised world we often buy goods and supplies from anywhere in the world based on quality or price criteria we have set. However, we often forget the environmental impact of shipping goods halfway across our planet. The concept of measuring the miles (or kilometres) travelled by a product from the producer to the consumer was first developed in the food supply chain, where the term 'food miles' was conceived. Food miles is now regularly used as a metric on food-packaging labels to make consumers aware of the fact that some food has travelled a long way (which might not always be necessary). Some research suggests that, on average, food travels between 1,500 and 2,500 miles (4,000 km) every time that it is delivered to the consumer, a distance which has increased by a quarter from the 1980s to today.

Measuring the distances that products or components have travelled will provide companies with insights into the environmental impact of their business activities.

Supply chain miles can be measured for both the demand side (i.e. for the products and goods a company buys from their suppliers) and the supply side (i.e. the products or services a company supplies to its customers).

How do I measure it?

Data collection method

Collecting data for supply chain miles can be done easily by putting the location of the beginning and end of the supply chain (on either the demand or the supply side) into a tool such as the Google Maps Distance Calculator, which will then calculate the distance. Alternatively, there are online tools available for measuring food miles which can be used in the same manner. Supply chain miles can be measured for individual products or components that you purchase or sell, or can be clustered (e.g. all supply chain miles for goods supplied to produce one product or all delivery miles for one product range).

Formula

> Supply chain miles = Distance between location of production and the location of the final delivery

Frequency

Product recycling rates are usually collected on an annual or six-monthly basis.

Source of the data

The location information for suppliers and customers can usually come from sales and purchasing databases.

Cost/effort in collecting the data

Unless automated through a software program that calculates supply miles, the costs for collecting data for this KPI can be quite high because of the manual effort required to collect and calculate the data.

Target setting/benchmarks

Because every supply chain is different, it is impossible to give actual targets or benchmarks here. The aim should always be to reduce or minimise supply chain miles.

Example Let's take an example of a manufacturing firm in Philadelphia, PA which is buying components from a supplier in Boston. The supplier will ship the goods by lorry from Boston to Philadelphia. Using Google Maps, the supply chain miles for this product is 319 miles.

Another example comes from the National Health Service (NHS) in the UK. The NHS supply chain has a depot in Bridgwater, Somerset which supplies vital medical equipment to hospitals around the south-west. From there, 60 vehicles make 500 deliveries a day to 3,000 locations such as hospitals and general practitioner practices. By mapping, measuring and reorganising the supply chain using a supply chain tool, hospitals in Bristol and Bath were able to save more than 10,400 delivery miles – that's about the distance from Bridgwater to Sydney in Australia.

Tips/warnings

When purchasing goods it can sometimes be tricky to identify the production location, especially when dealing with traders that act as middlemen between the supplier and the company. Invoice and sales details will often contain the location of the trader but not necessarily the location of the supplier.

Also, when calculating the distance you have a number of options, e.g. distance by road (following actual public roads) or distance by air (direct line between the two locations). The one to pick depends a little on the supply chain – if most of the delivery is made by lorry, for example, it would make sense to calculate distance by road. If, on the other hand, the product is flown from one city to the next it makes sense to use distance by air.

References

Erika Engelhaupt, Do food miles matter? *Environmental Science & Technology*, 42, 2008, p. 3482

www.organiclinker.com/food-miles.cfm

www.daftlogic.com/projects-google-maps-distance-calculator.htm

http://www.supplychain.nhs.uk/news/press-releases/2010/reducing-delivery-miles/

Waste reduction rate   73

> **Strategic perspective**
> Corporate social responsibility perspective
>
> **Key performance question this indicator helps to answer**
> To what extent are we minimising the amount of waste we generate?

Why is this indicator important?

We live in a world where resources are precious and where we can't afford to waste any. To that end there is a concerted effort by businesses and governments to reduce the waste we produce.

Any business will aim to reduce waste to a minimum, especially if you take the manufacturing industry where raw material cost is often around 60% of the manufacturing costs. However, waste is an important component of any business, and beyond the simple costs of wasted raw materials there are hidden waste costs such as disposal costs, the costs of producing the wasted product, lost production time, time lost on waste management, storage and clean-up costs, etc. Cost-effective waste minimisation is a valuable investment that pays dividends for any company.

According to waste minimisation expert Dr Robin Kent, waste is costing companies real money which is coming directly off their profits. He argues that at a gross margin of 7%, a reduction in waste costs by 1% is the equivalent of increasing turnover by over 14%.

Measuring and monitoring the amount of waste a company generates can give companies an insight into the efficiency and effectiveness of their operations as well as the environmental and social impact of these operations.

How do I measure it?

Data collection method

Waste can be measured simply by calculating the amount of raw material used in a company and subtracting the amount of raw material that was used in the finished goods. The difference between these two data sets can be classified as waste. The waste reduction rate is a percentage calculated by dividing the waste produced in the current period by the waste produced in the previous period of the same production output.

Formula

$$\text{Waste reduction rate} = \left[\frac{\text{Wasted raw material (in this period a)}}{\text{Wasted raw material (in the last period b)}} \right] \times 100$$

Where the production output in periods a and b is the same

Where Wasted raw material is (Raw − Raw in part)

Where Raw is the amount of raw material used in period x

Where Raw in part is the quantity of raw material in parts for period x, calculated by multiplying the amount of raw material per unit or product and the total number of products or units produced in period x.

Frequency

Usually savings levels are tracked on a quarterly basis but the frequency depends a little on the project time-frames – for example, if all projects have a long project timeline such as one or two years then it might make sense to report only after that period or to break the project up into shorter milestones that can be reported against.

Source of the data

The data for the raw material can usually be collected from the purchasing and manufacturing systems. However, the data for the amount of raw material used in the product or service are typically not available and require manual calculation or estimation.

Cost/effort in collecting the data

Costs for collecting data for this KPI can be quite high because of the sometimes complex and time-consuming nature of calculating the amount of raw materials used in the final product or service.

Target setting/benchmarks

As waste levels differ enormously between companies and sectors, it is not possible to provide meaningful benchmarks or targets for this KPI. It is best to generate baseline figures and aim to reduce them by, say, 10%.

> **Example** Let's look at an example of a machine manufacturer that wants to understand the waste reduction rate for aluminium:
>
> The amount of the main raw material (aluminium) used this year is 1,000 tonnes = Raw
>
> The amount of product (specialist machine) produced last year is 2,000 units
>
> The amount of the main raw material per (specialist machine) unit of product (aluminium) is 0.4 tonnes
>
> Quantity of main raw material in parts last year = (0.4 tonnes × 2,000) = 800 tonnes
>
> Wasted main raw material (aluminium) = 1,000 − 800 = 200 tonnes
>
> To get the waste reduction ratio we need to know the waste level of the previous 2,000 units, which in this case was 250 tonnes. The waste reduction ratio is therefore $\left(\frac{200}{250}\right) = 0.8 = -20\%$

Tips/warnings

Waste can be calculated for the entire company or maybe more meaningfully for individual products, supply chains or production lines. While waste can be expressed as e.g. 1,000 tonnes saved, it is also useful to express these savings in monetary terms, taking into account the direct and the major indirect costs.

In many cases it also makes sense to go beyond the basic raw material used and include items such as packaging.

References

www.resourcesmart.vic.gov.au/for_businesses/waste_and_recycling_2205.html

http://amproscorp.com/Benchmark.pdf

www.pcn.org/Technical%20Notes%20-%20Waste%20(1%20-%205).pdf

www.wrap.org.uk/downloads/Waste_Management_Guidance_Note_5.b7958fb7.5175.pdf

Waste recycling rate 74

> **Strategic perspective**
> Corporate social responsibility perspective
>
> **Key performance question this indicator helps to answer**
> To what extent are we recovering our waste for reuse or recycling?

Why is this indicator important?

For any company it is best to minimise waste or not to produce any waste at all, which we discussed in the waste reduction rate KPI (see page 333). However, as it is not always possible to eliminate waste completely, companies need to try to minimise the impact that the waste they are producing is having on the environment. When we produce waste that is sent to landfill sites or to incinerators, this has commercial as well as environmental implications.

By reusing or recycling the waste we produce we can not only reduce the environmental impact but also save costs. Cost savings can be generated from saved waste disposal costs, saved material costs (e.g. if you decide to reuse waste material) and generated income (if you are able to sell your waste for reuse or recycling by other companies).

Understanding the waste recycling rate over time is therefore a good indicator to show not only how much of the waste your company produced is being recycled or reused but also how this rate is rising towards the zero waste target that many businesses and governments strive for.

How do I measure it?

Data collection method

Collecting data for the waste recycling rate can be complex and usually requires some manual data collection and estimation work. In most cases it is not about being 100% accurate but about understanding key trends. In many cases companies look at specific types of waste and identify how much of this is sent for recycling or reuse. For example, if waste material is sold to other companies or sent for recycling there are usually records describing the weight or volume of material.

Formula

$$\text{Waste recycling rate} = \left[\frac{\text{Amount of waste recycled or reused}}{\text{Total waste produced}}\right] \times 100$$

As it is often difficult to determine all waste, companies often identify the main waste items or products and calculate the percentage for those. In order to get an overall average they can just combine the individual waste reduction rates.

Frequency

Waste recycling rates are usually collected on a quarterly or six-monthly basis.

Source of the data

The data will come from waste disposal and recycling paperwork and internal data systems. Where these data are not available manual estimations need to be conducted.

Cost/effort in collecting the data

Costs for collecting data for this KPI can be high because of the sometimes complex and time-consuming nature of calculating the waste recycling and reuse rates. The more data are available in systems or paperwork, the more that will reduce the data collection effort and cost.

Target setting/benchmarks

In order to minimise the environmental impact of operations, companies should aim to reuse or recycle all the waste they produce.

Governments have set targets to reduce the amount of waste sent to landfill sites. In the UK, for example, the target is that by 2015, waste sent to landfills should be 35% of that sent in 1995, and also that by 2015 a waste recycling and reuse rate of 67% should be achieved.

Example An example calculation comes from a food manufacturer that produces 1,000 tonnes of vegetable oil waste from their production per month. The company can now sell 800 tonnes of this used vegetable oil to a company that recycles it into fuel. Its waste recycling rate for vegetable oil is therefore $(800/1,000) \times 100 = 80\%$.

Take, for example, the YES Window Company, which set itself stringent targets for waste recycling. In its policy the company states: 'YES Window Company Ltd recognises the necessity to recycle as many waste products as we can, particularly the bulk of our waste which is glass, aluminium, wood, old PVCu and metal window frames. YES Window Company Ltd is proud to announce that we are currently recycling 94% of all our waste products.' Examples of its waste reduction efforts include producing its own bio-diesel from waste vegetable oil on its premises to run its fleet as well as recycling its glass, wood and metals.

Tips/warnings

Measuring the waste recycling rate can be a complex undertaking and in order to reduce effort companies can estimate the recycling rate based on known facts and information.

References

www.wrap.org.uk/downloads/Waste_Management_Guidance_Note_5.b7958fb7.5175.pdf

www.letsrecycle.com/news/latest-news/waste-management/uk-leads-europe-on-tyre-recycling

www.recycling-guide.org.uk/targets.html

www.zerowasteamerica.org/statistics.htm

www.pira-international.com/businessintelligence/measuring-the-recycling-rate-of-UK-magazines.aspx

www.yeswindow.co.uk/recycle/

Product recycling rate 75

> **Strategic perspective**
> Corporate social responsibility perspective
>
> **Key performance question this indicator helps to answer**
> To what extent are we minimising the environmental impact of the products we produce or sell?

Why is this indicator important?

With the previous KPIs we looked at waste reduction and waste recycling, which are concerned with minimising the environmental impact of production. However, recycling is also desirable for the products a company produces or sells.

Once products have come to the end of their life, the aim should be to recycle most if not all of them. There is now agreement among governments and business associations that product recycling is the responsibility of manufacturers. However, many companies selling products are now also measuring and reporting product recycling rates.

The product recycling rate will provide insights into the proportion of the products sold that were recycled or reused.

How do I measure it?

Data collection method

Collecting data for the product recycling rate can be complex and usually requires some manual data collection and estimation work.

Formula

$$\text{Product recycling rate} = \left[\frac{\text{Amount of products recycled or reused}}{\text{Total amount of products sold}}\right] \times 100$$

Frequency

Product recycling rates are usually collected on an annual or six-monthly basis.

Source of the data

While sales and production data can usually be obtained from the transaction or accounting system, the recycling rates are much harder to get. Collecting these data usually requires some research and estimation work. In some cases industry data are available for everyone to use.

Cost/effort in collecting the data

Costs for collecting data for this KPI can be high because of the sometimes complex and time-consuming nature of calculating the product recycling and reuse rates.

Target setting/benchmarks

Companies should aim to recycle or reduce 100% of their products. Most governments have set themselves targets for recycling. Take, for example, the Scottish government's zero waste ambitions, with a target of 70% recycling by 2025.

> **Example** A good example comes from the tyre industry. Approximately one tyre per person is discarded per year. Tyres are designed to be extremely durable in order to last in some of the harshest conditions possible. Landfilling or burning tyres for energy is not desirable as there are greener alternatives for recycling tyres into products such as basketball courts and shoes. In order to understand the product recycling rates, a number of tyre companies and industry bodies commissioned independent research which found that, in Europe, more than 87% of used tyres are now diverted from landfill.

A similar example comes from the magazine-publishing industry where the UK government has announced a new agreement with publishers to implement tough new recycling targets for the industry. Under the new standards 70% will be recycled by 2013. The voluntary arrangement was made in cooperation with the Periodical Publishers Association (PPA), which represents 90% of the UK's magazine publishers. Like the tyre example, the recycling rates are based on independent studies and research.

Tips/warnings

It is recommended that packaging should be included in the recycling calculation. This can be done as part of product recycling in cases where the product has a short life-span and the packaging becomes waste in the same period as the product becomes waste. It the product has a long life-span then it might make sense to produce two separate calculations, one for the product and another for the packaging.

References

www.wrap.org.uk/downloads/Waste_Management_Guidance_Note_5.b7958fb7.5175.pdf

www.greenconsumerguide.com/news2868.html

www.letsrecycle.com/news/latest-news/waste-management/uk-leads-europe-on-tyre-recycling

www.recycling-guide.org.uk/targets.html

www.zerowasteamerica.org/statistics.htm

www.pira-international.com/businessintelligence/measuring-the-recycling-rate-of-UK-magazines.aspx

www.yeswindow.co.uk/recycle/

Index

360-degree feedback score 289–93

absenteeism
    Bradford factor 285–8
accounts payable 65
    days payable outstanding (DPO) 62, 64
accounts receivable 65
    days sales outstanding (DSO) 62, 63–4
activity-based costing 105
advertising companies 51
aerospace manufacturers 227
airlines 99, 122, 124
Amazon 149, 160, 263
American Customer Satisfaction Index (ACSI) 98, 99–100
amortisation 21, 23
Anheuser-Busch 60
annual and annualised rate of return 42–3, 223
assets 139–40
    amortisation 21, 23
    depreciation 21, 23, 48
    return on (ROA) 49–51, 140
    ROCE and depreciated 48
Audi USA 176

Baidu 152, 153
balanced scorecard 266
banks 93, 99, 106, 113, 162–3
    Scotiabank 271–2
banner ads: cost per lead 145, 146
beta 35
beverage producers 30
Bing 152
Boots 94
Boston Consulting Group 133–4, 221
bounce rate and page views 155–8
Bradford factor 285–8
brand equity 91–2, 139–42
Brazil 319–20
buyback of shares 60

call centres 247, 278, 282, 296
    first contact resolution: contact and 251–4
capacity utilisation rate (CUR) 185–7
CAPEX to sales ratio 75–7
capital asset pricing model (CAPM) 35
capital structure see debt vs equity
car industry 93, 94–5, 99, 142, 176, 226, 231
carbon footprint 311–15
    data on conservation projects 325–7
carbon-trading system 321

cash conversion cycle (CCC) 61–5
cash cows 134
cash flow 23, 28
    cash conversion cycle (CCC) 61–5
    customer cash flows, NPV of 107–11
    inflation 48
    investment decisions 47
    working capital ratio 67–70
catering and leisure 278
change management 195
China 153
click-through rate (CTR) 148, 151–4
climate change see environment
clothing and leather manufacturers 227
Coca-Cola 141, 319–20
compensation see remuneration
conservation and improvement efforts
    savings levels due to 325–7
contact centres
    first contact resolution (FCR) 251–4
Convergys Corp 263
conversion rate 147–50
corporate social responsibility
    carbon footprint 311–15
    energy consumption 321–4
    product recycling rate 341–3
    savings levels due to conservation and improvement efforts 325–7
    Shared Planet 172
    supply chain miles 329–31
    waste recycling rate 337–9
    waste reduction rate 333–6
    water footprint 317–20
cost of capital
    economic value added (EVA) 7, 33–7
    return on capital employed (ROCE) and 48
cost of debt 35
cost per lead 143–6
Costa Rica 319–20
current position
    working capital ratio 67–70
customer complaints 121–5
customer engagement 117–20
customer lifetime value (CLV) 105, 106, 107–11
customer online engagement level 159–63
customer order cycle time 193–5
customer problems/questions
    first contact resolution (FCR) 251–4
customer profitability score 103–6
customer relationship management (CRM) 65, 114, 115, 252

customer retention rate (CRR) 91–5
customer satisfaction
    index (CSI) 97–101
    net promoter score (NPS) 85–9, 91–2
customer turnover rate 113–16

days inventory outstanding (DIO) 62, 63
days payable outstanding (DPO) 62, 64
days sales outstanding (DSO) 62, 63–4
debt vs equity
    debt-to-equity (D/E) ratio 57–9
    return on assets (ROA) 50, 51
    return on equity (ROE) 53, 55
debt-to-equity (D/E) ratio 57–9
delivery in full, on time (DIFOT) rate 197–200
depreciation 21, 23, 48
Digital Footprint Index (DFI) 170–1
DIO (days inventory outstanding) 62, 63
DMAIC principles 181–2
dogs (growth-share matrix) 134
downtime level, process or machine 247–9
DPO (days payable outstanding) 62, 64
DSO (days sales outstanding) 62, 63–4

e-mail marketing: cost per lead 144, 146
earned value (EV) metric 213–16
eBay 149
EBIT (earnings before interest and tax) 45
EBITDA (earnings before interest, taxes,
        depreciation and amortisation) 21–4
EBITDA Margin 24
economic value added (EVA) 7, 33–7
economies of scale 133–4
employee churn rate 277–80
employee engagement level 120, 268, 269–72
employee perspective
    360-degree feedback score 289–93
    absenteeism: Bradford factor 285–8
    employee churn rate 277–80
    employee engagement level 120, 268, 269–72
    employee satisfaction index 265–8
    employee tenure, average 281–4
    human capital value added (HCVA) 257–60
    revenue per employee (RPE) 261–4
    salary competitiveness ratio (SCR) 295–8
    staff advocacy score 273–6
    time to hire 299–301
    training return on investment 303–7
employee satisfaction index 265–8
employee tenure, average 281–4
energy consumption 321–4
    data on conservation projects 325–7
Enterprise Rent-A-Car 118, 301
enterprise resource planning (ERP) system 199
environment
    carbon footprint 311–15
    energy consumption 321–4
    product recycling rate 341–3
    savings levels due to conservation and
        improvement efforts 325–7

waste recycling rate 337–9
waste reduction rate 333–6
water footprint 317–20
equity
    return on (ROE) 53–5
equity cost of capital 35
equity vs debt *see* debt
Europe
    capacity utilisation rate (CUR) 187
exhibitions: cost per lead 145, 146
exit interviews 280
ExxonMobil 47

Facebook 169, 170, 172
    Klout score 175–7
financial perspective
    CAPEX to sales ratio 75–7
    cash conversion cycle (CCC) 61–5
    debt-to-equity (D/E) ratio 57–9
    EBITDA (earnings before interest, taxes,
        depreciation and amortisation) 21–4
    economic value added (EVA) 7, 33–7
    gross profit margin 13–16
    net profit 3–7
    net profit margin 9–11
    operating expense ratio (OER) 71–3
    operating profit margin 17–19
    price/earnings (P/E) ratio 79–81
    return on assets (ROA) 49–51, 140
    return on capital employed (ROCE) 45–8
    return on equity (ROE) 53–5
    return on investment (ROI) 39–43
    revenue growth rate 25–8
    total shareholder return (TSR) 29–31
    working capital ratio 67–70
financial services sector 113
    banks 93, 99, 106, 113, 162–3, 271–2
first contact resolution (FCR) 251–4
first pass yield (FPY) 229–32, 238
first to market advantage 226
focus groups 98, 99, 114, 120, 140
    employees 266
food miles 329–31
Ford Motor Company 142

Gallup 118, 119–20, 160, 270–1
gearing: debt-to-equity (D/E) ratio 57–9
General Electric/GE 181, 263
Google 142, 152, 153, 263
greenhouse gas emissions 311–15
gross profit margin 13–16

Hackett Group 195
Honeywell 181
hospitality industry 282
hospitals 217, 247, 331
hotels 99, 122, 278, 296
human capital value added (HCVA) 257–60

IBM 141

INDEX   345

inflation 48
innovation
  pipeline strength (IPS) 217–20
  return on innovation investment (ROI²) 221–3
insurance companies 106
intangible assets 139–40
  amortisation 21, 23
  brands 91–2, 139–42
intangible investments and return on investment (ROI) 40
Interbrand 140–2
International Organization for Standardization (ISO)
  carbon management 313–15
internet 117, 125, 273
  banner ads 145, 146
  conversion rate 147–50
  customer online engagement level 159–63
  e-mail marketing 144, 146
  Klout score 175–7
  online share of voice (OSOV) 165–8
  page views and bounce rate 155–8
  search engine optimisation (SEO) 152, 153, 158
  search engine rankings (by keyword) 151–4
  service provider sector 93
  social networking footprint 169–73
  webinars 145
inventory 65, 197
  days inventory outstanding (DIO) 62, 63
  process waste level 190–1
  shrinkage rate (ISR) 201–3
investment decisions
  cash flow 47
  ROCE: projects to finance 46

just-in-time production/supply chains 65, 197

Klout score 175–7

Lady Gaga 177
landfill sites 337, 338, 342
lean production 65
  process waste level 189–92
leisure and catering 278
leverage: debt-to-equity (D/E) ratio 57–9
LinkedIn 172, 273
  Klout score 175–7
losses
  forward P/E ratio 81
loyalty cards 94

machine or process downtime level 247–9
macro ROI 40
magazine-publishing industry 343
manufacturing companies 51, 75, 185, 193, 221
  cars 93, 94–5, 99, 142, 176, 226, 231
  energy consumption 322–3, 326–7
  product recycling 341
  rework level 233, 234, 235–6
  time to market 227

total quality management (TQM) 233, 237–8
  waste reduction rate 333
market, entering a new 27–8
market growth rate 129–31
market share, relative 133–7
marketing and sales perspective
  brand equity 91–2, 139–42
  click-through rate (CTR) 148, 151–4
  conversion rate 147–50
  cost per lead 143–6
  customer online engagement level 159–63
  Klout score 175–7
  market growth rate 129–31
  online share of voice (OSOV) 165–8
  page views and bounce rate 155–8
  relative market share 133–7
  search engine rankings (by keyword) 151–4
  social networking footprint 169–73
markup 15
micro ROI 40
Microsoft 142, 263
milestone dates 227–8
mining companies 51
mobile phone sector 93, 107, 114, 225
  Vodafone 323
Motorola 181

Nestlé 322–3, 326–7
net profit 3–7
net profit margin 9–11
net promoter score (NPS) 85–9, 91–2
Nextel Communications 306–7
Nielsen Company 161, 169, 172
Nottingham Trent University 323

Obama, Barack 177, 301
online share of voice (OSOV) 165–8
operating expense ratio (OER) 71–3
operating profit margin 17–19
operational processes and supply chain perspective
  capacity utilisation rate (CUR) 185–7
  delivery in full, on time (DIFOT) rate 197–200
  earned value (EV) metric 213–16
  first contact resolution (FCR) 251–4
  first pass yield (FPY) 229–32, 238
  innovation pipeline strength (IPS) 217–20
  inventory shrinkage rate (ISR) 201–3
  order fulfilment cycle time (OFCT) 193–5
  overall equipment effectiveness (OEE) 241–5
  process or machine downtime level 247–9
  process waste level 189–92
  project cost variance (PCV) 209–11
  project schedule variance (PSV) 205–8
  quality index 237–40
  return on innovation investment (ROI²) 221–3
  rework level 233–6
  Six Sigma level 181–4
  time to market 225–8
order fulfilment cycle time (OFCT) 193–5

346   INDEX

overall equipment effectiveness (OEE) 241–5
overhead costs 7

packaging 343
page views and bounce rate 155–8
pharmaceutical companies 72, 217, 218, 221
Portakabin 192
power bases 195
price/earnings (P/E) ratio 79–81
prime mover advantage 226
prison service in UK 287–8
privacy 111, 172
problem child products 134
process or machine downtime level 247–9
process waste level 189–92
product recalls 228
product recycling rate 341–3
profit, net 3–7
profit margin 226
    gross 13–16
    net 9–11
    operating 17–19
profit/payroll ratio 263
profit/return, rate of 39–43
project cost variance (PCV) 209–11
project schedule variance (PSV) 205–8
public sector 97–8, 99, 300, 301, 323
publishers, magazine 343
purchase of own shares 60

quality index 237–40
question mark products 134

Radian 6 platform 165, 166
rate of return/profit 39–43
recessions 57
recycling rate
    product 341–3
    waste 337–9
relative market share 133–7
remuneration 31, 34
    salary competitiveness ratio (SCR) 295–8
reputation 140, 228, 312
research and development (R&D) costs 72, 73, 217, 218, 221
restaurants 93, 120
retailing 89, 278
    supermarkets 114, 197, 296
    see also individual companies
return on assets (ROA) 49–51, 140
return on average capital employed (ROACE) 45, 47
return on capital employed (ROCE) 45–8
return on equity (ROE) 53–5
return on innovation investment (ROI^2) 221–3
return on investment (ROI) 39–43
return on investment, training 303–7
return on sales/net profit margin 9–11
revenue growth rate 25–8
revenue per employee (RPE) 261–4
rework level 233–6

risk appetite 37

salary/remuneration 31, 34
    salary competitiveness ratio (SCR) 295–8
sales perspective see marketing and sales
Satistar 195
savings levels due to conservation and improvement efforts 325–7
Scotiabank 271–2
Scotland 342
search engine optimisation (SEO) 152, 153, 158
search engine rankings (by keyword) 151–4
services sector 51, 75, 185, 193, 278–9
    downtime 247
    quality 237–8
    rework level 233, 234
share buybacks 60
Simmons Research 161
Six Sigma level 181–4
small companies 24
Social Mention platform 165–6, 167
social networking footprint 169–73
software companies 51
spinoffs 60
staff advocacy score 273–6
Starbucks Coffee Company 170, 171–2
stars (growth-share matrix) 134
start-up mode 27–8
steel companies 50–1
Stern-Stewart 33
stock see inventory
stock/share price 312
    price/earnings (P/E) ratio 79–81
    working capital position 70
supermarkets 114, 197, 296
supply chain
    miles 329–31
    operational processes and supply chain perspective see separate entry
    water footprint 320
Supply Chain Council 195

tangible assets 139–40
    depreciation 21, 23, 48
tax 51
    pre-tax and post-tax P/E ratio 81
telecom companies 94, 99, 113, 114
    mobile phone sector 93, 107, 114, 225, 323
telemarketing: cost per lead 145, 146
360-degree feedback score 289–93
time to hire 299–301
time to market 225–8
tobacco companies 30
total quality management (TQM) 233, 237–8
total shareholder return (TSR) 29–31
Towers Watson 270
training return on investment 303–7
trends and trend data 46, 87, 131, 268, 271
Twitter 169, 172
    Klout score 175–7

Unilever 31
United Kingdom 287–8, 321, 331, 338
    Nottingham Trent University 323
    recycling 338, 342, 343
United States 153, 177, 202–3, 282
    capacity utilisation rate (CUR) 187
    time to hire in public sector 300, 301
    water footprint 319–20
utilities 30

value-for-money analysis 327
Verizon Wireless 115
Vodafone 323

WACC (weighted average cost of capital) 35
Wal-Mart 18, 94, 263
waste
    process waste level 189–92
    recycling rate 337–9
    reduction rate 333–6
water footprint 317–20
    data on conservation projects 325–7
    supply-chain 320
webinars: cost per lead 145
Western Union 60
whisky manufacturer 203
working capital ratio 67–70

Xerox 118, 233

Yahoo 152
YES Window Company 339
YouTube 172

Zappos 89

INDEX